The Freedom of Spring

MELINDA HEALD

PAGE PUBLISHING, INC.
New York, NY

First originally published by Page Publishing, Inc. 2018

ISBN 978-1-64214-402-4 (Paperback)
ISBN 978-1-64214-403-1 (Digital)

Printed in the United States of America

Chapter 1

It might have been a strange name to have if another person had it. It had been bestowed upon her nineteen years ago by her mother because of the day of her birth. And her mother, who died shortly afterward, was firm in her last request. Those who knew her came to realize it was a perfect name, for she was always alive, warm, fun filled, and as fresh as new-mown hay, or wild mountain flowers. Her hair was a glistening warmed chestnut, and her skin as white as milk. Her smile was full and happy, and she found good in most everyone she came across. Her eyes were wide in their innocence, green with tawny-yellow specks. She was not without temper, for when she saw injustices, her eyes could blaze with fire, and the chestnut hair surrounding her face seemed to help fuel the flames. She had a slim, supple body that attracted most male attention, for it was not so slim as to fool anyone of her womanliness. She had been raised in the strictest Victorian sense, that of Boston, by an old-maid aunt. Yes, she was a breath of fresh, clean air, corn-silk sky, and vivid vitality. Her name was an odd one. Her name was Spring.

Spring shut her eyes to the yellow glare that invaded the inside of the stagecoach. It seemed that her bones would shake apart as the coach bounced over the hard, rutted trail.

"Mrs. Butler," she said to the large, plump woman across from her, "whenever is this bone-jarring conveyance going to arrive in Morgan's Hill?"

"Spring," came the reply, "it'll be soon enough. You don't realize how lucky we are to have traveled in the way we have. Why, I remember . . ." And she proceeded to tell Spring again of the months it took her and her doctor husband to come west by wagon train, the heat, the fear of Indian attacks, sickness, and other travails that befell the various families on their way across the plains of the United States. Spring pretended to listen, for Mrs. Butler, her chaperone, was a good-hearted soul and was at times entertaining.

Spring's mind drifted as she listened to the drone of the older woman's voice. She thought of the events that led up to her being in the Colorado territory.

Aunt Emma, her guardian for most of her life, had died suddenly. It had been such a shock, for there they had been, eating their breakfast in the large formal dining room at Beacon Hill. Aunt Emma had laughed at some anecdote Spring was telling her about her six-year-old charge when she was a governess. A slice of ham had caught in Emma's windpipe and she choked to death before Spring's tawny-green eyes.

It happened so fast that Emma was gone before the younger woman could leap from her chair and call for help.

Spring was at a total loss, for Aunt Emma had meant everything to her, and so it seemed a stroke of luck, or coincidence, that a telegram arrived from her father, Colonel Allan Ames, who headed the United States Army cavalry at Fort Frontier, about one hundred miles east of Denver. The telegram, arriving on the day of Aunt Emma's funeral, said that the fort's schoolteacher had moved east to Independence, and someone was needed to teach the few children living at the fort.

Spring disposed of the house she'd grown up in, and gathered her resources and began making her way west. She traveled by train as far as Chicago, where she met Mrs. Butler, who was on her way back to the fort and its doctor. They'd continued by train to Fort Laramie, and then by stagecoach.

"So now, dear, just count your lucky stars you've had things so easy. Once we get to the fort, things won't be quite so comfortable as they were in Boston."

"Hmm," was Spring's reaction to Mrs. Butler's recitation of the trials and tribulations of past pioneers. The first time she' heard it, she had listened with all her avid attention, for she was eager to learn of new things. But now, she just wanted to be free of the confines of the trains and coaches. Then she asked, "Would you please tell me about my father again? I'm rather nervous about seeing him after fourteen years."

"Well, you don't need to be apprehensive, dear," the plump woman began, adjusting her black bonnet on her graying hair. "Your father can be formidable. He has to be, as he's responsible for all the men under his command. But he's a fair man, does his job well."

Spring did not mention to Mrs. Butler, nor indeed had she done so to anyone, ever, of the resentment she'd buried deep within her. When she was five years of age, her father left her in the capable hands of his older sister to take a position in the cavalry. He'd been a dashing young lieutenant then. But his need to be a father to his young daughter had fallen short of his need to fulfill his destiny. At least that was how Spring had viewed his departure and subsequent absence from her life. She knew that if other suitable options had been available to her when her aunt died, she would've snapped them up immediately, rather than grab at the straws her father held out to her. Of course, she was rather curious to see him again, and to also meet the young lieutenant she'd been corresponding with for the past six months.

"Morgan's Hill!" the voice of the driver atop the wagon rang out.

Spring set her bonnet on her head, tucking her thick curls under the crown. She tied the bow under her chin and tried to see the town out the window of the right side of the vehicle.

Morgan's Hill was a small settlement, and very rough. It was the closest piece of civilization to Fort Frontier; and though it was unrefined, Spring was extremely happy to remove herself from the jolting stagecoach and walk around on her own two feet.

There were four soldiers to meet and greet the two ladies, who had been the only passengers.

"Oh, John, so nice to see you again!" Mrs. Butler exclaimed to a trim young officer standing slightly at attention. The three other men remained in the background. "Spring, this is Lieutenant John Granville. John, Miss Ames, the colonel's daughter."

Spring had not related to her chaperone that she was already letter acquainted with Lieutenant Granville. It had come about because he'd written her a thank-you for having attended the funeral of his grandfather in Concord, Massachusetts.

"Miss Ames," the lieutenant said, tipping his hat to her.

"Lieutenant." Spring nodded her head and smiled. She was so relieved to be out in the open air again that her usual effervescence spilled over into her face and voice. John Granville, brown eyes set in a narrow but handsome face, took this as a sign of encouragement on her part. Perhaps her coming might make this drab country not quite so dreary or his nights so boring. He hadn't realized his correspondent was such a beauty.

"Well, ladies, I've gotten you a room at the one hotel here. We'll start out for the fort in the morning."

"You mean it's too far to get there today?" Spring asked with disappointment.

"It's another ten miles, Miss Ames," Granville answered, gesturing for the three privates with him to gather up the baggage, most of which contained the fancy Eastern outfits belonging to Spring. He went on, as he led the travel-weary women to the hotel, "We'll be at the fort in time for lunch, though. After a good night's sleep, I'm sure you'll feel much better than if we tried to go on now."

"John's right, Spring," Mrs. Butler put in. "Tomorrow is soon enough."

In reality, Spring was just anxious to get the reunion with her father over with. Well, she'd waited fourteen years; she guessed she could wait one more night. At this point, she was much too concerned about the meeting with her father to notice the light that had entered John Granville's eyes as they rested on her. Besides, their letters had always remained on strictly friendly terms.

To Spring, the large, dark-colored fort was an intrusion on the otherwise plain, golden prairie landscape. It loomed on the horizon as the wagon carrying the two women, their luggage, and Lieutenant Granville trundled forward. The three privates served as lookouts for any trouble from Indians.

"I'm surprised at how big the fort is," Spring commented. She held her canary-yellow parasol over herself and Mrs. Butler.

John Granville, being the kind of man he was, rose immediately to the occasion and began to tell her about her new home. "The fort," he began, "is also called a stockade. The walls on most forts of this kind are at least ten feet high."

"These walls must be taller than that," Spring replied, gazing at the structure as they drew closer.

"Yes, these walls are about sixteen feet high, and the front and back walls are about one hundred feet in length while the side walls are about sixty. You needn't worry, Miss Ames. You will be perfectly safe within the walls." He gave her a reassuring smile.

"I'm not really worried," she answered. "What's that building on the right side?"

"That's called the blockhouse. There's one on the diagonal corner in the back," he replied. He was feeling quite pleased to be able to instruct this Eastern novice, this beautiful young woman, about the fort. He wanted to appear knowledgeable and capable in her eyes. "Each one can hold approximately thirty men. On the other side of each wall, there's a walkway eleven feet off the ground that runs around the whole of the inside. Guards patrol at all times."

By this time, the wagon approached the double front doors of Fort Frontier. Someone inside called out a signal, and the doors parted inward to let them pass through. Everywhere Spring looked on the inside, there were men dressed in blue uniforms. In the center was a small platform out of which rose a tall pole boasting the stars and stripes of the United States. There were barrack-like buildings along the back wall, and along the right side were horse stalls and equipment for the care of these animals. She was glad to see three or four other women. All had turned out to see the colonel's daughter and to greet Mrs. Butler.

The wagon pulled to a stop, and Spring looked down into the tired gray eyes of an attractive but definitely older man than she expected.

"Colonel Ames, sir," Lieutenant Granville stated, jumping down from his seat on the wagon. He saluted smartly, and the salute was returned. "Your daughter, sir."

Spring was unable to move. This was not how she wished to meet her father again after all these years. There were too many eyes on her, eyes she was not even aware of. She vaguely heard Mrs. Butler greeting her husband on the other side of the wagon.

Clearing her throat, she managed to say, "Hello, Father."

"Hello, Spring. Let me help you down." Colonel Ames held up his hands and held Spring's slender waist to lift her down. He smiled and gave her a perfunctory kiss on the cheek. Then he turned to the group of interested people around them.

"I'm sure you will all excuse us as my daughter and I need to get reacquainted." He placed his hand around her and moved her across the open center area to what looked like a small double cabin to the left of the fort's front doors.

Spring's satin-slippered feet kicked up little puffs of dust, and the hem of her yellow ruffled dress picked up the dust, and it remained there.

"These are my quarters, dear," he said to her. "You will be staying next door with the Butlers, as they have a small second bedroom. Was Mrs. Butler an adequate chaperone?"

"Yes, more than that, Father. A friend too," she replied as they entered a neatly organized room complete with a desk, chairs, maps, and books. This obviously was the colonel's office. Another room to the back served as his bedroom. "I will enjoy staying with them."

"Sit down, sit down," he invited, waving her to a chair as he went behind his desk and sat back.

"No, Father, if you don't mind. I've been sitting for so long it feels wonderful to stretch my legs. I'll just remain standing." She moved to one of the front windows and glanced out. The crowd had dispersed, but there were still a good number of people out, each involved in some sort of activity. She saw the inner walkway halfway up the thick-timbered walls of the stockade and the men patrolling back and forth.

Colonel Ames took a pipe, slowly tamping down the tobacco before lighting it. He was quite surprised at the delicate, fragile beauty of this stranger. Now that he had seen her, he felt he'd erred in bringing her out to this rough, uncivilized country. He felt she was totally unprepared for it all.

"I was sorry to hear of Emma's death," he remarked casually. "It was impossible for me to come to the funeral."

"I was greatly saddened," Spring answered, turning from the window. She untied her bonnet's ribbons from under her chin and removed it. The light from the window highlighted the loosened tendrils of her hair, and it shimmered about her head.

"Well, I'm glad you chose to come out here to give me a hand."

Spring walked back to the desk and faced her father squarely. "I must tell you, Father, that if I'd really had a choice, it wouldn't have been to come here to give you a hand." Her voice was soft and low. Her words came from deep in her soul, which left no doubt in Colonel Ames's mind as to her meaning, and yet she spoke without anger or hatred.

He gazed up at her and took the pipe from between his teeth. She had a strong character, so similar to her mother, he had to admit. He smiled slightly and said with candor, "Well, I do understand your feelings in the matter, Spring. I was never a father to you. I've been completely selfish, thinking only of my needs. You have every right to resent my treatment of you and to even hate me. I can only apologize to you for it and hope you will allow me to make amends in whatever way possible."

The gray eyes bore into Spring's green ones, and she could see he was sincere. She was taken aback by his quick capitulation to her position and was momentarily at a loss for words. Then, realizing she had no one else in the world to whom she belonged, she felt a burden lift from her shoulders that had been there many years. She went around the desk, knelt beside her father's knee, and laid her cheek against the rough fabric of his uniform

"Father, I never wanted to hate you. I do not hate you." She felt his hand on the back of her head in a tender gesture. "The girls at school always questioned your whereabouts and if you should be doing what you were doing. And sometimes," she went on, raising her face to look into his, "they questioned whether or not you even existed at all." Tears glistened on her long eyelashes.

Colonel Ames caressed her cheek and smiled down at her. "Well, dear, for all the slights you received because of me, I'm sorry. Deeply sorry. I now intend to try to rectify my nonexistence in your life. Now, stand up and square your shoulders."

Spring brought herself to her full five feet, three inches, and her father rose beside her.

"Yes, Father, I intend to put all that behind me now, for this is a new life for me." She made a little curtsy to him.

"I can see why your mother insisted on calling you Spring," he replied with gravity. "It seems you are able to renew yourself with vigor, no matter what!"

"I'm not so sure about that, but I do give it a try anyway," the girl answered, seriously.

"How about a tour of your new home?" Father asked. "I'll call Lieutenant Granville in here. I'm sure he won't mind doing that after luncheon."

"I'd like that. He seems to be very good at his job. He knows quite a bit about the area and Indians." Spring felt she would be quite comfortable with him, as they already had their bond of friendship between them.

"He's a little headstrong. It hasn't gotten him into serious trouble yet, but I'm sure it'll all work out." The colonel was talking more to himself than to Spring, so she made no comment.

Spring was surprised by the compact little community held within the fort walls. Almost every basic need was supplied to all who lived there. John Granville showed her the place where she would be teaching the four white children and three Indian ones beginning the next Monday. The same room also served as the chapel on Sunday mornings.

Only a small portion of this room was actually used for the classroom. The rest of the time, the troops, officers, and families met there for their dining needs.

There was an old piano pushed into one corner, and it was quite dust covered. Spring ran her fingers over the yellowed keys and plunked a few notes. It wasn't too badly out of tune.

"Does someone play this?" she asked.

"There's no one here now who does," John answered her. "In fact, in the last two years I've been here, I've never heard anyone play it. I believe you mentioned in one of your letters that you play."

"Yes, I've had lessons for almost all my life. Do you think someone could be found to dust it, inside and out?"

The lieutenant slapped his gloves against his blue pants leg. Anxious to please her, he said, "If I can't, I'll do it myself."

"Well, it's just that I can't imagine Sunday services without music," she replied, smiling shyly, her cheeks dimpling. "Is there anything else to show me?"

"Just the high walk around the inside of the fort. But I'm not sure you want to go up there."

They walked outside into the glaring sunlit afternoon, and Spring once again raised her yellow ruffled parasol.

"Lieutenant, I'm a very curious person. I'd like to see everything there is to see, especially now, while I have such a knowledgeable escort. What is that noise?" Her attention was drawn to a repeated snapping or cracking sound.

John Granville took her elbow and he led her to some steep, wooden steps ascending to the upper walkway. "That sound is the reason why I didn't want to take you up here. The sound is coming from your father's scout, Whip Saunders. I'll introduce you to him shortly, but I think you'll find him most . . . um… offensive."

At the top level, they went to the edge, and Spring could see for what seemed to be miles. Rolling golden hills to the west and flat prairie lands to the east as far as she could see, meeting a corn silk–blue sky, holding no clouds.

"It's all so empty," she murmured to herself in awe, remembering the crowded city streets of Boston. Bustling people, loud wagons on cobbled streets, shouts of street vendors, tall buildings, and lush green foliage in the parks and surrounding family homes. "It's all so, so vast."

She felt John's hand on her arm once more, and they began to stroll along the parapet. The cracking sounds became louder, and after rounding the inside corner of the blockhouse, they stopped behind an un-uniformed man wearing leather breeches and shirt. The shirt was sweat-stained from the exertion of his activity, which consisted of swinging a fifteen-foot bullwhip. The instrument was thick at the end held in the man's hand, made of rawhide, the lash tapering to a plaited end. Every time the man swung the whip, it landed precisely on target, which happened to be a series of bullets lined up on the walk a calculated distance in front of him.

He stopped to realign the targets, removing his gray Stetson hat with red and gray feathers stuck in the hat band. Spring was amazed by the color of the man's hair, for it was almost white, and thought he must be quite old.

"Saunders."

The flat statement of his name by Lieutenant Granville caused the muscular man to turn quickly around.

Cold blue eyes in a ruggedly tanned handsome face swept over John briefly and then settled with intensity on Spring.

"May I present Miss Ames, the colonel's daughter."

Through tight lips covered nearly completely by a thick dark moustache, the man called Whip Saunders said, "Get rid of that damn thing!"

Startled, Spring's eyes opened wide, and she blurted, "I beg your pardon?"

"That yellow thing you're carrying," he answered. "You have alerted the whole Arapaho nation you've arrived by waving that bloody thing around. What's the matter with you, Granville? You've been out here long enough to know those Indians are attracted to all manner of things." Whip wound up the leather whip.

Granville flushed hotly and cleared his throat. "I never thought," he began.

"Of course not. You never do. Well?" The cold gaze settled once more on Spring, raking over her in a look that missed nothing of her feminine allure. When she failed to move, still startled by the man's reactions, he lost patience, stepped back, and skillfully aimed the whip at the top of her parasol's metal tip. Her shade was jerked out of her hand, and the umbrella skittered over the edge of the boardwalk and disappeared from view to the dusty ground below.

"How dare you," she demanded, at last finding her voice.

"Yes, you have the nerve, sir!" John said tightly, stepping forward.

Whip Saunders now spoke in a soft, deep voice that held no rancor. "I dare, Miss Ames, because I have a responsibility here to all those who abide here. Same as the young lieutenant, and since he's forgotten that, I have to act at the moment."

John was flustered, having been put to some shame in front of Spring by a man he obviously detested. He grabbed at Spring's arm, saying, "Let's go on, Miss Ames."

The other man glided between them and looked into Spring's face. "And what is your given name, Miss Ames?"

The ice-blue eyes were fringed with thick dark lashes, and it was then Spring really noticed that Saunders' hair was not truly white but lightened to almost whiteness in the sun, and his face was not an old man's; rather, the skin was smooth and unlined as on a young man.

She seemed mesmerized by his stare and, finally, wetting her lips, said, "Spring. My name is Spring." Her creamy-white face flooded red when he unexpectedly threw his head back, and his mouth opened in loud raucous laughter, showing even white teeth.

"Spring. That's the most absurd thing I ever heard," he managed to say. And then he realized he was speaking to a yellow-clad back as Lieutenant Granville led her away.

As for Spring, she had never felt so insulted in her whole life.

Chapter 2

Spring stormed into the Butlers' quarters, her tawny-specked green eyes blazing, her cheeks flushed with anger.

"Just who is that awful, obnoxious man?" she questioned Mrs. Butler, who had turned to face her when she'd flung open the door.

"What awful, obnoxious man?" The stout woman came to stand before her charge, concern on her face.

"That . . . that man with the whip. Look what he did to my parasol!" Spring stalked about the living room, brandishing the bent and torn umbrella like a sword.

"Spring, stand still, for heaven's sake."

The younger woman made a visible effort to calm herself, but her heaving chest belied her true emotions.

Mrs. Butler tried to hide a smile. "Did Davey do that?"

"Davey? I don't think that is what John—I mean Lieutenant Granville—called him."

"I'm sure he was introduced as Whip Saunders to you. But his given name is David. Now, come along, my dear. You are exhausted. I have a light snack for you, and then you may lie down to rest."

Spring noticed that her friend's voice had softened imperceptibly, and she looked at her intently. Not wanting to drop the matter, she said, "It sounds as if you like that disrespectful, odious person."

"If you are speaking of Davey, yes, I do. He has many fine qualities, lots of responsibilities, and this fort is lucky to benefit from his expertise in Indian affairs. True, his manners may need working on, and I'm sorry he damaged your parasol, but I'm sure he wouldn't have done so if he hadn't thought it necessary."

They entered Spring's small bedroom. The shutters were closed against the warm May afternoon, and it was cooler in there.

"I must say, I'm quite surprised at your choice of friends, Mrs. Butler. He was rude, and I don't like him," Spring persisted, throwing the ruined sunshade into the corner.

"I'm sure he was, Spring," Mrs. Butler consented. "Now, turn around and I'll loosen your dress and stays. Things are usually quiet in the afternoons, for it's much too warm to have much activity."

After eating, Spring took the pins out of her hair, unwound it, and let it cascade to her waist. She removed her dress, the four heavy petticoats and her stays, which she abhorred. At last, free from all the hindrances, she lay on the bed in cotton drawers and a chemise. She never slept in the afternoon, unless she was ill, and she didn't think she would now. However, she was very much mistaken.

*   *   *

Dressed in blue satin with shoes and reticule to match, her chestnut hair neatly rearranged upon her head, Spring approached the open door to her father's office. Hearing voices inside, she stopped in time to hear John's words.

"And it went toppling over the edge. Needless to say, colonel, your daughter was extremely upset over the incident, and as a gentleman, I ask—no, sir, I demand that Saunders make an apology and in future—"

"Yes, well, Lieutenant, I've heard what Mr. Saunders's explanation is, and though I agree his manner toward Spring was a bit unorthodox, I do believe he's correct that we all should remain as unobtrusive as possible. You should've learned that by now."

"But, sir," John began.

Spring, listening outside the room, knew she shouldn't be eavesdropping. She was about to step away when she heard the soft voice of the man, Whip Saunders. It kept her rooted in place.

"If you will permit me, sir, to offer you and Miss Ames an apology. I'm in hopes that will put an end to the young lieutenant's protests." That was the second time Mr. Saunders had referred to John as young, Spring realized. To her inexperienced knowledge, John seemed educated enough in western ways, and not at all young or lacking.

"I accept your apology, Dave, though none is needed for my sake. As for my daughter, you may do as you feel is right.

"I'll trust your judgment, as always." The colonel nodded a dismissal to him, leaving John open-mouthed. Saunders had come out on top again. Well, he'd just have to come up with some way to raise himself in the eyes of Colonel Ames.

Spring backed up a few steps and then proceeded forward, meeting the dreadful Mr. Saunders as he emerged from the office, alone. His appearance had changed in that he no longer wore his leather outfit from the early afternoon. Now he wore a pale-blue broadcloth suit with a white ruffled shirt and black boots that would've shown if not for the thin layer of dust across the toes. The very blond hair, which fell in a natural middle part, was brushed back on both sides, leaving the ends in the back to curl around his coat collar. His cheekbones were high and smoothly shaven, the darker moustache neatly trimmed. Spring became aware of the slight indentation of his squared chin, which angled off to his fine jawline. His blue eyes were moderately set over his long, slightly crooked nose. He was, Spring realized, one of the most handsome men she'd ever met.

"Ah, Miss Ames," he spoke easily. "I was coming to look for you."

"Oh? And what, may I ask, would you need to see me for, Mr. Saunders?" Spring's arched eyebrows lifted higher, and she drew herself up as well.

"I would like to offer you my sincere apology for the way I treated your sunshade today. I hope you will forgive me."

Spring turned away and walked a few steps toward the courtyard. Over her shoulder, she said, "It's completely ruined."

"I'll replace it," he stated simply, moving close behind her.

"No, no, that's all right." Nervously, she stepped away from him, and then faced him. She did not want to be under any kind of obligation to him. "Thank you very much, Mr. Saunders. I do forgive you. And believe it or not, I understand your important position here."

The sun setting now sent a few orange-gold rays to rest on Spring's bountiful hair, burnishing it and setting it aglow. David found himself wanting to get his hands into it, but instead, he shoved them into his trouser pockets. She saw the way he was looking at her, and she cleared her throat. She wanted to be done with this man.

"Mr. Saunders, now that you've apologized and I've accepted, and as we have no further interests in common, I trust we need not have any further conversation."

David rocked on his black-booted heels. Spring was unable to look away from his face, those captivating eyes boring into hers. She was surprised when his face relaxed into a smile, and he said, "As you say, Spring." His voice broke into a deep, gentle, rolling laugh, and it carried across the inner compound as he turned and made his way to the dining hall.

*　　*　　*

Spring sat poised at the piano. She set her hands in motion. The room was silent except for notes filling the air. She forgot her tiredness and the dreams that had penetrated her unconsciousness the night before. She forgot the sound of cracking whips and haunting ice-blue eyes.

The uniformed soldiers and what families were present were very appreciative of the music spilling forth from the young woman's graceful fingers. Then an unnoticed shadow filled the doorway. David Saunders, back from an hour's hard ride from the town of Morgan's Hill, viewed Spring in a new light.

Previously, he'd seen her as a pretty piece of fluff from the East, wrapped up as a gay package in her fancy finery. He thought her stuck up and righteous. But now, he had to admit she wasn't just pretty. She was beautiful. And there was something more in her soul and mind than pretty clothes and stitchery. The way she was playing the piano told him she was a woman filled with emotion, and one of intelligence too.

17

He realized that her name, Spring, was not an absurdity after all. It fit her exactly. For there she sat at the piano, the tune "Amazing Grace" sounding forth. Her small head was slightly tilted, the curve of her rose-tinted cheek silhouetted against the window. There was a small smile on her soft pink lips, her wide-set eyes were shut, letting the long fringe of her lashes brush her cheeks.

The emotion of her green-clad body, the graceful arch of her slender fingers on the keys, the morning sun haloing her sunburnt curls under the small hat reminded him of newly blossoming flowers bursting forth through snow-laden mountainsides. Yes, she reminded him of spring.

He stayed by the door until the service was over, and then stood apart, watching while everyone gave her compliments for her abilities in music. He saw that many of the younger men continued to gawk at her even after introductions had been made. At last, he made his own way forward and came to stand before Colonel Ames, who was standing by Spring.

In a quiet but far-carrying voice, David said, "Let me compliment you on your daughter's expertise at the piano, sir. It really brightens up the place to hear music well played." He purposely kept his gaze from Spring's face.

"Well, thank you, Dave. But why don't you tell her yourself?" the colonel queried.

"Oh, I would like to. However, I am following her explicit instructions never to have a conversation with her again." David Saunders kept his face serious, his voice solemn, but the few who knew him well would have been able to detect the twinkle in his eye.

The buzz of voices in the large room halted. Spring was so embarrassed she wished she could drop from sight. Her fine, delicate features flushed, and she was unable to meet those eyes for several seconds. At last, she met them haughtily. She decided to ignore what he'd said to her father.

"I see you have one redeeming quality, Mr. Saunders. That's your appreciation for music. Now"—she glanced at her father—"if I have your permission, Lieutenant Granville has asked me to go riding with him after we eat."

To her chagrin, Father turned again to Whip Saunders. "You've been outside, Dave. What is your opinion?"

"Surely, Father, you can trust Lieutenant Granville's judgment," Spring put in.

"To the contrary, colonel. If I were you, I would not trust Lieutenant Granville to take your daughter for a ride around the inside of the fort, much less the outside," David said dryly.

Spring began to retort, but Father silenced her with his hand. "Perhaps we can further discuss this in my office." He took Spring's arm, and together they moved to his quarters, out of earshot of the interested bystanders, and Saunders followed. Inside, Father took his chair behind his desk, while Saunders lounged sloppily in a chair opposite. Spring was trembling with rage and remained standing.

"Father, I don't see why we need this . . . this despicable man's opinion to decide whether or not I go riding. I am a skilled horse-woman." She clenched her hands tightly at her sides. David Saunders was not unaware of the rapid rise and fall of Spring's breast in her dress's low-cut green bodice.

"Hmm." Her father took out his pipe and prepared it for smoking. "Now, Dave, I wasn't quite able to determine why you said what you did. Would you explain further?"

The younger man straightened up a little in his chair. He brushed his hair back from his tanned face. "Colonel, you are aware of what I think of the lieutenant's abilities. However, I'm afraid I spoke out of turn a few moments ago. At the moment, it probably is safe for them to go riding for a while—a short while and not too far. Without a parasol."

"Father, I still don't see why I have to let this man dictate my activities, or why—"

"You may go for a short while and not far, or not at all," Father interrupted Spring, giving her a nod of dismissal.

She turned to glare through her green eyes at David Saunders, who remained relaxed and aloof to her anger. Knowing, however, that it would do her no good to continue with an argument, she turned on her satin heels and left the room to have a bite to eat before changing into her riding clothes and meeting John for their ride.

The sun's rays streamed down upon Spring's velvet brown shoulders as she sat upon the dappled-gray mare. Below her, she could see John and the three Indian men gesturing back and forth. It had seemed that he knew exactly where he wanted to ride that afternoon, and it had made her extremely nervous when he left her to ride down the hill to converse with the savages.

Spring did not really think of them as savages, but that was what John called them. In fact, many Eastern people called them that. Spring, in her heart, knew that there was good in all people, no matter what was said or written about them.

All of a sudden, her back straightened. John was directing the attention of the man in charge to her. He even handed him an instrument with which to look through. She looked away, and at the same time heard horse hooves behind her. She glanced over her shoulder, and her heart sank when she saw David Saunders and two other soldiers bearing down on her.

"Just what are you doing?" she asked before he reined to a stop. "Are you checking up on me?"

"What the hell does he think he's doing?" Saunders's blue eyes iced over as he peered down the hill at John and the Indians. "You men, take Miss Ames back to the fort while I see what's going on."

"I will not be told to do anything more by you," Spring stated firmly.

He grabbed her arm in a tight grip, saying, "You will start back to the fort right now with these soldiers. And," he went on, addressing the two men, "if she gives you any trouble, tie her up and take her back by force." Not waiting to hear her explode with anger, he headed his sleek black horse down the hill to John Granville and the three Indian men.

Spring felt her gray mare being turned about, and the two soldiers took positions on either side of her. They rode at a quickened pace, which made her side saddle stance difficult to hold on to. She was too angry to speak, and besides, she didn't know these men at all. So she continued to try to hold on to her balance as well as her composure as best she could under the circumstances.

Meanwhile, David "Whip" Saunders made his way leisurely down the hill slope to meet the group below, wondering what in the world Lieutenant Granville would have to discuss with these men, especially Black Claw, an old acquaintance of his. Black Claw was one man who was after what he could get for himself rather than what was best for his tribe as a whole.

Arriving, David saw that John eyed him warily, and his gaze darted furtively between David and Black Claw. David began conversing with Black Claw in the language of the Arapaho. He used no hand gestures. John had been forced to use his hands, along with some Indian words he'd picked up here and there.

David did not learn much from the conversation. Black Claw was a secretive man, and had been since David first met him. There was no love lost between them. He thought to himself that the Indian and Granville were quite a bit alike in some respects. They were both out for themselves. Finally, their conversation ended, and David turned to John.

"I think you are through here now, lieutenant. Let's head back to the fort."

John looked over at Black Claw, wondering if he had made his points clear enough to him earlier, and wondering what Saunders had said about him. He nodded his head in Black Claw's direction, and the warrior gave him a thin smile. Then suddenly, the Arapaho wheeled his horse around and left in a cloud of dust.

John turned in the opposite direction and saw that Whip was already halfway up the hill. He saw too that Spring was no longer sitting atop the hill; and immediately, his heart began to pound. He had been not a little embarrassed to have Whip come in on his talk with the Indian Black Claw, but now he could foresee that he would be undergoing further humiliation with the colonel if he didn't straighten all this out with Whip Saunders.

"Hey, Saunders, wait up," he called and kneed his horse to a faster pace. Catching up, he asked, "Where is Miss Ames?"

"I sent her back with an armed escort. I sure don't know where you get off dragging her way out here and then leaving her on top of that hill in plain view of whatever evil may be out here. I sure don't get your gall, mister."

David's hat was pulled low over his forehead, and it was a good thing, for if John Granville had been able to see his eyes, he would certainly be chilled to the bone, and even in fear of his life.

"Well, uh, I can explain everything, if only you'd give me a chance." John was having trouble swallowing.

"I'm waiting, Granville. And listen to me, it'd better be a reasonable explanation, because if it's not, I'll go straight to the colonel and have you court-martialed for all the ridiculous stunts you've been pulling lately."

"Listen, Saunders, I'm damn sick and tired of you always being on my back. What's the matter with you, anyway? Are you trying to make me look bad in front of Miss Ames so's you can have first crack at her?"

David's harsh laugh cut through the late afternoon air. Then he pushed his hat back on his very blond hair and stared at Granville. John was startled when he saw the blue eyes almost white with anger. "I'm still waiting for your explanation, Granville, and I want to hear it now."

"Well, all right." John tried to calm himself, but his hands tightened on the horse's reins. "We were riding along and talking, you see. She's a very interesting person. Well, surely, you can see that."

"I'm not interested in Miss Ames's attributes. Get on with it." David was rapidly getting fed up with this man. "We . . . we just got to talking, you know, and, uh, we rode out much farther than I anticipated . . . yes, that's what happened. We just rode farther than I thought. So, well . . . we, all of a sudden, came to that hill, and I saw those renegades down the slope, and I thought I better go down and make sure that they were friendly, see?"

"So you left her all alone unprotected? What kind of a fool do you take me for?" David snapped.

"Well, maybe I shouldn't have done that . . ."

"I should say you sure as hell shouldn't have!"

"It all turned out okay, though," John protested. "She was all right when you found her, wasn't she?"

"Yes, you lucky bastard. But I really gave you more credit for intelligence than you've ever shown, Granville. You are one stupid man," David bit out.

"Give me one more chance," pleaded John, against his will, for he hated this man who always came out ahead of the game.

"Please don't tell the colonel, and I swear, I'll try to do better."

David rode silently for a while. He glanced sideways at Granville and saw he was sweating profusely and breathing heavily. He didn't trust him at all.

"What did you and Black Claw talk about?" he asked, finally.

"Nothing, really. I just showed him my white kerchief as I rode down to him and told him I was out having a peaceful ride with my lady friend."

"He believed you?"

"Well, he didn't attack either one of us, as you can see. Listen, if you promise not to tell the colonel, I'll apologize to Miss Ames about my carelessness. What do you say?"

John was ashamed to be groveling to this man. He would show him, and it wouldn't be long before the colonel thought he was the best man at the fort, not this Whip Saunders.

"I won't promise I won't ever tell, Granville. But if there are any more slipups on your part, no matter how trivial, you've had it!" David replied, at last. Then urging his black mare forward, he left John Granville behind, seething.

*　　*　　*

"Spring, Davey is here to see you," Dr. Butler said outside of her bedroom door.

"I'm sorry, but I'm too busy doing my work for tomorrow's classes," Spring answered him absently, reading to herself from a book on arithmetic. "Besides, I don't have anything to say to him anyway. I don't want to see him." She closed the book and rubbed her tired eyes. She had been getting things ready for her first day of classes, which would be the next day. And she'd been furious with him for his presumptuous behavior of that afternoon, so she had tried to immerse herself in the only thing that would take her mind off that terrible man.

"Spring," came Mrs. Butler's voice, "politeness behooves you to present yourself to Mr. Saunders right now."

"Mrs. Butler, I cannot abide the sight of that man. You know that," protested Spring.

"Come out."

"Please don't make me." Mrs. Butler entered without being invited. She saw Spring's tired beautiful face and felt some degree of sympathy. But she also knew David Saunders very well and knew that he wouldn't come to see her charge unless he felt it was necessary. She said to Spring, "If you won't do it for politeness' sake or for me, my dear, you must think of your father and all that he owes to Davey."

"What could anyone possibly owe to that person?" Spring questioned, jumping up from her chair at the small desk under the one and only window in the room. "He does nothing but humiliate John."

"I'm not going to argue with you any longer, darling. You just must come and see what he wants." Louise Butler turned away and left the room.

Spring was indignant. She did not wish to be put in this position of seeing someone who was mean and less than human.

Yes, that was it—he was less than human in his behavior. But she was staying in the Butler household and knew she must comply with the wishes of her chaperones. She glanced in the mirror and saw that her usually neat appearance was awry this evening: her chestnut hair had many tendrils waving about her small face. Well, she certainly was not going to primp on his account. She swept from the room, into the front room, and there she saw the object of her frustration sitting casually in one of the Butlers' most comfortable chairs.

When David saw Spring enter the room, his heart began to beat a little faster, something he was totally unaccustomed to. But then he saw the anger written upon her delicate features, and he gained quick control of himself. He stood and faced her.

"Miss Ames."

"What do you want to see me about?" she asked without preamble.

"I just wanted to make sure my men got you back to the fort without any trouble and safely." His eyes narrowed at her tone of voice.

"Well, you can see that I am fine. I would have been fine even if you hadn't come along to 'help out.' John Granville was taking very good care of me, despite what you may think." She pushed away the thoughts of her nervousness that she'd experienced sitting at the hill that afternoon.

"Miss Ames, John Granville may very well have gotten you killed today if I hadn't come along," David said easily.

"Oh, yes," Spring said sarcastically, clenching her hands in the folds of her peach dress, "you were magnificent coming to the rescue. And do you know what else I think, Mr. Saunders?" she asked, ignoring the look Mrs. Butler gave her.

"No, but I'm sure you'll tell me, Spring." He spoke to her in gentleness, without any ire at all. She didn't realize that he'd again used her given name.

"I think you enjoy humiliating people, Mr. Saunders."

"Spring!" Mrs. Butler exclaimed in shock.

"She's just tired, Dave," Dr. Butler put in, taking a step forward. Spring waved him away.

"I may be tired, but my tiredness comes from Mr. Saunders meddling in my affairs." She turned on David again, moving closer to him. "You enjoy humiliating John Granville because he's a lieutenant and you're a nobody. You try to make fools out of people, including me, making me feel silly because of my parasol and insulting me because of my name." It hit her then that he had used her name, and it had sounded nice on his lips. She brushed that thought aside too.

David looked at her intently and folded his muscular arms across his large chest. His eyes, fringed by their long dark lashes, remained blue and earnest.

"Of course you are entitled to your opinion, Spring, but only foolish people can be made to feel humiliated, as in the case of the young lieutenant. As for you, it was never my intent to humiliate you.

However, if you felt that way, your foolishness only comes from your lack of understanding of our ways out west. It's too bad Granville cannot claim the same excuse."

Spring's green eyes blazed brightly, and two red spots of color filled her cheeks. She stomped past him in rage and stopped at the front door. Turning at the last moment, she looked at the Butlers. She tried to subdue her anger.

"I must get some air. It is far too stuffy in here. Mr. Saunders, my only answer to you is that you must feel a special need to hold yourself above others so that you gain, in your own eyes, some sense of importance, to make yourself appear better than others. That's fine, except that I want no part of it, and again, I ask that we no longer have any kind of conversation." Without waiting for a comment from him, she swept out of the door and into the dark night, hoping to rid herself of the memory of his eyes in his handsome face and the soft way he had said her name.

Inside, Mrs. Butler was truly upset with Spring's rudeness. She said to David, "I'm really sorry about that. She shouldn't have spoken to you in that manner. She is very young, but that is no excuse."

"Don't worry about it, dear lady. Spring, it seems, has a temper to go along with that reddish hair. What bothers me, if anything does, is her unwarranted championing of John Granville."

"She appears to like him and is comfortable with him," Mrs. Butter said. "It's almost like they already knew each other."

"Dave, do you think you are being too hard on that young man?" Dr. Butler asked.

"No, sir, I don't. I don't trust him, especially after today. When I saw him speaking to Black Claw, it made my skin crawl. However, I promised the man that I wouldn't go tell on him to the colonel, if he apologized to Spring. So I would appreciate it if this little talk tonight didn't go any farther than these four walls."

"Well, if you think that's best, then you have our word," the doctor replied.

"Thanks." Turning to Louise Butler, he went on, "I don't know if they know each other or not, or how they could, but of one thing

I am sure. I'm positive he hasn't shown her his true colors. I'll turn in for the night now." He gave them a rare smile and then left.

Meanwhile, Spring had stormed once around the inner walls of the fort before she slowed her step to a more ladylike gait. Coming back around to her own quarters, she was hailed by John Granville.

"Hello, Miss Ames. I'm so glad to see that you arrived back here with no trouble. I want to apologize to you for any hardship you have undergone."

"John, I thought we agreed you and I were on a first-name basis. And I did arrive back safely, no thanks to Mr. Saunders. I was perfectly fine waiting for you. But let's forget about that, shall we?"

John took Spring's arm and guided her around to the corner of the Butlers' building. He liked the silky feel of her dress and the scent of her hair wafted to his nostrils, urging him to speak of it further. He took both her hands in his after turning her to face him.

"I was a little lax in my responsibility toward you, Spring. I want you to know it will never happen again." He tilted her head back and looked into her lovely face and knew he must have her at all cost. "Please give me the chance to make it up to you."

"John, of course I forgive you. There's really nothing to forgive. You've always treated me like a lady, unlike some around here."

Knowing whom she referred to, John was happy to know she disliked Whip Saunders. That would make it easier for him. "I think you and I are lucky, Spring. We aren't exactly strangers, though we've just met face-to-face. I feel as though we know each other quite well from our letters. What I actually meant when I asked you to let me make it up to you was I really want to take care of you."

Spring was startled by his implication, and she stared up in the darkness, trying to discern his features. The moon was on her face, and he could see how tired she looked. He decided to press his advantage.

"I'm not sure what you mean, John."

"I fell in love with you the moment you got off the stage last Friday, and I've thought of nothing else but you and . . . and how I want you to marry me."

Taken aback, Spring looked away and detected a slight shadowed movement on the porch and knew without a doubt it was Whip Saunders. She became angry at his eavesdropping and continued nosing into her affairs. For some unknown reason, she felt she wanted to punish him, so she turned back to John. Rashly and without further thought, she blurted out, "Yes, John, I'll marry you."

He grabbed her shoulders and roughly pulled her to him in a harsh embrace. Being held tightly against him, she could scarcely breathe; and when his hard mouth came down upon hers, making her teeth bite into her warm lips, she felt she would suffocate. Dizzily, she remembered all the chaste, proper kisses she'd received from men in Boston, on the cheek or the forehead, even the hand, and was grateful for them. She also remembered the whispers of her friends in the dark at school. They had speculated over the mysteries of life as a woman married, and realized this was what they must have meant when they said that men had their way with their wives without any regard for their feelings.

John pulled away at last, and Spring was able to gulp in the cool evening air. "You've made me very happy, Spring. I'll go talk to your father right away."

"No, no, John, please don't. I don't think he would agree to anything quite yet. Give it a few weeks. I haven't told him we've been writing, and I think he'd be too shocked by a sudden proposal."

He stared down at her face, but she seemed determined. In order not to press his luck, he consented to wait two weeks.

"John, I must go in, or the Butlers will be getting worried about me. Besides, I must get up early in order to teach my first classes tomorrow."

"All right, my darling," he said, walking her onto the porch to the door. Spring half expected to find Whip Saunders lurking in the darkness, but the porch was empty. When John tried to kiss her again, Spring was ready, and at the last moment, turned her face so that he caught the corner of her mouth.

"Good night, John. See you tomorrow." She slipped through the doorway without waiting for a reply. Picking up the lantern on the nearest table, she carried it quietly to her bedroom, wondering whatever possessed her to give John Granville a positive answer to his proposal. She knew without thinking about it that it was to show that snooping Mr. Saunders that he had absolutely no control over her life despite what he might think.

Chapter 3

Monday began a rather vigorous schedule for Spring, which did not allow much time for wondering about her rash promise to John or the reasons behind it. She awoke early every morning to the awful sounds of whip cracking in the distance and knew that Mr. Saunders must be practicing his aim.

After breakfasting, she went to the designated building used as the schoolroom and met with her seven pupils for three hours of reading, writing, and arithmetic, with spelling and a little music at the piano for good measure. The four white children, three from Major Kimball's family and one from another lieutenant's family, did not like being in the same room with the little Indian children who were living with an Indian woman who worked in the kitchen and laundry to earn her keep.

They were not very well kept—their hair hung in clumps and their bodies were noticeably unwashed. They sat huddled together when Spring allowed them to and the four other children would not go near them unless Spring asked one or two of the older ones to work with them on their handwriting or spelling. They did so, but extremely unwillingly. Spring felt that there could have been complaints about her forcing the two groups together if she was not the colonel's daughter. So she used it to her advantage, in that she was able to give each child more individual attention for their particular needs, while the others at their seats either worked alone on a certain subject or an older one helped a younger one.

When school was over for the day, Spring lunched with either her father or the Butlers and then retired to her room for the nap she now looked forward to each afternoon. After the hour or so was up, she went to her father's office to copy his illegible notes into her nice, neat schoolmistress hand. Many people came and went during the times she spent in a corner by the window. Most often, she was not even noticed; so quiet was she. Sometimes she wrote letters to senators, or even the president, as the colonel dictated them. It was an interesting job.

At about four in the afternoon, she would either go with Mrs. Butler to visit one of the few other ladies present at the fort and do some needlepoint, or she would spend an hour at the piano practicing songs she had committed to memory years ago.

Every day was full, and she fell asleep instantly each night. She walked a few times with John after dinner before retiring, with the excuse that she had to get her plans set for the next day's school work. She had to constantly stay out of his reach, and when this was impossible, she tried to fend off his aggressive advances as politely as possible.

Finally, one night, standing in the moonlight where he'd first proposed, she had to tell him that she wanted to be as discreet as they could, at least until her father was told of their intentions; and since that wouldn't be for a while yet, she didn't want the news to reach his ears by another source other than themselves. And that could happen very easily if they were seen by others. "I especially don't want my father told by Mr. Saunders. I'm sure you don't want that either," she ended.

"No, you are right about that. You're just so beautiful, but you are right. I'll try to behave myself. I have a small token of esteem for you that I hope you'll wear in honor of our promise to each other." He handed her a small package, which she opened with trembling fingers. Inside she found a thin, delicate gold ankle bracelet.

"It's lovely, John," she said. "But you shouldn't have."

"Just to remind you of your promise. Here, let me put it on, and I'll be happy to wait for your kisses until we tell your father."

She hesitated and then consented.

He knelt, and she felt his cold fingers on her ankle as he fastened the clasp. His fingers lingered a trifle longer than necessary. When he stood, he enfolded her gently in his arms.

"I love you, Spring," he told her softly.

Because of the way he held her and spoke to her, she thought for the first time that it would be all right to marry John Granville. "I'll remember my promise," she assured him. "I . . . I love you too." Again, shadowy eyes watched and ears heard.

At the beginning of the next week, Joshua Kimball, the ten-year-old son of the major, was giving Spring a very hard time about working with a six-year-old Indian called Two Stone.

"I just can't, Miss Ames," Joshua protested for the third time.

"It would help Two Stone very much, if you would."

"But . . . but . . . he stinks. Worse 'n usual, Miss Ames." Joshua screwed up his nose in distaste.

Spring arose from the table and went over where the three little ones sat. A very strange odor permeated the air around all of them. Well, if no one else was going to take care of this situation, she was going to have to give it a try. She motioned for them all to stay seated, and she went outside.

Seeing two privates nearby, she asked them to bring a tub of water and towels to the outside of the door of the schoolroom. They looked at her strangely but asked no questions.

In ten minutes, Spring was told that the tub was ready.

She gave the officers' children books to read, and then she gathered up the three odor-ridden Indians and took them outside. She saw that the privates had guessed what she was up to, for along with the tub of water was a thick bar of lye soap.

Without ceremony, she stripped the seven-year-old girl, lifted her up, and gently put her into the water.

Spring rolled up the sleeves of her white blouse and knelt beside the tub. As she was giving the girl a good washing, she talked to her softly and smiled her sweet smile. The girl was docile, and only clung to the sides of the tub when Spring pushed her back into the water to wet her hair. When she was through, Spring toweled her dry and had her dress. Then she repeated the undressing of the two small boys.

Two Stone's eyes were wary and watched every movement Spring made on his partner in the water. When he was out and dried, Spring began on Two Stone. Meanwhile, quite a crowd had gathered to watch the cleansing. Spring paid them no mind but continued on her mission, knowing that if the problem were not solved, she would get no teaching done.

Speaking to Two Stone, Spring finished the main washing and then began to take the boy back into the water for the washing of his thick, greasy hair, and that was when he let out a bloodcurdling scream that rent the air and caused Spring to draw back in alarm.

The boy's black eyes were wide with terror, and he grabbed hold of Spring's arms with a strength that a person half his age would not possess. He continued to scream in a haunted way that brought many more spectators out to see what all the noise was about, among them Whip Saunders.

Spring did not see him, for all her attention was focused on Two Stone as she tried desperately to calm him, though she was beginning to lose her patience at his obstinacy.

Suddenly, as she again pushed him back, he reached up and grabbed her abundant hair in his now-clean hands and pulled her with all his might, and she found herself falling almost headfirst into the tub with him. Water, being kicked and splashed around, cascaded onto her back and literally drenched her.

All at once, the hands released her hair, and she was able to sit back on her legs. She saw the person who came to help her and was chagrined to see David Saunders standing above her, holding Two Stone's hands.

"Step aside, Spring," came his deep voice. It commanded immediate obedience.

She stood and dried her hands on her dark-blue skirt and then tried to rearrange her disarrayed hair as she watched David kneel down beside the tub.

He started to talk to the obviously frightened boy in smooth, even tones, in a language Spring couldn't begin to comprehend. She noticed her father out in the crowd and was embarrassed to have brought this attention to herself and the child. Then her eyes were brought back to the tub, and it was as if by magic the boy's face and body relaxed, and he lay back in David Saunders's arms as David took the soap and gently washed the boy's hair. All the while, he spoke in an easy manner and the boy was able to smile up at him when his ordeal was over.

"I guess I must thank you again for helping me out," Spring said grudgingly, standing close beside David so no one else could hear.

He ignored her for a moment and said to the crowd still standing around, watching the scene, "The party is over, folks. Go back to your business."

"This was not a party, Mr. Saunders. I wasn't doing this to embarrass the children, as you might have done." Spring shaded her yellow-specked green eyes with her hand and looked up into his face.

"Oh, I'm sure you had a good reason," he said dryly.

"I couldn't work with them smelling the way they did. If their mother can't keep them clean, then for the good of the school and the other children, I have to take things into my own hands." He gave her a tight smile and took her elbow, not too gently, and guided her up the steps into the schoolroom. The others, who hadn't been able to resist the sounds from outside, were dismissed for the day; and now the room was empty.

"So the little savage renegades smelled, did they?" he asked.

"Yes, they did," she answered, pulling her arm from his grasp. "The other pupils didn't want to be near them. I had to do something." She drew herself up taller and faced him. Her blouse and skirt were damp and crumpled; her hair was falling out of its pins and hung in her face. He thought he had never seen a more desirable woman than at this moment.

She discerned his personal look, and her face blazed with color. "And," she went on hotly, "I don't think of them as savages or renegades."

"Well, if you don't, then you are the first Easterner who doesn't, with few exceptions. In fact, I know for a fact that your John Granville thinks so." He looked at her closely, and her eyes wavered.

"We're not discussing what he thinks at the moment," she replied, brushing her hair away from her cheeks. She moved away from him. "For your information, Mr. Saunders, I am not one who believes everything that is written. I am well aware of what news reporters have said about the Indian, and I personally don't believe all they have written, nor do I believe all the accounts written about how well the white man has treated them."

"Ah, there is a brain in that pretty head of yours, is there?" David asked, raising an eyebrow.

"Of course. Just because I'm a woman doesn't mean I don't have a brain," she snapped.

He let out a low, mirth-filled laugh that reached the corners of the room out from between his even white teeth. "You are right, Spring. So tell me, what do you think of the Indian?" He stuck his hands in his pockets and awaited her answer.

"I think of them as people, with certain needs and wants just like everyone else. There are bad ones and good ones alike. There is even some of each in them. Just like you, Mr. Saunders. I'm sure there is even good in you, if one took long enough to look for it."

David threw back his head and roared with laughter. "But as I said, Spring, there's an exception to everything. Perhaps I'm the exception."

"What's going on in here?" John entered the room just then and took in David's laughter-filled face and Spring's disheveled appearance. "You've been here alone long enough." He'd been kept outside talking to the colonel about matters they had previously discussed. He suspected he'd been kept purposefully.

"Nothing, John. We were just talking about the children." She turned back to David. "Well, thank you again, Mr. Saunders, for the help."

"What I wanted to tell you, Spring, was that Two Stone saw his mother drowned by some army soldiers a year ago, and that is what made him so afraid to go under the water."

Spring's face reflected the shock that went through her, and her slim hand rose to her mouth. "Oh my, I didn't know. I'm sorry."

"One less worthless Indian around," John put in.

"Yes, those without brains would think so. Isn't that correct, Spring?" David's blue eyes turned on her. She was still thinking of poor little Two Stone and the terrible fright she'd caused him. On the fringes of her thoughts, she realized John had said a thing that went against her honor. She also realized Mr. Saunders had asked her a question that would make her side with him against John. He had said her name in that soft, deep way again too. She shook her head and brought her gaze to his.

"Mr. Saunders, I have not given you the right to call me by my given name. After all, friends call each other by their first names, and we, to be truthful, are not friends, and not likely to be. Come along, John." She held out her hand to him, and John, giving David a smug look as they passed him, squeezed it tightly. He had won that little skirmish.

The next morning, when Spring awoke, something seemed not quite right. She lay there under the light sheet and blanket in the morning stillness. Yes, that was it, the stillness.

There was no constant cracking of that infernal whip. She thought that it was indeed strange that something so evil as that whip and what it could mean could become so much a part of one's life. And when it was no longer there, one missed it. Well, the sound of it anyway.

Dressing, she thought again of little Two Stone and the drowning of his mother. She would have to do something today to make it all up to him for frightening him so. She knew what it meant to be frightened of water.

But when she got to the classroom a while later, Two Stone approached her hesitantly and presented her with a nondescript wildflower. Afterward, he was so overcome with shyness that he scrambled back to his chair and hid his face.

Spring took out one of the pins in her hair and stuck the flower's stem into her curls and repinned it. Then she came to Two Stone.

"Two Stone," she said to the bowed head, "I want to thank you for the lovely flower. See how pretty it is in my hair?" She lifted his chin to look up, and she turned her head to its best advantage so he could see his gift in its new resting place. He gave a small smile.

The girl, Half Moon, gave him a nudge with her elbow.

Again with the elbow. Two Stone began to open his mouth and then ducked his head once more.

"What is it?" Spring asked.

"Two Stone says he is . . . is . . . sor . . . sor . . ." And then Half Moon uttered a word Spring didn't understand.

"Oh, he says he is sorry." Spring raised her eyebrows, and her forehead wrinkled in surprise. "Well, it is I who is sorry. I didn't mean to frighten you yesterday in the water. I hope we can be friends." She patted his head, and he glanced up at her with a big grin. Spring smiled in return and started the class work for the day.

As she began walking to her father's quarters after school for luncheon, she noticed that there seemed to be fewer men around and about the fort. She wondered if there was a specific reason for this.

Upon entering his office, she found her father busy with his mound of papers and maps, puffing on his pipe. She asked him about it.

He looked up at her and thought again of how lucky he was to have her out here, not only for her help, but for the beauty she lent to a drab existence.

"I gave several troops a furlough for a week in Morgan's Hill. Then I sent out a band of men to try to find two deserters who left sometime yesterday morning, probably during the little ruckus you had going with the children." He tempered his accusation with a wide grin, so she knew she really hadn't angered him.

"Did John go with them?" she asked.

"Yes, he went along with Dave. He's the best tracker around these parts and knows the Indian like the back of his hand. Two or three others went along as well. I didn't pick them out. John did that. This is the second time for these two fellows." He bit on his pipe for a moment and then asked, "Are you becoming enamored with John, Spring?"

Spring lowered her eyes momentarily, thinking of the hesitant words she'd spoken to John earlier, and then looked her father squarely in the face and answered truthfully.

"If you mean, am I in love with him, no, I am not. However, I . . . I . . . find him interesting."

"I hope not too interesting, dear. I would hope for something better for you."

"Father, he has been very nice and attentive to me, and I like him. That could lead to . . . something."

She felt guilty for not coming right out with the fact that she had consented to marry him. So she said, "Father, we . . . we have had correspondence since you telegraphed asking me to go to his grandfather's funeral. He wrote to thank me, and we've been writing ever since."

He raised his thick eyebrows at her. "There are much better men around here, darling girl. Much more trustworthy, loyal, and intelligent." He rose from the desk and came around to offer his arm to her. They proceeded to the Butlers.

"Well, if you are thinking of Mr. Saunders—" she began.

"Now that you mention it, yes, he does fit the description I just gave," he replied.

"Father, I find that man despicable, uncaring, rude beyond belief, and . . . and . . . a busybody!" Spring exclaimed as they entered next door.

"Ah, you must be talking about Dave," Dr. Butler said.

"You see, Father? Even Dr. Butler knows from my description to whom I am referring," Spring said with satisfaction.

"To the contrary, my dear," Dr. Butler said with a smile. "It's just that you are the only one I have ever heard speak of him in that manner. It is certainly not what I or Mrs. Butler think of him."

"You will all grant me the right to an opinion?" Spring asked sweetly, her cheeks dimpling, anxious to get on to other subjects.

"Yes, Spring," replied Father. "Even if you are wrong, you are entitled to your opinion." He mentally kicked himself for perhaps putting into motion a situation between John and Spring that he would have to stop.

Chapter 4

The next few days were peaceful and quiet for Spring. The situation in her classroom had improved. The children worked better together, and the Indian pupils came each day more presentable than before.

The afternoons and evenings were restful. Spring, though, felt herself looking for Mr. Saunders over her shoulder at times. He had always appeared when she least expected it, and to tell the truth, though she hated to admit it, she wondered where he was and what he was doing. She caught herself listening for the sound of that snapping whip—listening for that sound that would tell her he had returned.

She missed her walks after supper with John, but she did not miss his constant pursuit of her. Though he tried to keep away from her, when he did kiss her, she always received the rough handling with revulsion and remembered his one moment of gentleness with her. She asked herself why it couldn't be that way all the time between men and women.

At the end of the week, Spring was busy sitting in her father's office by the window at one side of the room, transcribing notes that had been written up several years ago about the Sandy Creek massacre. She was appalled at what had happened to the peaceful villages of the Arapaho and Cheyenne. The account she read described how a large army force in Colorado had ambushed and killed warriors, women, and children. The attack was unprovoked. Spring's heart ached for those people who were being driven from their lands at the hands of so-called civilized people. She thought the written account must be true, as it was signed by an army officer and an eyewitness.

She was so engrossed in what she was doing that she at first did not notice the commotion that began in the center court of the fort. Voices started to raise, and the hoof beats of several horses finally drew her attention to the happenings at hand rather than in 1864.

She glanced out the window and saw Whip Saunders on his shining black horse walking slowly to the post in the very center of the fort. Tied by ropes on their wrists, two soldiers walked behind him, if one could call their stumbling and jerking motions walking. There was John, and the others who had gone in pursuit of the way-ward soldiers, following.

They all dismounted and gathered in a small circle at the post.

As usual, something of this nature caused a crowd to gather without invitation. Spring could see her father walking briskly to Mr. Saunders to confer with him briefly. It seemed as if her father issued some orders, for the men were tied to the post. They could scarcely remain standing, and if their hands had not been tied to the post above their heads, they would have fallen to the dust-covered ground.

Before she knew it, Spring rose to her satin-slippered feet and ran outside to join the crowd. As she drew nearer the center, she saw that Mr. Saunders was uncoiling his evil lash, and Spring knew without asking questions what he intended to do with it.

She heard above the din of the crowd one of the soldiers begging for mercy while the other opposite just sagged against the post, tears streaming down his cheeks.

She reached the colonel's side as David stepped back the necessary steps in order to execute the punishment the deeds of these two soldiers warranted. She grabbed hold of her father's hand tightly.

"Father, you cannot allow this to happen. Please don't let Mr. Saunders whip those men. Can't you see they've been punished enough?"

Colonel Ames looked down at Spring's earnest face and would have liked to relent. He said to her quietly, "This is none of your business, Spring. Stay out of this." Then he extricated himself from her grasp and took several steps forward, until he stood by the post. He said in a loud voice so all could hear, "As you know, ladies and gentlemen, the punishment at this fort for desertion is to receive ten strokes of the whip for a second offense. As these men have committed this crime against the fort and its inhabitants for the second time, I now command Dave Saunders to administer their just punishment. Please remember"—and he looked straight at Spring—"this was taken out of my and your hands the moment these two men took their unauthorized leave. Dave, merit their chastisement."

Spring shuddered inside and without thinking, as David raised the whip high over his blond head, she raced to his side and grabbed hold of the offending arm. He gazed down in surprise.

"You can't do this, Mr. Saunders! It is cruel and not necessary. I'm sure these men have learned their lesson without you using the whip on them." She felt her hands being pried off his thick, muscular arm. He looked at her in sympathy, and then duty reasserted itself in his mind.

The blue eyes turned to ice, and she shivered in the warm afternoon sun. His fingers remained clasped around hers, and he squeezed them hard.

"Spring," he said in a coldly dead voice, very low and only for her ears, "you don't know what you are talking about. Go to your quarters." He loosened her hand and raised his arm again.

Spring was outraged by this scene. Maybe it was because she had just finished reading about the massacre and the uncivility of men. Maybe it was because of her feelings against this man. She didn't really know and had no time to analyze it in her own mind. She did know that she believed in kindness and mercy to others. She stepped forward and pushed him with all her strength, using both hands, as he extended the lash to the back of the closest man. The aim fell short, and David turned on her with fierce anger. Disregarding those around them, and John, who had come forward, David Saunders grabbed Spring in a viselike grip on her upper arms. He pulled her up on her toes and said into her face, "Get the hell out of here, or I'll use the whip on you! We have rules for civilians too, you know." He set her free, and she stumbled back into John's arms.

"You are a beast, Mr. Saunders. You're cruel and mean, and the fact that you seem to enjoy this humiliation of these men makes you all the more despicable." Only then did she notice her father standing next to them. The look he gave her was not that of a father but that of a commanding officer.

"Miss Ames," he said quietly, "Mr. Saunders would be well within his rights if he took the lash to you for interfering with his duties in the disciplining of these deserters. Now, I want you to stop making a spectacle of yourself and go to your quarters. Lieutenant Granville, please see that she gets there."

Spring's eyes blurred with unshed tears. "You are no better than he is, Father," she replied, and turning on her heel, she stormed across the courtyard. John had trouble in keeping up with her. She entered the front room, slamming the door behind her, leaving John on the front porch. Already, she could hear the whip cracking against flesh and the pitiful cries of the recipients. In her bedroom, she threw herself onto her bed and covered her head with the pillow. How could she have missed that sound all week? She knew she never wanted to hear it again.

Not only did Spring refuse to see John, Dr. Butler, and Mr. Saunders that afternoon, but she also refused to see and speak to her father. Mrs. Butler did not listen to any of her excuses but came into her room regardless of what Spring said. She lay on her bed, pleading a sick headache, and declined her dinner. How she longed for the pleasantries of Boston, the social events she so enjoyed, her many friends, her job as governess in prestigious homes.

Here in the Colorado territory, inside the fort, she felt trapped and unable to try her wings and be free. She was boxed in by her schedules, rules she didn't understand or want to understand, and by the mere fact of not being allowed to leave the four walls of the fort. It made for a very closed-in feeling within her.

The next several days, she kept to herself, speaking only when spoken to when she was out to church services or when working in her father's office or at the school. She had been completely embarrassed by what had happened to her before everyone at the fort. Her father was to blame for that, and so was that man. With such intensity did she dislike David Saunders that she was somewhat frightened by it. She blamed him for the rift that had now been created between her father and herself.

Strangely enough, her father seemed to have forgotten the incident and John, nor did the Butlers bring it up to her in any way. They were all back to their normal routines almost immediately. The colonel was particularly preoccupied with a special mission he was to ride on, taking many of the men with him; and he was getting all his papers and materials ready for that. John also seemed to be thinking more about other matters than Spring at the time, spending much time away from the fort.

So Spring felt able to wallow in the misery of her circumstances. However, her mind was not at rest, for she was beginning to form a plan of her own. She hoped to go to Denver soon, to live and perhaps take up some semblance of the same life she'd had back in Boston. All her inheritance had been transferred to a bank there. All that was left to do was find some way to get there.

Colonel Ames left in the middle of the week with a long column of soldiers behind him. He had absently kissed Spring good-bye and patted her on the shoulder, saying he would be back the next week. John was remaining at the fort, and Mr. Saunders was given several days' furlough. Life at the fort that day seemed boring and quiet.

*   *   *

Spring awoke with a start. What was it that awakened her? Everywhere there was silence—dark, velvet silence. She lay on her bed, straining her ears, but could hear nothing. She had no idea what time it was, but she knew it must be early morning. She had slept for quite a while.

There it was again, a soft scuffling and a thud. Her head jerked toward her door, and she dimly saw it was opening slowly. She could not see who was on the other side.

"Who is it?" she inquired. "Mrs. Butler, is something wrong?"

The door then burst open and swung back on its hinges, hitting the wall with a loud bang. Spring could not recognize who had entered the room, but she pulled herself up on the bed, clutching the bedclothes around her. She opened her mouth to scream when a rough hand was clamped over it, smothering any sounds in her throat. She frantically reached up to grab the hands away and felt long hair, for now her attacker was leaning over the bed. Heart racing madly, she clawed at the figure above her. She felt skin beneath her nails and knew she'd drawn blood. A man's voice let out a low growl, and he let go of her.

"Get out of here! Leave me alone!" she managed to beg, but she was pounced upon again, this time by the shoulders and dragged across the bed. Her white cotton nightgown tore at one shoulder. What was happening to her? Wild thoughts raced through her muddled head. She was brought against the man's chest, and the frightened Spring discerned beads and a bare chest. *Oh my God*, she cried in her mind, *we're being attacked by Indians!* She let out a bloodcurdling scream as she realized there was no one coming to her rescue. She remembered there were fewer men at the fort, but surely . . . Spring's head snapped back as a stinging blow fell on her face. Her hair, now wild about her head and streaming down her back, was seized in a tight fist, and she thought her head would break right off her slim neck, for the Indian was pulling it back as far as it would go.

He muttered to her, but she didn't comprehend his words. He seemed to be trying to tell or explain something to her. Now her feet were touching the floor, and she used the opportunity to kick his bare shin and push with all her might.

His hold slackened, and she turned to run. She got as far as the door when a hardened fist met her face again, and with a whimper, she sagged to the floor.

*   *   *

Spring did not know how long she had been lying huddled on the dust-filled buffalo skins in the hot tepee. She did know that it must be in the late afternoon, for the heat inside was unbearable. Someone, a young woman, had brought her some ground meal in a bowl earlier, but Spring could not bring herself to partake of it. The lace on her nightgown was torn around the neck, and one sleeve hung by a few threads at one shoulder. Her face was tender to the touch, and she could feel that one eye was closed completely by the swelling. She did not know where she was or what would become of her; but so far, she'd been left totally alone, and she was grateful for that much.

In the distance, she heard horses approaching; and then a moment later, there was a discussion outside of the tepee. She could not understand what was being said, and the sounds were being muffled by the flap at the front. She felt, rather than saw, the front opening become wider, and light streamed into the interior. She buried her head into the smelly robes and awaited her fate, heart pounding in her ears.

She heard soft footsteps come over to her, and a person knelt down beside her. Spring could not bring herself to look up. Her heart beat wildly, and her whole body shook.

"Spring, are you all right?" The voice was familiar, soft, and deep. Though it was not a voice she had responded to in the past, it was the voice of one whom she could've expected to show up. And he was welcome.

She raised her aching head and saw David through a curtain of tangled chestnut hair. He was peering down at her with sincere concern, reaching out his hand to brush her matted hair away from her face. Touching her eye gingerly, he asked, "Are you hurt anywhere else?"

Spring mutely shook her head, and rising on her knees, she fell against him. He caught her slim body in his arms and held her. Why didn't she talk to him? He saw her injury and thought it would not prevent her from speaking, but she was shaking uncontrollably, and his hold on her tightened.

"Don't worry," he said, "we'll be out of here in a bit. Can you stand?"

Without answering, she stood up, still clinging to his arm.

She looked small and vulnerable. He helped her outside, and together they went directly to his black mare, Aphrodite. Spring did not look around her, for she was afraid of what she might see. She was no longer as frightened in Mr. Saunders's care, for even if she did not like the man, she did respect him for his know-how and was glad for his coming to rescue her. She wondered why John had not come for her. He had been at the fort. Why hadn't he protected her at the time of her abduction?

Raised voices finally brought her attention to the scene around her. Mr. Saunders was arguing with a tall Indian, whose skin was not a lot darker than David's. He looked vaguely familiar to her; but in her fog of the moment, she did not try to figure out why. Another, older, man stood between the two younger men, and it was obvious he was the man in charge for he spoke roughly to the Indian, who, after a few uttered words and hand gestures in David's direction, turned on his heel and left to take up a position a short distance away. David then shook hands with the Chief and returned to Spring's side.

"I have only Aphrodite, so you will have to ride with me. I trust you will allow that?"

Spring only nodded her head instead of coming out with her usual barb, and David looked at her closely. Her one open green eye did not have its natural healthy sparkle, and it worried him. This whole experience had taken its toll on her, he knew; and if she did not give in to it or show some kind of emotion, it might scar her for life.

He placed his hands about her slim waist, feeling through the thin cotton of her garb the shapeliness of her feminine figure. It did not take much effort to lift her onto the saddle. He was about to climb up behind her when a female voice attracted his attention.

"Pale Eyes?" came the soft sound. He turned and saw a beautiful young woman, hair as black as midnight, running up behind him. Spring also turned at the sound and witnessed a very fond embrace between the two. She was surprised to feel resentment steal its way into her heart and did not want to see this greeting, especially when David lowered his head and kissed the young maiden deeply. But she couldn't turn her face away. The girl laughed up at him, show-ing even white teeth, and then she spoke. Again, Spring could not understand.

Then she noticed a small child in her arms, and it was offered to David for an inspection. He took the child in his big arms, cradling it gently. It had very light hair for an Indian, and its eyes were not brown but gray. David kissed the child and said a few words to the woman and handed back the child. Then he turned and climbed into the saddle behind Spring, placing his arms around her. As they started off, another shout stopped them, and Spring was astounded to look down and see Two Stone's big brown eyes staring up into hers.

It was the sight of the dear little boy that finally brought her to her senses. He held up to her a bright-green feather and gave her a grin that stretched from ear to ear.

"Hello, Two Stone," Spring said in a low voice. "Thank you for this gift. Are you staying here?" She used some hand gestures she'd learned in the schoolroom.

"Yes, Teacher. I stay, you go with Pale Eyes. He nice Pale Eyes." He waved his hand to the distance. "I like Teacher. ABC."

Tears welled up in Spring's eyes, and she brushed her mass of hair back from her face. Horror filled Two Stone's expression, and it was a few seconds before Spring realized her injuries must be the cause of it.

"Oh, I just hurt my eye. It's all right," she said. "Well, we must go. Bye, Two Stone. Stay well. Be good."

"Bye, Teacher," he replied, and then turning, he ran back to the woman who had cared for him at the fort. Spring had been unaware they had been brought here too. She gave him a wave, and it was returned.

Then, tiredly, she leaned against Mr. Saunders's massive chest, resting her aching head on his shoulder. They met one other man, waiting outside the village for David. No introductions were made, which was fine with Spring, for she was not up to being social.

They rode swiftly for several miles, and in silence. Slowly, Spring came to realize she was not dressed properly, that her white gown was hiked up to her knees and thin enough to be ineffectual. She rode sidesaddle, thanking David to herself for placing her that way on the horse. She wondered briefly if he had done that on purpose.

Off in the distance stood a lone tree, and as they came nearer, several more horsemen came into view. The three on the two horses made for the tree, and on arriving, greetings were exchanged.

The men climbed down to stretch, and David turned to Spring. "Do you wish to get down for a bit? We're going to be doing some hard riding before we bed down for the night. This will be your last chance."

"Aren't we going to the fort?" she asked David.

"No, we aren't. Are you getting down?"

"Yes."

He reached up to her waist, and when he pulled her off the horse, she fell against him; and for the second time, she was aware she was so very scantily dressed, covered by a torn nightie without a stitch on underneath. She drew away sharply and asked, "Why aren't you taking me back to the fort?"

He looked at her intently, the light-blue eyes wavering slightly. He did not know if she was ready for the truth. He did not want a hysterical woman on his hands right at the moment, if at all. She looked up into his face defiantly. "You don't have to be afraid to tell me, Mr. Saunders," she said, wrapping her arms about herself, trying to cover up as best she could. She could feel the stares of the other men behind her. "I won't faint or throw a tantrum."

He heaved a sigh. "Spring, there is no one left at the fort."

"What? How can that be? There has to be. John has to be there. Dr. and Mrs. Butler have to be there. My . . . my father is coming back there. They'll all be worried if I don't come back. Why won't you take me back?" All this was said with urgency.

"Spring," David took her by the elbow and walked with her to the other side of the tree so they could have some semblance of privacy. "The Indians, Arapahos, are the ones who came and took you away. The only others they took were the Indian children and the squaw."

"Well, then there should be the others left at the fort. I demand to be taken back there now."

David brushed his thick hair back from his forehead, a gesture that in the future would become familiar to Spring. "I told you there was no one there."

"What happened to them, then?" she queried, not really expecting the hard truth he now gave her.

"Some of the soldiers escaped. You are aware there was not a full detail left at the fort after your father left?" She nodded, mutely. "Those who put up a fight were either injured or killed. Dr. Butler was killed out in the court. When I arrived at the fort, about noon, everything had been ransacked. Bodies were lying all around. I . . . I found Mrs. Butler lying outside your bedroom door. She had tried to keep the Indian Black Claw away from you. She was alive when I got to her. She managed to keep herself going, until help came, though I don't know how she did it. She gave me what information she could for your rescue. She told me what happened to you. There had been no warning of the impending attack on the fort. It was a complete surprise."

He stopped to gaze at the young woman to see how his words were affecting her, but she stood straight-backed, arms wrapped about herself, staring out over the yellow prairie. "She . . . she died in my arms, begging me to find you and take care of you, because you know so little about the life out here. I liked her very much. She was a strong woman, and she was good to me." He stopped again. Spring said nothing. "I'm sorry. I know you cared about her."

Spring turned to him and said dully, "You don't know anything about me, Mr. Saunders. Well, what about my father? Surely, you are going to take me to him?"

David dug his hands into his pockets. She was taking everything so calmly. Was she really hearing all that he was saying? Her back to him again, he saw a proud young woman, disheveled though she was with torn gown, straggling hair, and bare feet. How strong was she?

"Well?" she asked.

He decided the best way was to come out with it and be done with it. Out of the corner of his eye, he saw Henry, the man who had waited outside the Indians' camp for him, signaling they must be on their way. David cleared his throat. "The Indians came upon them yesterday afternoon. Your father is dead."

"I don't believe you! I just found him again. He can't be dead!" she burst out.

Over her shoulder, she heard Henry say, "It's true, ma'am. I saw him myself. Besides, Dave would never lie to you about something like that."

Spring put her hands over her face. She swayed momentarily and then caught her balance. How could everyone she ever loved be dead in so short a time? There was no one in the world for her. She took some deep breaths, feeling David standing close to her. She stepped away and looked up at him. "Where's John? He was at the fort."

"That's a good question, Spring. No one's seen him since late yesterday afternoon. You didn't see him, did you?" Oddly enough, he hoped she had. Otherwise, all his suspicions would very well be unfounded.

"No," came her simple reply. "Where do you think he could be? Is he . . . is he dead, too?"

"He hasn't been found anywhere," David answered. He hesitated, and then said, "I think he was the cause of all this."

Spring's emotions finally snapped. "How dare you say such a horrible thing? John would no more do any of this than I would."

"I never trusted that man, Spring, and neither should've you. Your own father . . ." His words were met with a flying small fist hitting his stomach.

"No, stop! Don't speak of my father. You aren't worthy to even speak his name. As for John, you . . . you . . . aren't fit to wipe his boots!"

David grabbed her wrist, and now she saw his blue eyes turn to ice and his mouth tighten in a cruel line. "You know nothing of this man," he began.

Spring lashed out with her free hand, catching his cheek in a stinging blow. The sound cracked in the silence, and she was appalled by her own actions.

David seized her other wrist and now squeezed both in a vise-like grip. He pulled her close, wrapping her tightly in his arms, keeping her arms and hands captive. He felt the curve of her soft back beneath his hands, and it was almost as if she had nothing on; the gown was so thin in his rough hands. "You can't ever do that again, do you hear me? No woman has ever gotten away with it before, and don't think you will, if you try it again."

She gazed up at him with contempt. He marveled at her tenacity and realized she was not the simpering type of woman from the East he knew about from the past. He had to give her that much credit, especially under these trying circumstances.

"Well, I won't be around long enough, will I? You are going to take me to Denver, at least. I have money there and can well take care of myself," she hissed through her teeth.

She squirmed in his hold, but seeing the change come over his features when she did, she blushed hotly and remained still, except to peer up at him. His eyes, however, were still ice filled and his look was hard.

"We're going to Denver for one night before heading up the mountains to my home. But I'm not leaving you there. I'm taking you with me, as I promised Mrs. Butler." He let her go then and turned to walk to Aphrodite, who nickered softly at his approach.

"I'll run away from you. You can't make me stay where I don't want to. I'll get away from you in Denver, and if not there, sometime I'll get away." Her voice began to quaver, so she stopped speaking, not wanting to give in to the fear that was at last taking over.

David whirled back on her, and his look caused her body to shake as well. He spoke in a soft but deadly voice. "Don't even try it, Miss Ames. In fact, don't even entertain the thought."

In two strides, he was by her side and, taking her roughly in his arms, set her atop Aphrodite. Then he mounted the horse himself, and they all rode off to the southwest in the beginning dusk of evening.

Chapter 5

The next three days proved to be difficult ones for Spring. She endured riding next to David Saunders with dignity showing on the outside, but shamed beyond words on the inside.

He had to hold on to her so that she wouldn't fall off the horse, but in his holdings, she knew he could not miss the almost-nakedness of her. He did not take advantage of this, but her upbringing had taught her nice women never let a man see their legs above the ankle; and here she was, day after awful, hot day, with her legs bare to the knees, as the constant jouncing on horseback caused her gown to creep ever upward. She was forced to perform her daily ablutions within very near proximity of him and the other five who rode with them. She was not allowed to go far—not that she wanted to, for she had no shoes, and there were snakes and all manner of vermin out in the tall yellow prairie grasses. David always came with her and stood guard, watching for anything that might prove harmful, though he was gracious enough, she noticed, to turn his back.

Once, over particularly rough terrain, she had slipped forward, almost losing her balance to fall headlong onto the ground below. But David had made a quick grab for her, his hand taking hold of her breast. When she turned on him angrily for his impropriety, he only laughed and asked if she had rather taken a spill.

Saved again by Mr. Saunders. Would she ever be rid of him and the knowledge that she owed him her life?

She did not talk much to him, and listened less to the conversations between him and the others—Henry, Joe, Hap, BJ, and Jack. Once introduced to them, she kept herself and her thoughts from them. Riding in the hot sun caused great sleepiness. She let herself drift in and out of sleep, lying lazily in David's big arms, trying not to think of Aunt Emma, Mrs. Butler, her father, and John. She did not like to think of being alone in the world; she preferred to think of those at the fort as being alive and well, and that she would be seeing them one day soon.

The only serious thinking she did was about how she could leave Mr. Saunders once they reached Denver. He did not tell her where they would be staying, but she was determined to leave him and perhaps find John. Surely, he would come to her rescue in the end. After all, no one had seen that he was dead.

Nights were the worst of all. She was completely unaccustomed to cooking, much less on an open campfire; and so each evening, she sat and watched Hap working with the staples he'd brought for food. There was jerky, flour-and-water biscuits, very strong coffee—all of which did not appeal to Spring's taste. She ate little. Jack was a small man, not a lot larger than Spring, so he was able to lend her a red plaid shirt that came down to her thighs and offered a little more cover. Nights were cold, and though David had given up his bed-roll for her comfort, on the first night, she shivered uncontrollably. David, lying next to her on Aphrodite's blanket with his coat thrown over his chest, could feel her shaking and hear her chattering teeth.

"What's the matter?" he asked, not sure of her malady.

"N-nothing. I'm j-just fr-freezing."

Without further word, David moved over next to her and gathered her, bedroll and all, up into his arms and snuggled her against him. He placed his coat over both of them. At first, Spring was too shocked to say anything, and then her shame swept over her again, and knew it was indecent to be here lying next to a man she detested and was not married to. These things were just not done.

Even though she began to feel the warmth of his body steal through the material of the bedroll, and would have liked to partake of it, she said, "Mr. Saunders, I must ask you to move away from me."

"Why? Aren't you warmer?" he asked, surprised.

"Yes, but it just isn't proper for us . . . I mean . . . that you . . . we shouldn't be here like this. I wasn't raised like that," she finished lamely.

David's warm laugh reached her, and she felt his warm breath on her neck and cheek. "No, Spring, I'm sure you weren't. I seriously doubt if any of your upbringing could have prepared you for life out here." He pulled her closer against his chest and settled down for the night.

"Please," she protested, squirming in his arms. "Can't allow you to . . . to . . ."

"To what?" he asked, with irritation in his voice. "I can assure you I do not have any intention of molesting you."

Spring was almost embarrassed to tears, especially when she heard some soft chuckles from the others around the campfire. "It just isn't right, Mr. Saunders, please," she begged.

David heaved a large sigh and, turning away, said in a tired voice, "All right, suit yourself."

Spring lay huddled in a ball all night—so cold was she. She had to admit to herself that she had been much too hasty in asking him to move away.

The next few nights, she forgot her pride and asked if he might move closer. It was a good thing she could not see the smile that turned up the corners of his mouth, or the twinkle in his light-blue eyes, when he obliged her request.

The morning of the third day, the riders came in view of the majestic Rocky Mountains. As they rode closer, the gentle rolling hills became more pronounced, and the horses had to work harder to make the climb. Everyone was exhausted, for they had been riding as much as ten hours a day.

Spring did not sleep this day, for she was sore from her awkward position riding with David. Her back was very stiff; and her legs and her face, which was already throbbing with the pain from the two blows received at the hands of the Arapaho warriors, were sunburned from their exposure to the elements.

It was of great but pleasant surprise to David that she did not complain. Most women of her station, who had been brought up with all the comforts of the day, would be nagging and torturing his ears with complaints of their discomfort.

Whenever they rested, he could see she was in pain of some degree, for it took her many steps to straighten her back and walk normally. He had asked her if she hurt, and she had said no. But he knew.

She listened this day to the men talking of David's home in the mountains. She learned it was rather a substantial spread that raised several thousand heads of cattle and some horses, and that Henry had a wife named Lorna. They lived in their own place a half hour's walk from David's house.

The rest of the men lived in a bunkhouse together at the back of his home.

There was one other man who lived nearby, and that was Pap. She did not learn what relationship he had with David but could tell from the conversation that he was an important man in David's life. A woman named Mary lived with him, and she cooked for David in David's house.

It seemed an odd mix to Spring. She was glad that she would not be going along with them. She had decided that she would run away that night when they reached Denver.

The climb into the mountains continued, and at last, in the late evening, they saw the sky aglow with light and knew they were close.

"Those are the lights of the city of Denver," David explained, pointing toward the lightened sky. "It's funny how you can see them from this distance, but it has something to do with the clear mountain air. Soon you'll be able to hear the ruckus too."

"We stayin' at Molly's?" asked Joe.

"I sure hope so." No one could see Hap's grin in the darkness, but all, including Spring, could hear it in his voice. "After all, we won't be comin' back for quite a spell."

"Spring and I will be staying there," David replied. "If you want to, feel free. However, you may certainly go wherever you wish. Just so long as you are all able to hit the trail again tomorrow by seven. I want to reach the Haven by sundown tomorrow night."

The men gave their assent and quickened their animal's pace. David had Aphrodite hang back a bit.

"Why are we slowing down?" Spring asked.

"I just want to warn you, without embarrassment to you in front of the men. Molly's place is a rather . . . exclusive house where men of, shall we say, dubious character come to have some release from . . . from their normal routine. But Molly's a nice woman, and she'll take care of you tonight."

Spring was puzzled. If Molly was a nice person, why did men of 'dubious character' come to her house? "Why can't we just stay in a hotel? I can take care of myself there without help from anyone."

"I want to stay at Molly's. She's a friend of mine."

"But if she's going to have so many guests there . . .," Spring began.

David's laugh cut into her question. "You misunderstand, little girl. I guess I'll have to spell it out to you. Molly runs a house of ill repute, a house of prostitution, a whorehouse."

Spring sat up straighter, causing her back to ache all the more. She was unprepared for that revelation and did not want to be even close to a place like that.

"Well, I can't go to such a house. Take me to a hotel."

"I'm afraid that's out of the question. I'm going to Molly's, and you are going with me," he said firmly.

"But . . . but . . . I just won't be comfortable there. I'm not like those ladies. They are awful ladies to let . . . to do what they do." Her mind was in a turmoil, and she was angry that he would think to put her in such a position.

"Just what do you think they do?" David asked, enjoying her protestations.

"Well . . . well, I'm not sure, but," she went on with added inspiration, "I'm sure you do."

"Yes, I suppose I do. Let me set you straight on one thing, though. Those women who you say are so awful, are delightful, warm, and loving. Believe it or not, there are many wives out there who are cold, harsh, and ungiving."

"And what would you know about how a wife is or how she acts?" Spring demanded into the night.

"That, my dear, is no concern of yours." His tone indicated that he was through conversing with her, and they rode on in silence.

Spring could now hear the goings-on of the city, and though she could not see much, for they rode down a back alley, it sounded gay and high-spirited. She tried not to think of where she was being taken and the fall from grace she felt she was in, but repeating over and over in her head were David's words about the ladies living and working in this house of Molly's and, most of all, the words he'd uttered about cold wives.

She thought for sure he was wrong, for it seemed obvious to her he was the cold and unfeeling one and surely must treat women with far rougher methods than did John Granville. And John said he loved her. Look at the way Mr. Saunders had treated her, she thought. Much worse than John ever had; so if he married, it was Mr. Saunders who was the one at fault, not his wife.

David pulled up on Aphrodite's reins, bringing her to a halt at the back door of a rather large establishment from where came great bursts of laughter and gay, lighthearted music from a rinky-dink piano. He dismounted and then reached up to help her down. Spring stifled a groan, but not before David became aware of it. However, he gave no notice of it; and after giving some instructions to his men to take care of his mount, he turned to knock three times on the back door of the wooden building. The door opened a crack, emitting a sliver of light to cut its way into the dark alley.

"Molly's Leg o' Mutton," David said in a low voice. The door opened wider, and David came face-to-face with Molly's back door security guard, Hairy Harry. And indeed he was. The man had a lined face, what one could see of it, out of which glared hard brown eyes. One cheek protruded with a large wad of chewing tobacco, and a stream of dirty brown juice sluiced its way into the man's thick gray-filled beard, from the corner of his loose mouth. His hair hung to his shoulders, and he wore a sailor's cap atop the mess.

The clothes were sweat-stained and smelled as though they hadn't been washed for weeks. Spring could smell him, standing behind David in the night air.

"Hey, Whip, glad to see ya. Come on in." Hairy Harry stepped back to admit David, who also stepped back and took Spring by the arm. He pulled her around in front of him and gave her a little push. Being weak from so much riding and stiff from no exercise, she stumbled into the hallway and fell against the odious man. She pushed herself away in disgust, turning on David.

"You don't have to push. I can manage on my own, Mr. Saunders." She brushed her scraggly hair from her face and lifted her chin with dignity.

David had not meant to push her so forcibly, and, in fact, had not. He just now realized how weak she had really become. "Sorry, I didn't mean to be so rough," he apologized.

"I'm sure," she replied sarcastically. She drew herself up as tall as she could without moaning and drew the borrowed shirt about her. She watched David shut the alleyway door.

"What have we here, Whip? Have to beat the little bitch to get her in here?" Hairy Harry relocked the door, giving her the once-over with an inscrutable gaze. He carried a thick club with him for security and protection, for Molly did not like firearms in her house. He raised the club now and prodded Spring's breast with it. "I like to test the meat as it comes in," he added by way of explanation to Spring.

Angered at this assault, Spring knocked the club away from her chest. "Don't you dare touch me, you filthy—" And then her eyes opened in fear as the guard raised the club to bring it down on her shoulder.

David stepped forward quickly and, with an upraised hand, caught the club, at the same time forcing Harry back against the wall.

"This is not a girl for Molly, Harry," David said between his teeth. "This is a . . . a lady."

Harry knew he was no match for a man like Whip Saunders and immediately backed down.

"Okay, okay. But I ain't never seen no lady look like she does, all torn up and beat up. She don't look like no lady to me."

"Well, I am," said Spring, sagging by the door. Weariness, sadness, and loneliness were taking their toll on her, and she tried desperately to control her voice and tears.

David, seeing she was rapidly becoming undone, bid Harry to go find Molly, while he escorted "the lady" up to Molly's office. Giving Spring a last appraising look and shaking his head in disbelief, Harry sauntered off in the direction of the laughter and loud singing.

David approached Spring. "Come on, let's go upstairs. You'll feel much better after a good night's sleep in a real bed."

She moved with him toward the staircase on the right and began to climb. With each step, her body cried out in protest against the pain in her muscles. Her feet and legs were covered with scratches and bruises, and so cold as to be almost beyond feeling. Halfway up, she fell onto the banister.

"I don't think I can walk another step. I'll just sit here and rest. You go on."

David knew from the expression on her face that she was sincerely exhausted, and probably meant what she said. Yet he was not about to leave her alone there. Instead of going on, he swept her up off her aching feet and strode on up the wooden staircase and on into a large room. There he set her next to a chair. She collapsed into it gratefully.

"I really wish you hadn't done that," she said with some irritation.

"If you thought for one moment I was going to leave you on the stairs alone, you must think I'm a little on the crazy side," he answered over his shoulder. He stood with his back to her, gazing into the fire laid in a large hearth. The room had several overstuffed pieces of furniture covered in brightly flowered material. Two windows on the outside wall were draped with heavy brocade curtains, in front was a massive, ornate wooden desk that was highly polished. A big Persian rug covered the inlaid wood floor, and the bottoms of Spring's injured feet couldn't help but find comfort in the plush pile.

"Really, Mr. Saunders," Spring protested in a tired but disgusted voice, "I'm much too weary to go running off right now. But don't worry, when I get my chance, I'll take it."

He shifted his gaze to her. She looked small and tattered sitting in the huge chair, made for a large bulk of a man rather than a slim-bodied woman like Spring. He wondered if she'd ever look the same as she did the first time he'd seen her, dressed in yellow and waving that parasol around for all to see, ruffles everywhere, the low-cut bodice showing off a milky-white breast that rose and fell rapidly with anger. He wondered if, and hoped that, the bruises discoloring her face would heal up properly so that the smooth curve of her cheek would be as unflawed as before, and that both eyes would again be brought to his in intensity of feeling for whatever cause may be in her heart. He shook himself back to the present when he heard the door open, and he turned his look now on the newcomer.

Spring was shocked by what she saw. The blonde-haired lady who swept into the room was dressed in a vivid-pink robe that billowed out behind her. It was not tied at the waist and therefore gave full view to her buxom figure which was scantily clothed in what Spring would've called a corset; however this one was bright red with silver threads and bows embroidered into the material. It was low cut and showed an ample bosom, and her legs were stockinged in black, held up by black garters. She wore red high heels that made her seem taller than she actually was. Her face was a pretty one, though she rather ruined her looks by using quite a bit of heavy makeup, which covered up any natural good looks she had.

She held out her satin-covered arms to David, and Spring saw that each finger was wearing a ring of some type of glittering stone.

"Whip! Whip Saunders," she exclaimed, her red mouth opening up in a big grin. "Whatever are you doing here, and why have you kept yourself away from me for so long?" By that time, she had reached his side, and the two embraced heartily, without regard for Spring's presence. After several seconds of heavy kissing, David noticed Spring, at last, out of the corner of his eye. She was huddled down into the chair, making herself as invisible as possible. David stepped back from Molly and smiled down at her.

"It is good to see you, my girl, but for the moment, I want to introduce you to a friend of mine." He indicated Spring with a nod of his head. Spring peered up meekly in Molly's direction.

"My God, Whip, what did you do to this poor girl?" Molly breezed across to Spring and sat down on the arm of the chair. She pushed the young woman's hair back and gazed into Spring's face and then placed a warm arm about her shoulders.

Spring tried not to cringe away from this woman who did what she did for a living. Anything she'd ever heard about creatures like this one was nothing good. To look at her, Spring would guess that everything she had heard was true, but Molly's blue eyes were sincere, and her voice held words of sympathy. In her heart, Spring knew this woman was good, that she had a good soul.

"Mr. Saunders did not do this to me, Miss . . . Miss . . ."

"Just call me Molly, honey. Everyone else does."

"Well, he didn't do this to me, but we are definitely not friends," Spring explained.

"What? Whip not able to make friends with a woman? That seems almost too much to believe." She turned to David. "You must have done something to this young child to make her dislike you, Whip."

"Oh, I could tell you lots," Spring started. "To begin with—"

"Yes, to begin with, Molly," David interrupted, "could you find a bed for this poor child, perhaps a bath could be drawn? I'll tell you the whole story when we go downstairs for a few drinks."

"I can assure you, it'll be a completely biased story, Molly," Spring said, standing as Molly helped her to her feet.

"I have an open mind, dear. I don't believe everything all men tell me. However, Whip . . ." She left the rest of her sentence unfinished. "Come along, honey. What is your name?"

"It's Spring. Spring Ames."

"Spring. What an unusual name—but lovely. I think once you are cleaned up, you will look just like your name. Now," Molly said as she led her through a dark door on the far side of the room, "I'm going to let you use my room tonight, and I can promise you, you won't be disturbed."

They entered another large room, which boasted a large fireplace blazing with another fire. The walls were decorated with large tapestries in between which hung red velvet wallpaper. A big four-poster bed in the center of one wall was hung with sheer curtains from a ruffled canopy. On another wall was a mirror that covered half the wall. Spring went to stand in front of it.

Her eyes opened wide when she saw herself reflected in it. She was horrified by what she now saw looking back at her. David was also reflected in the mirror, lounging in the doorway; and Molly was pulling a fat braided cord, presumably to call one of her maids.

But Spring could not really focus on those other things when she was confronted by the ugly spectacle that was herself. A stranger stared back at her out of a sunburned, green-and-purple face, one eye half shut and one cheek with a blood-encrusted cut. The hair, which was her crowning glory, stuck out in all directions, most of it in clumps from lack of a good brushing and washing and, in reality, no care at all.

The red plaid shirt hung off one shoulder, showing the torn gown with a string of lace hanging from her neck. The bottom of the once snowy nightie was now ripped and dirty. She pulled up the gown a little and saw dirt-laden toes and ankles scratched and bruised. She felt completely defeated. How could she run away from David Saunders looking like an orphan? Oh God, that was exactly what she now was!

Well, she couldn't think of that now. It was all too much to bear—to look like she did and be absolutely alone too. She turned slowly from the looking glass and walked to the four-poster to sit at the bottom edge. To David, still watching her from the doorway, she looked small and forlorn, with her head leaning against the post and her shoulders slumped.

Suddenly he felt himself hurt for her, for what she had gone through and the realizations she would have to face.

This was a renewed experience for him, for he had always taken care of himself and had not usually been moved by other people's plights. But now his heart constricted in a way that surprised him. At first, when Mrs. Butler had begged him to find her and take care of her, to watch out for her, he had balked at the idea. After all, hadn't Spring kept telling him to mind his own business, that she could take care of herself? Her sharp tongue was not the most pleasant to listen to, and yet he had found that she had a sympathetic heart for those that were down and out, that her emotions were expressed so easily in her music and written all over that lovely face when she played. He did not want—indeed, he did not need the responsibility of her. Something had made him promise Mrs. Butler, and it wasn't just the fact that he had liked her and she'd been kind to him. There was something about Colonel Ames's daughter that caused him to strike out after her; and no matter how much trouble she was, he was going to take her to his home and look after her until . . . until what? He didn't know. Usually, his plans were pretty well defined, but for now, he would fulfill his obligations to Mrs. Butler and to his old friend, the colonel.

Molly's maid, upon receiving instructions to bring water for the tub in front of the roaring fireplace, left the room. Then Molly approached Spring.

"Well, Spring, after a nice hot bath, you get into this nightie and into bed here. No one will disturb you, and you should have a nice night's sleep." Molly sat next to her and patted her hand. "And don't worry, that bruise on your face will heal up fine. Believe me, I've had shiners worse than that one, and they do go away."

Spring looked at her in surprise. "You mean someone has hit you before?"

Molly gave a little laugh. "Yes, my dear. In my business, that just comes with the territory."

Spring glanced over at David. "Has he hit you?"

"Whip? Heavens no! He likes me. Now, here's Mavis, and she'll get you all fixed up in no time. Whip and I'll leave you alone for a while, and then I'll check on you later."

"Thank you, Molly."

David came over to her and, running his hand through his pale hair, said, "I'll check on you later too."

"That's not necessary, Mr. Saunders," Spring replied. "I'll be fine."

"That's not why I'll be checking on you, Spring," he answered dryly. Then, putting his arm around Molly's shoulders, they left the room.

*   *   *

Molly sat forward at the table, leaning her chin on her hands. Eyeing David shrewdly, she said seriously, "Well, it sounds as if you kind of like that girl upstairs."

"What do you mean by that?" he asked, leaning back in his chair and brushing his hand over his face. He took a deep draft from his glass of beer.

"Oh, I don't know, Whip. You tell me all these things about her innocence of the west, her nasty little cracks at you, her engagement to this John Granville, all in a disgusted manner, and yet I can tell from your voice, when you call her by her name, Spring . . ."

"It's an absurd name."

"Just by the way you say it," Molly continued as though he hadn't interrupted, "I can tell that you don't dislike her as you like to make it sound. I think you do." She smiled at him.

"Molly, my girl, I must admit I admire her courage and strength, but she has a waspish manner and is definitely a child. I like my women loving, not cold and unyielding, as she is."

She eyed him curiously, wondering briefly if he wasn't thinking of someone other than Spring. Then she said, "Ah, Whip, darling, you doth protest too much. But I don't want to argue with you, at least not now. Let me go up and see how it goes, and I'll meet you in the violet room." She arose from her chair and then turned back. "That is, if you so desire?"

"Try to keep me away," he replied.

*   *   *

Spring lay in the large bed, warm for the first time at night in what seemed forever. She now felt more human and able to face what lay ahead, namely, her escape. Her chestnut hair had been washed and brushed by Mavis until it shone like autumn leaves on a sunlit day, and it fanned out behind her small head on the pillow. She snuggled down beneath the covers and heaved a sigh of relief and began to relax.

64

The door opened softly, and Molly entered. Spring wondered how a woman so nice to a stranger could do what she did, and even stay with it after being hit in the face upon occasion.

"My little Spring, how do you feel now?" asked the blonde madam in a cheerful voice.

"I feel much better now, thank you. You have been very kind to me. I appreciate it very much."

"Well, honey, I might not be so kind if another gentleman had asked me for the same favor, but since it was Whip, how could I refuse?" Molly sat on the edge of the bed and picked up a handful of Spring's abundant hair. "You have lovely hair, so thick and shiny. I can see why Whip thinks he must be responsible for you."

"Oh, him." Spring waved her hand, as if brushing him away. "I really can't stand the man. He's very egotistical and self-righteous. I don't suppose he told you all the awful things he's done to me?"

"You mean saving your life?" Molly asked, blue eyes twinkling.

"I guess he did do that, and believe me, I am grateful. But ever since we met, he's tried to run my life. I want to stay here in Denver, but he insists on taking me into the mountains to his cabin. I don't want to go. I have money of my own and can take care of myself."

"Listen, sweetie, if Whip Saunders insisted I go to the mountains with him, I wouldn't hesitate one second." And Molly let out a loud laugh.

"Do you really like him that much?" Spring asked, incredulously.

"You bet. He's one of the finest men I know."

Spring did not know what to make of it. Everyone seemed to think a lot of David Saunders, except for John Granville—and herself, of course. So she asked this good friend of David's what she thought.

"Why do so many people like him? I think he's just awful."

Molly gave Spring an appraising look. She was so young and had so much to learn. "Answer me this, Spring," Molly commanded. "Do you like the people who like Whip?"

"Yes. I loved my father and thought very highly of Dr. and Mrs. Butler. You obviously like him, and I do like you, though I didn't think I would." Spring was thinking and did not see the corner of

Molly's mouth quirk up in mirth. "The men we rode in with, who live up in the mountains with Mr. Saunders, respect him and seem to like him. And they were nice to me. There was Two Stone. He liked and trusted him."

"Two Stone?" Molly inquired.

"A little Indian boy at the fort. He was in my class at the school," Spring explained.

"There, you see?" Molly asked, rising from the bed.

"See what? I don't understand," Spring said.

"Well, my child, if you like his friends and they are good people, and these good people like Whip, then he can't be all bad, now, can he?" Molly walked toward the door and then turned back once more. "He is a good man. I don't think you have anything to worry about. Now have a good sleep. I'll see you in the morning." The pink satin robe disappeared through the door.

Spring thought about what Molly had said and was just beginning to concede that Molly might perhaps be a little right in her assessment of David when he walked into the room with Mavis, each of them carrying two buckets of steaming water, which they poured into the galvanized tub by the fireplace.

"Just what do you think you are doing?" Spring demanded, sitting up in the bed, clutching the blankets to her throat.

"I'm going to take a bath, what does it look like?"

"But you can't do that in here," she protested.

"Why not?"

"Because . . . because . . . I'm in here."

"Oh, that won't bother me, Spring. I won't mind you being here." He began to strip off his shirt and then stood looking into the fireplace. Two more girls entered with more water.

"Well, it will bother me, and I mind very much."

Giggling, the two girls left, and David turned his back on Spring, unfastening his britches and beginning to move them down over his hips.

With a little cry of frustration and embarrassment, Spring dove under the covers and covered her head with the pillow. But it did not drown out the laughter that filled the room, or the splashes of water coming from the tub. No matter what anyone said or thought, they would not change her mind about Mr. Saunders being a rude, obnoxious man!

*   *   *

Spring stole out of the bed. The fire had burned down low on the grate, and a soft orange glow filled the quiet room. On the mantle was an old gilt clock that read three thirty. It was time to make her move. Mavis had brought some clothes for her to wear the following morning and left them on a chair by the door. Without noise, Spring gathered them up and brought them back to the hearth for what little light there was to dress. She was not a little appalled to see totally unfeminine attire. There was a white cotton camisole and a pair of drawers, but not one other item of proper underclothes for a woman. No stays or corset or stockings. Not that she enjoyed being constricted by those things. But still. There was a pair of men's socks and a lady's blue lace blouse, high at the neck and long in the sleeves, which was quite attractive; but worst of all, there was no skirt at all, just a pair of small men's blue denim pants. Well, there was nothing for it but to dress in what there was and get out of there.

She pulled the pants on and noticed they fit rather snugly, and showed every line she possessed. Oh God, how would she ever be able to present herself at a hotel looking like some cow hand? For her feet, there was also a pair of soft leather boot-type shoes that tied at the ankle, the likes of which she had not seen before; but they were very comfortable, and she was glad not to be barefoot anymore.

She brushed her hair back and caught it behind her head with a piece of silk ribbon she found in the top drawer of Molly's dresser, promising herself she would return it someday, in the near future.

At last ready, she went to the door and let herself in quietly through to the office. There was no one there. The house in general had quieted considerably, and except for some where suspicious sounds were coming from some of the rooms as she passed them in the hallway, Spring saw no one. Step by step she inched her way down the staircase and found herself at the back door.

Hairy Harry was nowhere to be seen, and Spring was much relieved. She tried the knob on the door and realized it was locked, and there was no key to be found to open it. She would just have to try her luck at the front door. She had to make her getaway now, for tomorrow would be too late. Fortunately, her shoes did not make any sound on the wooden planks of the floor, and so she made her way easily into the large front room, where there was a long bar and many tables and chairs. Spring did not want to take the time, nor did she truly want to know what this room really looked like, so she did not bother to investigate further. She made haste to the front, where two lanterns glowed by the double doors. Behind her, a door opened from an open hallway that ran across the top half of the room, and this hallway led to a front staircase that led to the very room Spring now stood in. She stood still, scarcely able to breathe, her heart racing madly. She looked up and saw Molly standing in the doorway of the room upstairs. She seemed to be peering into the dark shadows below. She turned back into the room and spoke to someone behind her. Then David appeared in the door.

However, he did not stop there; he came out into the hallway and leaned over the railing and looked over it into the darkness. The only thing Spring could see that he had on was a pair of pants, and the light from the violet room behind played across his bare back and white-blond hair.

"I don't see anything, Molly," David's deep voice drifted down to Spring. "Are you sure you heard something?"

Unexpectedly, from somewhere, a draft of air came whistling through the big room, causing the lantern wicks to flare up momentarily. It was for a breath of a second, but it was long enough for David's sharp blue eyes to pick out Spring's slim figure and fire-lit hair. Instantly, he was down the hall, and Spring, her legs turning to water, turned at the door and frantically twisted the knobs back and forth in her hands, to no avail. David, halfway down the stairs, vaulted over the banister onto the floor and, with catlike swiftness, was behind her and grabbing her by the shoulders.

"What the hell do you think you are doing?" he demanded between clenched teeth.

"What does it look like, Mr. Saunders?" Spring hissed back. He turned her about and took her wrists in a viselike grip. "I'm trying to get away from you!"

"I told you before, Spring, not to try anything like this, and I meant it." He picked her up roughly and threw her over his muscular shoulder like a sack of potatoes. She kicked and yelled, bringing some of the other ladies and their friends to their doorways. David seemed oblivious to them and her feeble attempts to get down. That is, until she took it into her head to scratch his back with her nails. He swore under his breath, but continued to mount the stairs three at a time. At last, she was thrown bodily onto Molly's bed. Molly had followed them into her room. David crossed to her, asking her to leave him alone with Spring. Then, with the door shut against any intruders, he advanced to the bed and stood over her. Something in his face told her she better not try anything else—at least not for the moment. His eyes had iced over, and a muscle twitched in his jaw repeatedly. He was breathing heavily, and his fair-haired chest rose and fell in heated anger.

"You little bitch, I ought to—"

"You ought to what?" she asked daringly, eyes wide in fright. "Are you going to beat me now, or . . . or rape me?"

Suddenly, David's anger left him, and his body visibly relaxed. "No, neither. But I want to know exactly what you intended to do, and if you don't tell me the truth, I'll do one of your two suggestions, both of which sound very tempting to me."

"You wouldn't dare." Spring, genuinely alarmed now at the look in his eyes, pulled herself up on the bed.

"Do you want to test me?" David asked in a wickedly calm voice.

"No," she answered. "No, I don't. Well, if you must know, I was going to a hotel to get a room. Tomorrow, I was going to the bank to get some of my money, and then find a job teaching or something."

"So," he mused, sitting on the bed next to her, "you had it all planned out, didn't you?"

She nodded, biting her lip and drawing away.

"Can you imagine what anyone would think of you when they saw your face like that? Do you have any identification? How do you think you could take your money, even part of it, out of the bank without any identification?"

Spring had not thought of that aspect. All she had been concerned about was getting away from David. He saw that these thoughts hadn't entered her mind.

"Pretty stupid, huh?" He arose from the bed. "Spring, I don't want you to try to leave again. I promise you, I won't go easy on you if you do."

She looked up defiantly, and her face held determination. "That is, if you catch me when I try again."

He sighed. "Just please don't try. Mark my words. Now get some rest. We have a long ride ahead of us tomorrow." He sighed, turned on his bare feet, and left the room.

David stalked into Molly's office with his hands jammed into his pockets. Damnation! Just what he needed, to babysit the colonel's daughter. He should just let her go and to hell with her. But staring into the dying embers of the fireplace, he saw Mrs. Butler's pleading face and knew he couldn't put her out on her own. She wasn't ready yet to survive on her own. Spring didn't know the first thing about the rough living of people, especially men, out west; and David felt sure she would fall victim to some gold digger sooner or later, or even worse. He shuddered at the thought.

God, what a mess. Women were considerably more trouble than they were worth. At one time, he was not willing to think so, but he had been taught well in his lifetime that one could not trust them. They were not stable, and Spring had just shown him those very traits.

The scratches on his lower back began to burn and he reached around and rubbed his hands over them. Traces of blood that oozed from the marks were barely visible in the dim light. If he was smart, he would let her go, he thought again; but he knew he couldn't. And it wasn't just Mrs. Butler's pleading eyes and voice or the memories of Colonel Ames's trust in him that caused David "Whip" Saunders to want to keep Spring with him. She was spunky, and she stood up for herself. She showed strong character; she was intelligent. But it wasn't that either. Somewhere deep in the recesses of his mind, David knew he had to keep her with him.

For no one was going to leave him again. What he said, he meant. He didn't voice these thoughts aloud, and so, because of that, the thought really wasn't there, for he knew that wasn't the way to be. A fair man he had always been, and that idea wasn't fair at all.

Chapter 6

The next morning found Spring standing outside Molly's back door, thanking her for her great hospitality. She and David had already had an argument about the clothes he'd arranged for her to wear. She considered them totally inappropriate for a young woman, and he thought them absolutely practical. And then when he said he wanted her to get on his mount because he couldn't trust her to stay with him on the ride, she had gotten furious with him and said it didn't matter at all, that just because he got her up to his cabin didn't mean she would stay there.

Behind David, she thought about their harsh words as she clung to his waist. Unfortunately, the only thing to hold on to was his middle, now that she rode astride Aphrodite, thanks to her attire. She was tired of fighting with him all the time. Now he was the only one she knew in this wilderness, and she wished that they could get along. However, he seemed to exasperate her at every turn. Most people in her life had always been warmed by her bright, happy smile; but lately, she couldn't seem to bring one to her face, especially to him. She would never be able to smile at him. She sighed heavily.

Two of David's friends had ridden off ahead of the rest to alert those at Saunders's Haven of their imminent arrival and to tell them to prepare a place for Spring to stay. Always wanting to share at least a little in plans that concerned herself, Spring's ire was again raised, but this time she managed to bite her tongue and not say a word as she watched Hap and BJ disappear in the distance.

Crossing the south Platte River had taken quite a bit of thought that morning as the winter runoff from the heavy snows left parts of the river too deep for crossing without mishap. However, after a thorough search, they found an area that was fairly fordable, and the horses made their way single-file down into the wide flat river west of Denver.

Spring was more than a little frightened, and she hung on to David with a mighty grip. Her legs also tightened around the black mare's back; and sensing the young girl's fright, Aphrodite danced sideways in the water.

"Spring," David warned as he felt her arms clench his middle in alarm, "you've got to relax. You are scaring Aphrodite."

"I . . . I . . . can't help it," she said, her teeth beginning to chatter. "I never learned how to swim, and I'm afraid of the water."

"Oh, all right," he said with exasperation. He turned the skittish horse around and took her back up onto the bank. He called across the rushing water to the others to go on ahead, and he brought his leg forward over the horse's head and slid to the ground. "Come on down here." He held up his arms to Spring, and she placed her hands on his wide shoulders, as she was lifted to the ground. Soft curling tendrils of hair whispered around her small head in the early morning breeze.

"Spring," David said to her, tilting her chin up so he could look into her eyes, "I'm surprised at you. Here you've been attacked by Indians and kidnapped in the middle of the night, and it didn't seem to alarm you over much, and now just because we are crossing a little stream, you become scared as a rabbit."

"You call that a little stream?" she asked, pointing a slim finger in the direction of the wide river.

"Well, how do you propose we get across?" he asked.

"Why don't you go and leave me here?" Spring suggested.

David sharply drew in his breath. *Here we go again*, was his thought. He turned her to face him and, placing both his hands on either side of her face, forced her to look up at him. She took both his wrists in her hands but could not remove his hands from her face. She gazed haughtily into the blue eyes that could so easily turn to ice and turn one's blood to water. But at this moment, his eyes were warm and, she admitted to herself, very nice to look into.

"I don't want to have this conversation again, about you getting away or running away. You are staying with me, and that is that."

"Do you always get your way, Mr. Saunders?" she questioned, her eyes searching his face.

He peered down at her lovely mouth pouting, though he actually thought about kissing it before he pushed the thought away. He was not going to, did not want to, get involved with her.

"In a word, my dear, no. I do not. Perhaps sometime you may leave, but for now, you will come with me."

"All right," she conceded. "But that doesn't mean I have to like it."

She was surprised when he replied, "Nor will I. Now, it may make it easier if I take you up front instead of behind." Without further ado, he whisked her up on the saddle and joined her in a matter of seconds. They began again into the water, and she heard him speaking softly to Aphrodite words of calm; and when she was carrying them out, he started to speak into Spring's ear to calm her fears as well. Spring became lulled by his voice, and even though the water crept higher and higher, she managed to let him guide the horse across the river without further trouble.

Once on the other side, she remained sitting where she was; and, filled with great relief, she leaned against his chest and laid her head on his shoulder. She remained that way for the greater part of the day.

Their ascent of the front range of the Rocky Mountains was not altogether slow, as David and his men had passed that way many times and the pathway was clear cut. Some parts of the path were smooth and dust covered, and other parts boasted rocks where slides had occurred. The width of these trails was wide enough to let a wagon pass through, sometimes the wheels coming quite close to the rocky cliffs or shrubs and trees. All about were majestic mountain peaks rising to over fourteen thousand feet above sea level. David pointed out various peaks that still showed remnants of the winter's snows in cracks and crevices high above them. Mountain streams tumbled beside them to the river below, and when they stopped to rest, the riders and horses drank deeply from them.

For the first time in a long time, it seemed to David that he saw Spring's face light up with pleasure when she tasted her first drops of ice-cold mountain water. It reminded him of the time he had seen her playing the piano at the fort during Sunday services, unaware of his eyes upon her. The sheer innocence and pleasure of something enjoyable made his heart feel lighter than it had in weeks.

"There's nothing else like it anywhere on this earth, that sweet taste of clear water," he commented to her, kneeling at her booted feet to fill his canteen. She looked down into the stream and saw trout swimming about and laughed out loud. He glanced at her in surprise. "Well, well, isn't that a nice sound?"

"What's that?" she asked, scooping more water up in her closed fingers and bringing it to her lips.

"Your laugh, it sounds very nice."

She colored and looked away. "I'm human, Mr. Saunders. I do laugh when there is something worth being happy over: I've never tasted such good water nor have I seen fish swimming in a mountain stream before."

"The life up here will make you laugh a lot then, Miss Ames," Jack said, behind her. "We're all one big happy family up at Saunders's Haven. You'll see."

Spring did not reply but inclined her head and gave him a half smile. After all, he wasn't to blame for her situation or for what his boss did or didn't do. Noontime, they ate more of the biscuits and some canned meat and beans that Henry had bought in town before they left that morning. Spring again refused the coffee, for she had never developed a taste for it and thought it bitter.

She preferred to drink the water they had stored up earlier.

She walked a little way from the group of men to the edge of a steep gorge and peered out over the canyon below. They had been climbing for some time now, and David said that soon they would reach the summit of their climb and start down into his valley. The men, in various relaxed positions around the campfire, watched the slim, soft-hipped woman as she walked to the cliff's edge.

"God, Dave, are you sure you want to bring her up here?" Henry asked, eyeing her rounded curves with an appreciative eye.

"No, but I made a promise just like I told all of you. She's just a girl in trouble, and I liked her father, so in payment for all his kindness to me, I think I ought to help the girl out."

"She ain't no girl, Dave," Joe shot back. "If you don't want anything to do with her, how about giving me leave to try my hand at her."

"Or a few other things, heh?" asked Jack.

"Listen," David said, fixing steely eyes on them. "Leave her alone. She's very inexperienced."

"Since when did you care about that?" Jack asked, seriously.

"Since now, Jack. You all know I give you enough time in the city to do what you need to do, and you may marry whenever you wish and come up here to live. But leave her alone. Besides, she promised to marry that Lieutenant Granville who disappeared the night she was taken by the Indian Black Claw. He gave her a gold ankle bracelet that she's still wearing on her left ankle as a token of his esteem and so-called love for her."

"How do you know all that?" Joe asked.

"Around the fort, nothing much got by me. But I happened to be standing by her quarters when she accepted his proposal and the bracelet another time. I don't think she knows anyone else knew of it."

"Maybe she's changed her mind about it," suggested Henry.

"I think she'd take the bracelet off if she was through thinking of Granville in the way of a husband," David answered derisively.

"You don't like him much, do you?" Henry questioned.

"Hell, no, I don't trust him either . Besides, I strongly suspect, from what I got out of old Chief Mighty Elk, that Granville had quite a bit to do with her abduction. However, she does not know anything about that, so mum's the word." David stretched and got up.

"Hey, Dave," Jack interjected again, "if you don't want anything to do with Spring, why can't we try to give her a tumble?"

David turned his look on the men. "I'm sure Henry does not have any designs on Spring, what with his lovely wife, Lorna, waiting at home with a big kiss and you know what else." The men chuckled.

"But as for Spring, she's a lady, and the rest of us are no gentlemen. Let's leave well enough alone, all right?" His tone told them there was no more to be said on the subject, and he moved across to where she stood gazing out over the miraculous view. In his estimation, his view of her was just about as miraculous as when he took in her straight back in the blue silk blouse with lace trim and the tight pants that left nothing to the imagination. Her abundant chestnut hair was tied back with the blue ribbon of Molly's, and it hung down her slender back almost to her waist. It curled softly at the bottom. Seeing her profile from the left side, he saw the purple bruise had begun to subside somewhat and parts of it were turning greenish yellow. Despite the disfiguration, she remained a delightful sight.

"Pretty up here, isn't it!" he said, breaking the silence.

"Yes, it is. Oh, what is that?" She pointed to a large bird in the distance.

"A little hard to tell from here, but I think it's a hawk of some kind. There are many birds of prey up here. The ones I like to see are the eagles. I could watch them all day."

"I hope to see one while I'm here," she said softly. She did not say it with the intent to antagonize him, and he realized it right away. Another thing he realized was that this was one of the first conversations they'd had that had not been fraught with angry or sarcastic words.

"You probably will. There's one in particular I'd like you to see." He took his hat off and stroked the two little feathers in the hat band.

Bending, she removed from the inside of her soft boot the bright-green feather Two Stone had given her when she last saw him. "Would you keep this for me? I wouldn't want to lose it." She was embarrassed to ask him.

"Of course," he answered, taking the feather from her fingertips and placing it in his hat band. His own fingers touched hers briefly, and she drew her hand away, as if burned. He hoped that wouldn't break the spell of their civility toward each other, so he went on quickly, as if no touch had occurred.

"See that mountain range to the south?" He pointed with his long finger over the canyon below to the purple edifice in the distance. "That's the Sangre de Cristo Range. That and the range of mountains we're on right now form what is called a mountain wall that faces the Great Plains to the east. We have many of the highest peaks in this area alone. That high one over there"—his finger moved to the right—"covered on top with snow, is Mt. Evans. And that one"—he moved his finger again—"is Pikes Peak."

"What does Sangre de Cristo mean?" she queried.

"It's Spanish for 'blood of Christ.'"

She looked with interest and listened intently to all he told her. She was an apt pupil and learned quickly. She also had an extremely good memory, and as they rode on toward Saunders's Haven, she memorized details of the trail they followed, noting rock formations and shapes of trees. Someday soon, she would be needing this information, and it would have to be before she forgot what she was seeing now.

Spring was not a vengeful person. She forgave people easily when they showed her they were willing to go halfway in making amends with her. She knew David was capable at what he did and did not deny it. But except for her Aunt Emma, she had made most of her own decisions and deeply resented this stranger taking over her life. In her individuality and independence of life, she honestly felt she could make it on her own. And she was very determined to do so.

The rocks and trees opened up before them and over Aphrodite's ears, Spring saw below, bright-green rolling hills that folded in upon one another to form soft ridges.

These ridges were filled with trees and shrubs as green or greener than the hills. From this distance, it looked as if the hills had been covered with a velvet blanket that would be heavenly to lie upon.

This was Saunders's Haven, and in the middle of a meadow-like area stood several tall aspen trees. To the right of these was not a dark one-room cabin, as Spring had come to expect, but a white-framed cottage with a veranda extending itself completely around it. Behind this cottage stood the barn, also painted white with a black shingled roof. It was quite a bit larger than the house. Farther up one of the sloping hills was a low-roofed barracks-like building that housed the unmarried men. Even a bit farther was the one-room affair that kept

Pap and Mary at night. There were also fences in different areas used for penning the horses, fowl, and various other animals used to keep the Haven running smoothly.

"Heaven on earth," David commented in Spring's ear as they sat atop the last hill looking down upon the valley.

Surrounding this valley on all sides were the stately peaks, purple, blue-gray blendings of the grand Rocky Mountains. The sky was just beginning to color in the west beyond the sharp points of snow-capped tops, rose upon amber, and there was a good chill in the air.

"It is lovely," Spring answered, turning her head to him. Beauty was never lost on her, and she could not deny it to David even if she had wanted to.

They descended the hills, making their way to the white house. Up close, Spring saw it was larger than she had thought from where she'd first seen it. There were red window boxes at the three windows along the front and a red door. Steps led up to this door upon which now stood an older woman than herself, and taller. She wore a rose shirtwaist dress, devoid of the many petticoats women of the day usually wore in the cities, and her brown hair was pulled back in a simple bun. Her apron was fresh, and her face held a welcoming smile on a clear, glad countenance.

Beside her, a step lower, stood a taller man of about fifty years of age. His thick hair was graying, and the lines in his face were, at the moment, crinkled up in a large grin, his mouth showing strong big teeth.

Arriving at the house, at last, David dismounted and embraced the man in a large hug.

"Hi ya, Pap. Kept the home fires burning for me again, did you?" He then took off his gray hat, now boasting the three feathers, and took Mary in his big arms and planted kisses all over her face. Mary giggled and held him tightly.

"Ah, Davey, it is good to have you home again. It's been too long this time." She pushed him away from her and then stepped back, looking in the direction of Spring, who still sat on Aphrodite. "Are you going to introduce us to your lady friend?"

"Yes, I'm sorry." He went back down the steps to Spring and encircled her waist with his hands to lift her off the horse. She looked down into his face and saw that it had become very relaxed, and his eyes were merry and not at all cold. She could tell he was happy to be home. She felt his strong hands on her body and, startled by her thoughts, realized just how attractive a man he really was. "Pap and Mary, this is Colonel Ames's daughter, Spring. She'll be staying with us. I hope you have the room fixed up for her, Mary. She's quite exhausted from the trip up here, and I'd like to see her get a good night's rest."

"Of course, Davey. I knew you wouldn't mind her staying in the bedroom. Hap and BJ got here about three and said you'd be bringing a lady with you." Mary gave Spring a tender smile, and Spring was relieved, for she felt in her heart that she would have at least one friend here.

"Hello, Mary, Pap. I do want you to know that I appreciate everything you've done in preparation for my coming. However, I am not planning to be here long." She gave David a sidelong glance. David's face remained calm, and he said nothing.

"My, you are the prettiest thing that's come this way in a long time," Pap commented. "Even with that shiner."

"Mr. Saunders didn't give that to me," Spring hastened to assure them.

"Oh, we know that," Pap said in return. "Hap said you ran into an Indian."

Spring's head tilted back, and she gave a little laugh. "Well, hardly that."

"Besides, we know Davey would never hit a woman, right, Pap?" Mary obviously thought David Saunders was almost a god and had him high on a pedestal.

David replaced his hat on his blond head and grunted. "Don't spoil my reputation, Mary. I don't hit women, Spring—leastways not unless they deserve it." He gave her a penetrating stare and then said to Mary, "I'm going to put Aphrodite to bed and have a look around. Would you please get Spring settled?"

Mr. Saunders!" Spring exploded. "I'm not a child, and I refuse to be treated as such. I can certainly settle myself."

David ignored her, which was hard for him to do. Instead, he asked Pap, "Where's Suzie? She always comes out to greet me now."

"She's in the family way, Dave," Pap answered. Spring watched the two men disappear around the corner of the house to check on Suzie, the red setter. She felt at a loss, that here she was now, trapped within the walls of these mountains. Would she ever be free?

The women went through the front door, and Spring was pleasantly surprised to see what her present accommodations would be. The front room was paneled in light pine. There was a big fieldstone fireplace on the opposite wall, but what made this one different than any she had seen was that it opened through to the kitchen, which was on the other side. To the right of the fireplace was a five-foot-wide bookcase that stood from floor to ceiling, filled with literature from the classics, to poetry to novels. Some of the books were many years old, such as Homer's *Iliad* and *The Odyssey*, and Dante's *Divine Comedy*. Others that fell immediately to Spring's eye were Grimm's Fairy Tales, two new books by Mark Twain, *The Innocents Abroad* and "The Celebrated Jumping Frog of Calaveras County." But there was more to see than a tantalizing array of books. Two big comfortable chairs sat opposite each other in front of the hearth, and a small table sat to one side of them, holding a large hurricane lantern for ease of reading after dark. A varicolored braided rug covered almost the whole area in front of the fireplace. A small wooden table, along with two spindle-backed chairs, stood by the window to the right of the door. To the left under the other front window stood an impressive wooden desk polished to a dull sheen.

Through a wide doorway, Spring saw a dining room with a china closet against the wall and an oval table sided by six cane chairs. Mary led her to the kitchen, which contained some of the most modern conveniences she had ever seen and stared at them unbelievingly, as it seemed very strange that a mountain home could boast such luxury.

"How in the world did all of this get up here?" she couldn't help but ask Mary, as the older woman went to the wood-burning stove to check on the evening meal.

"Davey wanted the best," she answered, somewhat evasively.

"But why?" Spring questioned. "He's only a man. He wouldn't want all of this. This is the kind of home a man would bring his wife to."

Mary did not comment but busied herself at the stove.

Then turning at last, she said, "Let's go into the storeroom for a moment. Anytime you need something, you'll probably find it in here."

She opened a door off to the side of the fireplace, and again Spring was dazzled. Barrels of flour and sugar, sacks of corn, and other dried goods were stacked on the floor. On the shelves were candles of all shapes and sizes, soaps already molded, materials of various colors, prints, and thickness were on bolts to be used for clothing or linens. Jars of preserves and canned vegetables lined the shelves.

"It's like a miniature store in here," Spring said in amazement.

"We have to keep up with the supplies, for someone only goes to town once every three months or so to do some buying. As you go along, you might want to make a list of the things you'd like to have so you won't be in want."

"I won't be here that long, Mary," Spring put in again.

Mary smiled at her and, taking her waist in her hand, turned her about and led her to the bedroom. "Well, you just got here, so let's not talk about your leaving now. Besides, it's nice to have another woman about the place."

"Don't you ever see Lorna, Henry's wife?"

"About once a week, I guess, but that's not the same as having someone here all the time. Here's your room."

Mary opened a door beside the lavish bookcase in the front room, and Spring's tawny-green eyes now took in a rather massive bed covered with a quilted spread of red, white, and blue squares. The bed also boasted a brass head and footboard. A small table was by one side. Two windows in this room were hung with fluffy white curtains. A large wardrobe stood in one corner to her left, and another door opened off in the far corner.

"What's in here?" Spring asked.

"That's the bathroom. Here, let me show you."

Inside was a small washstand holding a blue flower–sprigged pitcher and bowl. Above this was an oval gilt-framed mirror. A silver-handled brush sat on the stand's marble top. A considerable claw-foot metal tub sat to the right. And there was a smaller rendition of a wood-burning stove in the corner holding buckets of water already warming for her bath. A hand pump was erected over one end of the tub so a person did not have to hand-carry water for the purposes of personal cleanliness.

Lastly, there was a rack holding several buff-colored towels and washcloths.

"This is really remarkable. It's hard for me to imagine that Mr. Saunders would actually build a place like this for himself. Did he buy it from someone else?" Spring asked, shifting her look to Mary, who appeared a little uncomfortable with the question.

"No, he built all this himself, with Pap's help."

"But how long has it been here?"

"About five years, I think. I'm not sure, as I've only been up here for four."

"Oh, is that how long you and Pap have been married?" She walked over to the window and looked outside. Dusk had come quickly to the valley, and a sliver of a moon shone high in the purple twilight.

"Pap and I are not married," Mary replied simply, folding down the counterpane on the bed.

"But . . . but . . ." Spring raised her hand to her throat and found that it did not help her swallow any better around the dry lump that suddenly formed there. "But don't you . . . I mean I thought you and he stayed together."

Mary's face suddenly glowed with happiness, and her eyes lit up with love. "Yes, we do. Marriage is something that never occurred to us, I guess. We love each other, and a preacher and a piece of paper won't change that. Anyway, up here no one cares, and it doesn't hurt anyone. Does that bother you?"

Spring again looked out the window. In her heart, it did bother her. She was sure Aunt Emma would have had something to say about Spring being in the company of someone who openly lived with a man without the benefit of marriage. But then, Molly had been so gracious to her, and Mary seemed nice too. Everything seemed to be getting so confusing. Her world was all topsy-turvy. Mary waited quietly for her answer.

The chestnut-haired girl regarded the happiness, the tenderness in Mary's face, and she visibly relaxed. Spring glanced around the room, and then her eyes came back to Mary.

"No, I guess not," she murmured.

"Good, I'm glad. I want to be friends. Now why don't you lie down for a while until I get the others rounded up for supper, and then we'll eat."

"Is there something I can do to help?" Spring, asked, not forgetting her manners.

"No, I've got everything under control." She left, closing the door softly behind her. Spring hurried over and saw that she could not lock it for there was no key. She went back to the bed and smoothed her hand over the bright quilt before taking off her soft boots to lie down.

She tucked the pillow under her head. The last thought in her head was that without a key, she would have no defense against Mr. Saunders making of her what Pap had made of Mary.

But Mary didn't look unhappy. Why was everything falling apart?

*   *   *

David lit the lamp on the table and gazed down at the slender form curled up on his bed. The long hair, still tied back by the blue ribbon, lay across her arm and shoulder.

One graceful hand cradled her cheek on the pillow, and the soft, pink lips were slightly parted. He could not see the bruises on her face, and her skin had taken on a golden, creamy glow from the lantern's light. A beautiful girl, Spring Ames was. Was his heart actually beating a little faster at the sight of her lying so preciously innocent on his bed? He turned abruptly away and went back to the dining room.

"She's napping. Feed her later," he said, not meaning to sound as brusque as he did.

"All right, Davey," Mary said.

"Gettin' to ya, is she?" Pap asked.

"No!" David then lowered his voice. "No, she is not. I . . . I don't have room in my life for a woman. Anyway, she has a tongue that cuts like a knife."

"Sounds like she's right up your alley," Pap gave him a small smile.

"Pap, lay off. Like I said, I don't want her in my life."

"Like it or not, want it or not, boy, she's in your life. You brought her into it yourself."

David's eyes turned color. Pap was about the only one who could not be squelched by those changes. But Mary didn't want either of them to argue.

"Davey, Spring sounded a little suspicious about the extent you went to, to make this place so nice. I didn't tell her anything, but—"

"If I think she ought to be told, I'll tell her. But I don't see how that could possibly make any difference to her, and I certainly don't want to talk about it, much less be reminded. Let's eat. It's good to be home, and this stew sure looks good."

David dug into his bowl. Pap gave Mary a look under his shaggy gray eyebrows but said nothing. However, the look she returned was in total agreement with him.

Later, after eating alone, Spring told Mary that she would be retiring for the night. Her nap had done little to relieve her exhaustion, and she was hoping that by tomorrow she would be back to normal. She thanked Mary for the food and then made her way to the bedroom, closing the door behind her. She placed another log in the fireplace opposite the bed and undressed slowly.

She felt so lethargic. Her eyes felt dry and parched, and there was a big lump in her throat that she could scarcely swallow around.

"Maybe I'm coming down with something," she murmured to herself, slipping a warm flannel robe on. After bathing and pulling a borrowed nightie over her head, she took the silver-handled brush in her hand. Peering closely at it, she could see that the brush was not an imitation of silver, for it was delicately cool and silky in her hand.

Spring knelt in front of the hearth, feeling the warmth of the blaze on her body, and she gained partial comfort from it. Her long hair loosened, and she began to brush it vigorously, until it sparkled and snapped with electricity. She did not hear the door open behind her; she was so intent on grooming her soft tresses.

David stood in the open doorway, viewing the most lovely sight he had ever seen. The firelight glistened through the abundant mane, setting Spring's chestnut locks aglow. The shorter tendrils became like sparkles of gold making a halo above her head. As she leaned over, brushing in continuous strokes, the light shined through the gown she wore, making visible the slim body he had held against him for four long days. His stomach tightened as he viewed her small but firm breasts silhouetted against the flames, and unbidden, desire for her filled his very being.

Her arms tiring, she sat back on her knees to stare into the fire. Gold, orange, and yellow flames licked upward; and in the middle of them, she suddenly saw Aunt Emma's face; her father looking at her with pipe in his mouth; Mrs. Butler's happy, red-cheeked face; John's handsome features. Where had they all gone? Rare tears slipped down from under the fringe of her eyelashes and down her cheeks, falling unheeded onto the folded hands in her lap.

From deep within her, her grief welled up inside and spilled over into the shadowy room. Her body became racked with sobs, and she shook convulsively, now hiding her face in her hands and rocking back and forth in her pain and sorrow.

She cried for those whom she had lost, and she cried for herself. She thought of all the people she had loved and who, for some reason or another, had come to leave her. And now, she was alone, utterly and completely alone.

Mary appeared at David's side, and she touched his arm, wanting him to move aside so she could go to Spring's aid.

But he stayed her progress and backed away, softly closing the door on Spring's suffering.

In the kitchen, Mary turned on David with displeasure. "Davey, you can't be so hardhearted as all that. Surely you could see the girl was hurting."

"Yes, I could see, and believe it or not, I'm hurting for her. But I've been riding with her for four days, and she's not once given any indication that she's accepted her losses. Now I can see that she has, and it's good for her to get it out of her system. She's a strong person, and I think she'd be embarrassed if we horned in on her grief."

"Well . . ." Mary hesitated.

"Believe me, Mary, I know her. She has a will and a mind of her own. She would consider any of that kind of display a sign of weakness."

"I'll bow to your wisdom, Davey. There's Pap now, waiting for me, so I'll go on up the hill." She stopped at the door and looked over at the blond-haired man standing by the sink drinking a cup of coffee. "Davey, you won't . . . you won't do anything to her tonight, will you?"

David gave her a baleful stare and set his cup down. He thought briefly of the wild desire that had invaded his body a short moment ago and tossed it aside. "No, I don't plan to do anything to her, by your meaning, ever, so don't worry. Now good night."

She left, and he turned off a lantern's wick on the cooking table. Turning, he went to the bedroom door and knocked.

"Who is it?" came a small voice.

"David."

"What do you want?"

David entered the room, seeing enormous green eyes staring at him from the big bed.

"I came to get a few things," he answered, going to the massive wardrobe. He pulled out a few articles of clothing. "Are you warm enough?"

"Yes, I'm fine."

He peered at her in the near darkness and saw her face was calm and there were no traces of tears on the smooth skin of her face.

"Good. I hope you sleep well."

"This is your room, isn't it?"

"Yes, it is. It's all mine." He said it simply, without conceit.

"Well, you don't plan to sleep in here, do you?" she asked tensely.

The corners of his moustache turned up slightly. "No, my girl, I'll not. I'll sleep up in the loft, which is above you, so don't be afraid if you hear bumps in the night."

Spring was greatly relieved. She was too tired to try to save her virtue for John tonight—that is, if she ever saw him again. David saw her body release the tension, and again, his gut tightened. So he turned away and walked to the door.

"Mr. Saunders?"

"What?"

"Just remember, I'm not your girl, and I'm not your friend, and I won't be staying here long."

"How could I forget with your constant reminders? Good night, Spring." And he went out the door and closed it, hearing her "Good night, Mr. Saunders" in his ears.

Chapter 7

The next morning, Spring arrived in the kitchen feeling much rested. She found Mary busily kneading a mound of creamcolored dough on the cooking table.

"Hello there. Sleep well?" Mary asked cheerfully.

"Yes, I feel like I can face the day for the first time in quite a few days. No, I'm not hungry," Spring said as Mary stopped her work to get a plate and fork. "I don't eat much in the mornings. Usually, I just have a cup of tea."

"Tea? Goodness, I don't think we have any in the storeroom. I suppose we could gather some herbs for tea," Mary commented. "You must write that on your list."

Spring made no mention of the fact that she wasn't staying long enough to warrant a list, for she didn't want to bring it up again. She sat at the dining table and watched Mary's quick hands handle the dough. She herself had no experience in the kitchen at all. She had never had to do it, so she hadn't learned.

She picked up a biscuit from a batch made that morning and sitting on a plate in the middle of the table. She broke off a piece and popped it into her mouth.

"Mary," she ventured to ask, "do you suppose we, I mean you, could help me make a dress or a skirt? I don't like these pants, and I really wish I had some stays or something." She spread her hands. "I don't feel dressed, you know?"

"We could sew up some skirts and blouses, but as for stays . . ." She paused, thinking of the trunks of clothes up in the loft and then quickly discarding the idea. "Aren't you more comfortable without them? Things are pretty informal up here."

Spring thought a moment and realized she hadn't missed the stays themselves but the constriction of them. "Well, I guess so, but I feel, I don't know, loose and, oh, different."

"What do you mean different?" David asked, coming in the back door. He had been out since dawn looking over the immediate area and chopping a new supply of wood. His shirt was opened halfway down his chest, and Spring could see perspiration glistening on the golden hairs. He raked his fingers through his hair, and it fell back to its natural place.

Spring averted her eyes to Mary.

Mary replied, "Oh, the land is different out here."

David arched his brows. "Got any coffee, Mary? Are you finding everything you need, Spring?" He sat at the head of the table and picked up the last biscuit. Mary set a cup of the steaming liquid in front of him.

"Yes, Mr. Saunders. Everything but a piano," she answered, rising and taking the remnants of her breakfast off the table and carrying it to the kitchen counter.

"Piano! Goodness, what would you do with a piano?" Mary asked incredulously.

"Spring is quite an accomplished pianist," David supplied around a mouthful of biscuit.

"That's the only thing we have in common, an appreciation of music," Spring put in.

Unexpectedly, the door flew open, and Pap said, "Suzie's in labor. Want to come and help out?"

David stood up, brushed his hands across his pants. "You bet. Don't want to let my dog do the job all alone." He turned to leave.

"May I come?" Spring asked.

"Well . . ." David glanced at her and hesitated.

"Oh, I don't think you want to do that," Mary hurriedly said. "You've probably never seen pups born before."

"Why not? I'd like to see some puppies born."

"But, Spring . . ." Mary began.

"Let her come," David intervened. "Most girls know very little about these things, sin that it is." He turned and joined Pap who was walking across the yard to the barn.

Mary shrugged her shoulders, and Spring followed the men briskly.

Looking at her from the window, Mary decided they should get her into some skirts as soon as possible. A girl like Spring in pants like that—it was as if she wore a second skin.

A half hour later, Spring sat in the cool barn on a mat of hay, with the dog's head resting trustingly on her knee.

She was mostly red setter and golden retriever, and her coat was the same shade of chestnut as Spring's hair.

David was rather surprised at Suzie's easy acceptance of Spring, for Suzie was his dog, his protector. She did not cotton up to everyone, and especially now, when she was in pain, there seemed to be a special bond developing between the young woman and the young dog.

Spring knew next to nothing about birth, how it began or ended. But when she saw the dog whimpering, her heart contracted in sympathy. David told her to stay back, but the frightened look in the dog's luminous brown eyes caused Spring to disregard David's advice. She knelt by Suzie, stroking the soft, silky fur and speaking to her in low, comforting tones.

As the hour wore on, Suzie's contractions came closer and closer together, and she cried in her throat, her large belly straining to be rid of her burden.

Spring could barely stand seeing the dog in such pain, and at last, lashed out, "Can't you do something for her?"

David knelt on one knee. "Everything is going as it should. I know it's hard to watch, but you can leave if you can't take it."

Spring raked him with her jade eyes. "You are a heartless beast. You don't care how much she hurts!"

"I do care, Spring," David broke in with earnest sincerity. "But this is taking its natural course."

"I would pity any woman who was your wife!" she hissed at him.

David jerked back as if he'd been slapped, his face contorting angrily, the blue of his eyes whitening in his tanned face. Pap, seeing the danger signals, stepped forward.

"Let's pay attention to the situation at hand, shall we? Spring, we've birthed many animals. We know what we are doing."

She looked up into Pap's warning glance and bit her lip. She was acutely ashamed for her harsh words. "I'm sorry, Mr. Saunders. I shouldn't have said that."

David grunted and turned his attention to Suzie, who had reared up her head. Her whole body tensed and then shook with great strength. Suddenly, out in the hay shot a small brown bundle wrapped in what appeared to be a little clear bag.

"Move back, Spring," Pap said. "Suzie's got another job to do."

Spring watched in horrified fascination from the edge of Suzie's nest as Suzie took the object in her teeth and bit into the sack, freeing the small pup. Then she proceeded to lick and lick her offspring until it was free of the embryotic materials. Lastly, Suzie took the pup in her mouth and moved it to her teats, where the animal began to suckle almost immediately.

David watched the process with satisfaction. Contrary to Spring's belief, he felt it totally unfair for the female of any species to have to bear the burden of nurturing the unborn and then to bring it forth in great pain. He wished there was some way to make it easier for Suzie, but realistically, he knew Suzie knew it was something natural only for her to accomplish. She took it in her stride, and David resigned himself to those aspects of nature.

He now looked at Spring. Her face appeared dazed by what she was witnessing, and he thought Mary may have been right to want to keep her out of the barn. He thought it ridiculous that women were shielded from the aspects of their lives that were so much a part of them. In those terms, he guessed, after all, it was best she experienced this act of delivery, for someday, she would go through it herself.

Spring stood, hands clenched at her sides under folded arms. Despite her inadequacy of offering solace to a pain-ridden creature, she tried to think mainly of that rather than the large-bellied dog with the trusting eyes that had contorted in agony and released a small bundle from somewhere near her tail. Spring did not want to think about where or wonder how any female happened to find herself in this situation. Shadowy whispers from the past filled her ears.

Girls talking in low tones in the darkness, giggling, never really knowing, but speculating on male-female relationships. Molly's house with sounds emanating from behind closed doors—what did it mean, and what happened?

"Here she goes again," Pap said, breaking into her thoughts. Once more, Suzie began the process of expelling her young onto the now-bloodstained hay and bringing it to feed.

"She's bleeding!" Spring exclaimed, grabbing David by the ann. "Help her!"

"Spring, it's all right, believe me. That's part of the whole thing." David tried to be reassuring.

"Why don't you go back to the house?" Pap put in.

"No, I've got to stay. Suzie needs someone who is sympathetic to her ordeal," Spring said angrily.

The men glanced at each other, and Pap shrugged. *Knows her own mind, that one does,* he thought.

Patiently, the three waited, and then presently, a third pup appeared, followed shortly by the last one. Suzie bit off the sack and began to lick and clean up its fur. Then she stopped. She did not finish the job but now lay contentedly on her bed of hay, resting, while the three pups fed.

"What's the matter?" Spring asked, moving forward. "Why did she stop? Is this one dead?"

David didn't answer but bent to pick up the small fluff of dog. A runt, to be sure. He handed it to Pap. "Take care of it."

"What? What's wrong?" Spring looked into David's face, anxiety furrowing her delicate brow. She turned to Pap, and retrieved the tiny pup, holding it closely in her hands against her breast. "What is Pap going to do with Suzie's dog?" she demanded, the tawny specks in the green of her eyes shooting off sparks of anger.

"It's a runt, honey," David said, taking her cupped hands in his own. "It's going to die. Suzie knows it's going to, that's why she let it alone. It's too small to suckle, and the other pups, being stronger, won't let it near the mother. Besides, it will very easily get smothered by their bodies. It's survival of the fittest out here. Everyone must do what they can to survive." He gazed down into her upturned face and saw how shocked she was. Her breathing came short and in fast gasps and, standing closely as they were, her breast pressed, without her notice, against his hands. "Let Pap do quickly what nature will take its own sweet time doing, so the pup won't suffer."

Spring's mind seemed enmeshed in a fog of cotton, for she couldn't think clearly. They wanted to kill the puppy?

He couldn't mean that, could he? At last she found her tongue. "You mean . . . kill it?"

"Yes, honey, that's what I mean. It'll be more merciful in the long run."

It was as if Spring had been struck in the stomach. She lurched away from him and shut her eyes. How she despised him. There was nothing just about him, nothing good.

"I'm not going to let either of you touch this dog." She spoke slowly through her teeth, as if speaking to a slowminded child. "Mr. Saunders, you speak of mercy. You who would show no mercy to two men and laid the whip on them, you who give no further chances to those who are begging for them. You're so damned self-righteous, you know all the answers, giving no credence to anyone else's ideas or opinions. No! I won't let you kill this dog. I'm going to care for it. I'm sick of death and dying. Why bring on the death of something that could live?" Her voice shook with such deep emotion, and she was ashamed for letting him bring her to such a state.

The barn was silent and warm, and presently David cleared his throat. "Take the pup in to Mary. Have her get you a piece of material that has a soft nap on it. Sit with the pup on the porch in the sun, and rub it up good. Have Mary warm up a little milk. You will have to spoon-feed the little critter, a bit at a time. Got all that?"

Spring was so grateful she almost collapsed from her tense stance. Her face relaxed slightly, and the blaze of anger retreated from her eyes. She turned abruptly and left the barn. David went back over to peer down at Suzie and her litter.

"That pup's going to die," Pap stated, matter-of-factly.

David heaved a sigh and brushed his hand across his eyes.

"Yes, I know. But when she looked at me like that . . . I couldn't say no. I had to let her try."

Pap laid a hand across David's shoulders. He understood.

David had tried and tried before, three years ago, to do whatever he could to please a woman, even many times against his better judgment. It was all for love, and look what it got him. Nothing but heartache and the promise to himself that he would never love again. It seemed as though that promise was crumbling, even if David would not admit it.

Chapter 8

The rest of the afternoon, Spring sat on the back porch with the pup, rubbing it and trying to feed it. It seemed so small and fragile, almost as if her handling would make the animal fall apart.

The sun was warm on her head and back, and finally Mary came out with a gray bonnet. "We aren't going to have you turn into one big freckle," she said. Mary gazed down at the young woman for many moments after Spring tied the bonnet onto her chestnut head, covering the long braid she'd wrapped around her crown. It made her sad to think that all Spring's work and care for Suzie's offspring would probably lead to nothing.

Mary then went inside to the storeroom and found a bright-hued bolt of material of yellow broadcloth that had small green flowers interspersed throughout. She wanted to get started on a skirt for the girl right away. She spread the material on the dining table, and then she pulled the rope that hung from the ceiling in the corner of the room, and a door opened, releasing a ladder to the loft above. She pulled up her skirt and began the climb. It had been a long time since she'd been up in the loft, but this time, she had an excuse.

Up there, she saw where David had placed his bedroll atop a thin mattress on one side of the large open, slant-ceilinged room. On the whole, it appeared fairly clean and free of cobwebs. In another corner, she found the trunk she was looking for and opened it.

Inside were clothes, beautiful ones from the finest stores and of the latest styles that had been popular several years ago. There was lingerie so thin one could see through it and so soft and silky to the touch that it was fit for a person of royalty.

That was how she had been treated, the one love of Davey's life, like a queen. Mary pushed thoughts of Isabel away, for she didn't like to think of what she had done to Davey. Instead, she dug among the fineries for some patterns she had packed away in there herself. Finding one for a skirt, a petticoat, and a blouse, she shut the lid and grabbed the dressmaker's form standing close by and came back down the ladder. Then she set to work on the skirt for Spring.

Outside, Spring became drowsy and leaned against the post at the porch corner. She tried to feed the little animal some of the warmed milk Mary had prepared but didn't think she'd gotten much inside. The pup was now asleep.

Some of the men she had ridden with into Saunders's Haven rode up, two ropes around the neck of what was obviously a wild horse. The magnificent animal reared up on its back legs over and over, pulling on the rope, wanting to be free.

The ropes strained against the action, the men struggled to subdue the stallion. David strode out from the barn across the yard to the corral opposite and opened the white gate, and Joe and Hap rode in, dragging the horse after them. Once inside, they removed the ropes and left the corral, taking their horses to the barn. David and Pap hung on the fence watching the stallion—a chocolate brown, its coat shimmering in the sunlight—pace back and forth in front of them. Its eyes seemed wide and wild and angry.

It seemed unfair to Spring to pen an animal of such spirit when it obviously wanted and needed to be free to run where he would, over the mountaintops and into the canyons. She did not realize that she was also thinking of herself in the same light.

"How's the pup doing?" David asked, shading her with his body against the sun.

Spring started. She must have dozed off. "Oh, it's still living. What are you going to do with that horse?"

"We're going to break it, tame it."

"It wants to be free," she said, keeping her face averted, her voice calm.

"Yes, he does." He sat beside her on the porch. "This one, though, has caused me quite a bit of trouble. He ranges up and down the hills with his mares behind him, calling to every other horse I've owned for several years now. In fact, a few of mine have broken away and run with his group now. Once he's broken, we can go and get back what is mine. Yes, he has indeed been a lot of trouble, but that will stop now."

"You sound as if you hate him for what he's done, and now you want to show him who's boss by breaking his spirit." Her voice still had the quality of calmness of moments ago, but David detected that underneath lay her sense of mercy for the downtrodden of the world and her need to do what she could to assuage it.

"He is spirited. I don't want to take that away from him."

"Then let him go free."

"No, I can't do that."

"Just like me," she said, her voice finally taking on the old edge. "You must hate me too, because I've caused you so much trouble."

David was taken aback by this new thought of hers. He said in his deep, soft voice that took on a tone she had not heard from him before, "Spring, I don't hate you. I've never said so, and if I've acted in such a way to make you think so, then I'm sorry. I've always tried to act in your best interest."

He picked up the pup from her lap and held the scrap of fluff in his big hand, stroking its back with his finger.

"What makes you think what you're doing, keeping me prisoner, is in my best interest?" she asked, watching how gently he handled the pup.

"I think we've discussed that before. Anyway, you could leave sometime, but not yet. I'll let you know."

He gave her back her charge and went in to the house, returning shortly with some sugar cubes, and went over to the corral. He remained there the rest of the day, talking softly to the stallion, who eyed him warily. At the close of the day, the huge animal, at last, slowly approached David and took the sugar in his lips before galloping over to the farthest corner.

The next morning, Spring repeated what she had been doing for the dog all the previous day, but he appeared weaker, if that was possible. She stopped long enough to try on the skirt Mary had made her, and she was happy to have it. Brought up as she had been with all the amenities of a wealthy young woman in Boston, she was not used to wearing the same garments day after day. Naturally, her clothes had not been homemade, but Mary was quite a good seamstress, and therefore, Spring found no fault with the yellow skirt Mary turned out.

After drinking some herb tea made from a mint plant growing in the back flower box under the kitchen window, Spring placed the pup in her apron pocket, which she wore to help cover up her legs in the tight denim pants, and went over to the corral.

The stallion gave the impression that he was calmer than the day before and shied away from David only halfheartedly. Hap, Joe, Pap, and Henry were hanging over the fence watching David work with the wild steed. They watched in open admiration. As the day wore on, Spring walked over at various intervals to see what progress was being made.

She recognized David's expertise with the horse and saw again the gentleness and respect he gave the animal. Perhaps he was better with animals than he was with people.

Part of the day she spent on the porch with the pup in her lap, spoon-feeding it every half hour but getting more on the outside of it than the inside. She talked to it in a whispered voice that carried through the open window to Mary's ears.

"You have to live, little one. Please be strong and live. If you live, I'll have you be my dog, and no one can take you away except yourself. I'll let you go if you have to go, but if you want to stay, I'll love you. Please, please live."

At one point, in the late afternoon, Suzie ventured forth from the barn, leaving her other three strong pups for the first time. She came and laid her satiny black nose on Spring's knee, looking up into her face with her enormous brown eyes.

It was as if she was begging Spring's forgiveness for not caring for her own child. She sniffed at the minute creature and gave it a lukewarm lick and then nosed Spring's hand up onto her head. Spring smiled down at Suzie.

"It's all right, girl. I'm going to help your baby live, and then I'll bring it to you. You go on back to the others."

She patted the dog's head, and then Suzie headed back to the barn.

That evening, Spring placed the puppy in the small sewing box she had fixed up for it and placed it by the fireplace to keep it warm for the night. The puppy had whined against her cheek, before Spring left it for the night, and even perked up a bit, giving Spring a reason to hope.

Upon awaking the next day, Spring rose quickly from her bed and went to the box. The little scrap of fur was lying stiffly on the material used as a cushion, and when Spring touched it, it was cold and very dead. Spring stared down at it in a trance, unbelievingly, at first.

"Why did you have to die?" she asked into the empty room. "Everything and everyone has to die. Everyone I love. I wanted you to live. I tried to help you." And then she remembered her words to the pup yesterday: *I'll let you go if you have to go.* She guessed the pup had to go.

Mary had finished Spring's petticoat and pale-green blouse late the previous evening, and Spring decided to wear her new clothes that day. She felt rather sick to her stomach over the death of the pup, but as in the past, she closed her mind and heart to it, for the moment, and concentrated solely on herself.

In front of the mirror in the bathroom, she dressed her hair with great care, brushing it until it gleamed and then pinned it up in an extremely attractive bun.

Taking the box in her hands, she left the bedroom, passed through the front room, and out the back door. Mary said good morning to her, but Spring didn't hear her, leaving Mary to gaze after her in silence.

Spring looked about the yard, dazzled by the beaming sunlight streaming down. Then she saw David working with the horse again. She slowly crossed the yard to the corral. David's back was to her. This morning, he was going to try to get a bridle on the horse. He felt her stare and turned.

He was surprised to see her in feminine attire, liking very definitely what he saw. The pale green of her blouse brought out the green of her eyes, and her head was haloed with her bright, clean hair, which was done up so neatly. But there was something about her look that was vulnerable, a look that hadn't been present since he'd brought her here the first day and he'd witnessed her private grief that first night. Then he saw the little box. He turned from the horse and draped the bridle over the fencepost and came out of the corral.

She looked up at his handsome face, seeing the squared chin, the hard plains of his cheeks, the blue eyes that could turn so cold. At last she spoke, her words barely getting past the lump in her constricted throat. "You were right. It died." She shoved the box in his hands. David turned and handed the box to Pap, who was standing, close by.

He took her hand in his. "Come with me," he said, leading her down past the corral, away from the house. They walked in silence, and she did not draw her hand away from his. He held it loosely, but she felt some comfort from it."

They stopped on a hummock overlooking a stand of trees sloping down the steep hillside and coming to the edge of a clear-blue mountain lake. Around the lake rose blue-gray, rock-hard mountains, and it was beautiful in its massive, unrelenting way.

The soft late-May breeze blew across the bluff where they stood—a tall, confident, physically fit man and a small-boned, delicate form of a woman.

David hurt for Spring. Once more, that feeling arose in him, a feeling he had not felt for several years—hurt for a woman. But this time it was different, in that this woman was a strong-willed, intelligent woman with a vivid personality and qualities for survival that the other woman did not possess. He did not feel sorry for Spring as he had felt pity for the other, for he knew that Spring did not feel sorry for herself and would think less of anyone who would cater to her in such a way.

He saw the roundness of her cheek, the slight bloom of a rose in it, the small nose curving gently upward, and the soft, full lips that trembled despite her effort to control them. He turned her to him and took her face in his hands, tilting her head back until he could see all of her face.

"I'm sorry about the pup. I know how much you wanted to save it."

"I shouldn't have tried," she answered, her eyes bright with unshed tears.

"Yes, I think you should have tried. We never know what will work and what won't unless we try." He smoothed her cheeks with his thumbs. They felt rough on her silken skin. They were work hands, again giving her comfort.

"But you told me it wouldn't live. You all told me." She bowed her head, and he wanted to gather her into his arms and hold her, but he forced himself to stand with his arms at his sides.

"I'm not always right, believe me. I've made mistakes, but the only way I ever found out what would work was to try. You must do that too."

She looked up at him, and tendrils of her chestnut hair filtered about her face. She heaved a sigh of confusion. He was being so nice to her, and yet she couldn't let that keep her from her decision to leave, now that the pup was dead.

She glanced away from his handsome features and looked out across the rows of mountains fading into the distance.

"Your face is practically all healed," he said, "except for the cut." He traced it with his forefinger. "But I think it will be nearly unnoticeable in a few days."

Spring raised her hand to her face. "That's funny, I haven't even given any thought to my face in all this time. I'm a little vain, you know."

They turned to walk back up to the yard. "You have a right to be," he replied. They continued to the house in silence, and then he set out for the corral.

"Mr. Saunders," she called out to him. "Thanks."

"For what?" he asked.

"For not saying 'I told you so.'" Then Spring turned quickly and went into the house.

Mary was nowhere to be seen, so Spring went to the bedroom to make preparations for her departure. Now that she had some female attire, she would not be looked at in a strange manner in Denver and therefore call attention to herself.

She rolled her skirts and accessories in a blanket, which she would use for cover later when it got cooler; and she also took the silver-handled hairbrush to sell for money. She didn't have a cent to her name at present, or anything of value; and though she hated to steal, she felt she had no choice There was also the horse she would have to take. She didn't know yet if she would try to sell it or somehow get it back to Mr. Saunders.

She changed back into the hat and pants, but knew she would be more comfortable riding that way. Then she gathered her bundle and looked about the room where she'd spent the last several nights. It was a very nice room, one that any woman would be grateful to have and share with someone she loved.

Well, she must make her move now, while everyone was occupied with other things, and be gone for as long as possible before anyone realized she was missing.

In the kitchen, she picked up a few slices of thick bread and pumped herself with a bottle of water. There was also some meat left over from last night's supper, which she took from cold storage. On the side of the house, Mary was working in the garden, weeding and picking vegetables for the afternoon meal. The rest of the household was at the corral, watching David's progress with the wild stallion.

No one noticed her as she made her way across the yard to the cool, shadowed barn. Suzie rose from her bed with her sleeping pups and followed her into one of the horse stalls, where she quickly blanketed and saddled a horse. Thank goodness for all the riding lessons when she was growing up, she thought.

Suzie rubbed against Spring's leg as she worked; and when she finished tying her bedroll onto the back of the saddle, she stooped to pet the animal's head.

"I'm sorry, Suzie," she whispered, "but I failed you with your baby. He died in the night."

Suzie licked Spring's hand and raised her paw. Spring took it in her hand and gave it a shake. "Bye now, and don't tell anyone I'm leaving." She mounted the mare and rode quietly out the back door of the barn.

Keeping to the trees on the far side and keeping the house between herself and the garden and the corral, Spring found the trail leading out of Saunders's Haven. Her memory was serving her well, for there ahead was the sharp bend in the path with the sharp protruding rocks overhead. Past that hurdle now, she urged her mount to as great a speed as was possible.

Spring was very nervous about leaving. She knew she was safe up in the mountains—at least safe from the kinds of situations that a city many times offered up to inexperienced young women of her status. Mr. Saunders had not made any advances toward her, but she had noticed how some of the other hands had watched her from beneath their hat brims; and though she thought that they probably stayed away from her due to some word on David's part, what was he saving her for? Himself? No, her chances were much better in Denver, and the quicker she got there, the better. She did not know how she would live through Mr. Saunders's anger when he caught her.

No, that wasn't right. *If* he caught her.

She rode for over an hour and was getting hungry. She saw the place in the pass where along one side, a steep cliff rose almost straight up from the ground and on the other side was a steep drop to a canyon below. It was only wide enough to permit a wagon to pass by with extreme caution. It was at this point that a few rocks were dislodged from above the horse and rider, causing the mount to rear up and flare its nostrils in fear. On a ledge above was a mountain lion in a leaping position. Spring slid off the horse's back just as the cougar jumped onto the horse.

The horse screamed in terror, bucked, and reared up, waving its forelegs in the air. The sleek-coated tawny-brown cat lent its own voice to the fray, but stayed atop the horse, biting into its neck.

Not waiting to see what would happen, Spring somehow found the strength and courage to stand up shakily and try to scramble up the steep mountain cliff. Her soft boots did not grab into the rocky crevices at all well, but sheer panic and fear kept her moving upward, however slowly. She heard below her the horse scream again. Then silence. Looking briefly over her shoulder to the trail, she saw it empty of the horse and the mountain lion standing, its sides heaving, peering over the edge of the cliff.

Thinking that the horse must have gone over the rim, Spring grabbed roots and branches of bushes that stuck out of the side of the rock wall she was climbing. More loose pebbles and stones fell to the trail below, drawing the attention of the brown cat to Spring clawing her way to the ledge from where the cat had jumped.

She reached it at last, not noticing her cut and bruised hands, or her wildly beating heart in her chest. However, her pounding heart was drumming so loudly in her ears that she almost couldn't hear the cat's growling as it turned and padded its way across the path to where Spring had begun her climb moments before.

She edged her way farther up on the thin shelf of rock, all the while keeping a wary eye on the deadly cat. Suddenly, Spring's loosened long red-gold hair entangled itself in a thick bramble bush right above her shoulder. The more she tried to pull her head away, the more ensnared she became. The cat inched its way up the face of the cliff, and Spring realized that in her hurry to leave, she had brought no weapons, though she didn't know how to use a gun. And now that she was rendered almost immoveable, she was at the mercy of the cougar.

She picked up loose stones that lay within reach, throwing them at the advancing cat, to no avail.

The yellow-eyed cat bared its teeth as it crept forward. When at last she saw the animal crouch to spring, her legs turned to water, and her mouth dried in horror. However, she opened her lips and let out a wild scream that sent the birds flying from the trees and rent the silent afternoon air with a sound of complete despair. For a brief moment, the cougar checked its motion and then leapt forward in a powerfully muscled bound.

Spring braced herself for the assault. But then a sharp crack sounded, and it was several seconds before she opened her eyes to see why the wildcat hadn't landed on her. She looked down to the trail and was not surprised to see David, along with Pap and Henry, staring up at her. Her relief at finding herself still alive and breathing quickly engulfed her, and she could have sat down, her legs were trembling so, if her hair had been free to allow her to do so. Instead, she sagged against the stone wall and gulped great breaths of air, trying to swallow the fear in her dry throat.

At last, she looked down closely at David, and under his tan, his face was a dark, ruddy color, and his eyes were colorless behind his long dark eyelashes. Now she was afraid again, but for an entirely different reason.

"Come down from there," David commanded, his voice deadly quiet and calm.

"I . . . I can't. My hair is caught. I can't . . . can't move."

He muttered something under his breath and dismounted.

Pap and Henry also dismounted and went to look at the wildcat lying dead at the bottom of the cliff.

"Where's the horse?" Pap questioned.

"I . . . I . . . don't know for sure. I think he, she went over the edge," she said in a small voice. Pap and Henry went over to the ledge and descended to a small platform of stone where the horse lay.

Spring turned her attention back to David's advance up the mountainside.

He climbed with a deadly purpose, and she wondered whether death by a panther would not have been preferable to his wrath. When he reached her, which he did with more ease than she had reaching this spot, he removed a knife from a sheath hanging from his leather belt. He started to disentangle her hair and found it totally riddled with thorns.

"I'm going to have to cut your hair," he said unfeelingly.

"No, you can't do that!" she exclaimed.

"Well, damn your pretty hide, then you'll just have to remain up here for the mate of that cat down there." He made a move to leave her.

"No, don't leave me. Cut it if you must, but don't butcher it."

He gave her a baleful stare and began to chop at her hair. He himself hated to cut the gorgeous sunburnt tresses, and when he was through, there was a good eight inches of the fine stuff remaining in the bush. Then he led her down the cliff to the pathway.

Reaching the bottom, he suddenly turned on her in such a rage as she had not seen him display before. He grabbed her shoulders and shook her so hard her teeth rattled in her head.

"You lying, conniving little bitch!" he hissed into her face. "I trusted you!"

"I never lied to you, Mr. Saunders," she managed to say without biting her tongue. "I always told you I'd leave you, that you couldn't make me stay. I never lied to you about that."

"And I told you I'd let you go sometime. I'd let you know when."

"Why does everything have to be done on your time table?" she questioned hotly. "You are not my master or my father. You are not my—" A shot rang out, disturbing the birds that had settled once again in the trees.

"Goddamn it to hell! They had to kill Joker. You killed that horse just as if you pushed it over the cliff yourself. That's what this little sojourn of yours cost me, plus nearly killing yourself along with the horse. When I get you home, you're going to regret it!" He grabbed her about her waist and swung her up onto the saddle and mounted behind her, turning Aphrodite around in what seemed to be one fluid motion.

Pap and Henry reappeared, carrying saddle, blanket, bridle, and the blanket roll containing Spring's clothes. David and Spring headed back in the direction from which they had come, leaving the others to follow after they'd gotten Spring's gear arranged on their own mounts.

It did not seem long before they were riding into Saunders's Haven once more. On the last stretch, David spurred his horse to a faster gait. Arriving at the front door, he jumped down, pulling Spring roughly to the ground. Mary stood at the door.

"Oh, Spring, thank God you are all right. You had us all so worried. If Suzie hadn't told us you were gone . . ."

David seized Spring's wrist in a bone-crushing grip and pulled her up the stairs into the house. She didn't have time to say anything to Mary or wonder how Suzie could have possibly told them she had left. She was too busy trying to remain on her feet, for David was dragging her through the living room and into the bedroom in such a fashion as to almost pull her arm out of its socket. She tripped at the last, and he hauled her up and threw her bodily on the bed.

Mary appeared at the door. "Davey, what are you going to do?" She was genuinely concerned. "Don't hurt her, Davey."

David stormed across the room and slammed the door in her face, yelling for her to get out of the house and stay out until he said she could return.

When he turned back to Spring, she was standing by the bed, her hair hanging at different lengths, hands on her slim but gently rounded hips, her small but firm breasts heaving against the new white blouse tucked into the skintight pants. Two spots of red glowed hotly in her cheeks, and her wide-set green eyes blazed with indignation.

"You despicable cad! You have no right to treat me like some spoiled child. How dare you drag me in here?"

"I'll show you exactly what rights I have, young lady," he replied grimly, striding to her side. He again lifted her off her feet and tossed her unceremoniously onto the bed.

Before she had a chance to move, he was atop her, straddling her legs so she couldn't kick at him or twist away. She slapped at his hands and chest and tried to sit up. Seizing her wrists, he pulled her arms above her head, and she was rendered motionless.

"I'll scream," she threatened. "I swear to God, I'll scream my head off."

"Go right ahead, dear Spring. But let me assure you, it will be to no avail. This is my house. My word is law here, and everyone here knows that and adheres to that fact."

"Mary . . ."

"Mary, much as she may like to, will not come to your rescue. I am in charge here. Get that through your head."

Spring felt such frustration as she had never known before take hold of her insides and well up within her. He was right, of course. There was no one anywhere for her.

Relaxing for a second, he loosened his hold, and she suddenly freed one hand, giving him two stinging blows across his smooth, hard cheek. "I will leave here, I will, I will, I will. That's a promise, Mr. Saunders."

He loosened her other hand. Never in his life had he met with such a strong-willed female, and all he wanted to do was throttle those familiar words out of her throat. Instead, he took her shoulders in a heavy, hard grasp, digging his fingers into the softness of her arms. Almost losing control in his blind rage and remembrance of past years, he shook her up and down on the bed, until Spring was gasping for air and her head fell back, causing her to nearly lose consciousness. Her body became slack in his hands, and finally, he noticed how faint she had become.

Shocked, he stopped shaking her and gently laid her back on the bed, resting beside her, his breath coming in short gasps from his throat. One leg lay across her thighs, but she lay docile beside him, her eyes closed, her head turned away from him.

Calm now, he took her chin and turned her head in his direction. He saw where she had bitten her lip and a trickle of blood oozed out on her swollen lip. He wiped it with the tip of his finger, and her eyes fluttered open.

"I'm sorry," he said softly. "The only excuse I have is that I guess it makes me crazy when you say you're going to leave me."

Deeply overcome, Spring perceived that this man was greatly troubled by his feelings and his reactions to her deeds and words. She also knew she could never make an escape without his stopping her. He knew too much, and she knew too little.

"Are you all right?" he asked when she didn't speak.

She cleared her throat. "Yes, I'm all right. But I want you to know I wasn't leaving you. I was just going, that's all."

"If you leave this place, for whatever reason, you'll be leaving me." His face seemed vacant, as though he was speaking to someone in another time. "Please say you won't try to leave me again." He touched her cheek. "Please, Isabel."

The name startled them both, and he looked at Spring as Spring for the first time since they entered the room. His eyes came into focus on her, and he gave his head a small shake.

Corning to his senses, he spoke again. "Spring, as a favor to Mrs. Butler, promise me you'll stay," he asked, sitting up on the bed, his back to her.

"I need to find John. I don't think he's dead, and when we find each other, I'm going to marry him," she answered.

His back stiffened, and he brushed his hair back in the familiar gesture. "I'll help you find him, if that's what you really want." He said this quietly.

The room was dark now, and a chill pervaded the air.

She wasn't sure she wanted to marry John, if he was ever found. However, Spring wanted David to realize he could not control her, even if she didn't try to get away again.

"I don't like you," she said to his back.

He gave a little laugh, harsh and short. "Well, that's your pre-rogative." He arose and went to the door.

"Mr. Saunders, I promise I won't try to run away again. I'll let you know before I leave next time."

"Thank you," he answered softly and left her alone.

Spring lay on the bed devoid of feeling. What a long day it had been. It was a day that could hardly bear thinking of. First the pup had died. Then the gentle understanding of Mr. Saunders. Then the ride on the trail that almost led to her death at the sharp claws and teeth of a mountain lion, if Mr. Saunders hadn't saved her. Then the physical battle with him. And lastly, being called Isabel. Who was Isabel?

Mary came into the room carrying her bedroll. She was horri-fied by Spring's appearance and quickly got her into a bath to soak and wash her hair, promising she would do her best to straighten up the ragged cuts of David's knife. Pap had explained to her what had happened on the trail, and though she sympathized with Spring, her willfulness had almost cost her her life and caused a horse to lose its life. She remained kind and helpful but did not talk against David, as Spring thought she might.

At last, Spring asked her, "Who is Isabel?"

Mary was surprised at the question, but outwardly, she stayed calm and forthright. "She was Davey's wife."

"Where is she now?" Spring asked, incredulous at the news.

"She's dead. Now if you want to ask any more about her, it is not my place to say. You must ask Davey."

"I don't think he'd tell me. I'm not a close confidant." Spring sighed and closed her eyes. But she did know that Isabel must have tried to leave Mr. Saunders and he wouldn't let her. Well, she really couldn't, blame Isabel, and she said so to Mary.

Mary turned on her, her eyes piercing. "Sometimes you speak before you know what you are saying. You have a lot to learn about people, about Davey." She blinked back salty tears and drew herself up. "Just because you come from a la-di-da existence back East doesn't give you the right to look down your nose at things you don't understand, and it doesn't seem as if you want to understand."

Totally abashed, Spring murmured an apology, and was left to finish her bath in solitude.

*   *   *

When David had left the bedroom, he wandered out back, telling Mary she could go back in and see to Spring's needs before beginning supper.

He could not believe how vividly the memories of Isabel and their stormy marriage had replaced reality those few moments ago. He had actually called her Isabel, uttered the name aloud. It was the first time he'd given voice to that name since the night he'd gone out with the rest of the men to hunt for her in the wintery darkness.

She had always wanted to leave too, but for different reasons than the young woman he had left lying on his bed.

And she had been weak, weak. Spring was not weak. She was strong and intelligent, and she fought back. Nothing would ever get her down to where Isabel had been, and though Isabel had been beautiful, in her white but translucent way, her ideas had not been beautiful. He had called her his snow maiden, her hair as white as his own was in the spring and summer months, her eyes a pale gray, and her personality was like snow too. Pure, white, clear ice. And his deep love for her could not thaw her out.

Spring was not in any way the same, except for her wanting to leave. But why did he want her to stay? David walked over to the corral and watched the big stallion paw the ground and then dash away to the far side of the enclosure. Was he falling in love with her? No, he never wanted to love anyone again, not after Isabel. But contrary to his hard exterior, David was a warm-blooded, healthy male who could tell very well that Spring looked warm and inviting, that she would be soft and pliable in his arms. Even in a bedraggled state, she appeared sensual, and she was gentle and merciful, compassionate and passionate, except where he was concerned. She did not like him and wanted to marry that ridiculous John Granville. He felt sure Granville was the very reason for Spring being in her present situation, so why did he want her when she was just a hundred and ten pounds of trouble and responsibility that he really didn't want to have? God, that question was driving him crazy. He would have to guard his feelings very carefully.

He looked up at the stars. They seemed so close when up in the mountains. The wind lifted and sang its melody through the treetops. He hoped she wouldn't try to leave again. He very much hoped she wouldn't.

Chapter 9

Three days later, Spring awoke to the sound of a heavy rain falling onto the roof and slanting against the windowpanes of the bedroom.

She lay there listening to the comforting sound as it broke into the gray dawn of morning. She was warm and safe, and though she spent the past days in almost complete solitude, she felt content. After Mary had spoken to her in David's defense, Spring had kept to herself more than ever. She wasn't angry at Mary for having said what she had, but it was more out of shame for her own harsh judgment of David Saunders. It was apparent he had built this very lovely home for a wife that for some reason was no longer alive and had not wanted to be here with him. He had begged her to stay, again, through Spring. She had seen the hurt and anguish in those haunting blue eyes. He must truly love Isabel to still think of her and want her to be with him, was her conclusion.

She also thought of that awful thing she had said to him about pitying anyone who was his wife and saying to Mary that she couldn't blame anyone for wanting to leave him. Her face burned with mortification for her outlandish behavior. By what right did she have to say such things about events that she had no knowledge of? She never had tried to understand David, or tried to get to know him, what he was like or what his life had been. He was held in such high esteem by so many; and she knew without a doubt that if their first meeting had been under different circumstances, she would have been impressed by his rugged good looks, the slightly crooked nose, the brilliant blue of his eyes, the white blond hair contrasting so vividly with the darker moustache. If he had been dressed in the blue broadcloth suit with the ruffled shirt, as he had been the night he had apologized to her for ruining her parasol, instead of cracking that whip in his sweat-stained leather attire, she knew she would have been very favorably attracted to him.

But those were only outward attributes. There was the self-assurance that got under her skin. He was right about everything, and for some reason, that made her angry. She was always in situations that caused him to think less of her, and she didn't like that feeling of having to defend herself to him. And then there was John. She had only agreed to marry him because she knew David was standing in the shadows, listening in on their conversation. So, foolishly, she had accepted the ankle bracelet she still wore, and without losing more face in front of him, she was still determined to marry John and show David Saunders he did not have control of her life.

She did not try to analyze why she needed or wanted to prove that to herself, or to him. She did not even let it enter her mind that David "Whip" Saunders had become so important to her that she had to emotionally and mentally push him out of her life in this way.

She did not realize that David watched her every time she was outside working in the garden that she had taken over from Mary, or hanging out wash on the clothesline, and when walking about the yard. He watched her to see that she did not try to run away, but also because she was so lovely to see. He always appeared to be busy, so she did not suspect his avid interest in her, and she did not know that the more visible she was, the more he wanted to see her.

This morning, she did not smell breakfast cooking as usual, and so she arose and dressed hurriedly to see if something was amiss. When she arrived in the kitchen, she saw David kneeling by the cooking stove, putting fuel inside to get it going for the day. He lit the kindling and stood.

"Is Mary ill?" she asked, causing him to start.

"Oh, no," he replied, turning around slowly. "We have an understanding that whenever it rains, she gets a little free time, and she can remain in her quarters with Pap."

"Then she won't be down here until the rain lets up?"

"We all have a lazy day when it rains like this. It's too messy outside to do much. By the way, I meant to tell you, I think Mary did a pretty neat job on your hair the other night."

"Oh, thank you," she answered, turning to look out the back-door window. She saw rivulets of water running down the slopes of the hills and draining across the yard. Dark, gray clouds covered the mountaintops and hung in the valleys between them. It was a dismal day, and the prospect of having to be with Mr. Saunders all by herself made Spring a little uneasy. "It's awfully short, though. I can't remember having it this short for many years."

"Well," he said, taking the coffeepot and readying it for the stove, "it'll grow back and be as beautiful as ever."

Spring glanced quickly over to him, but his back was to her, and she couldn't tell if he had been paying her a compliment or just reassuring her.

"What do you want for breakfast?" he asked, now taking plates from the shelf.

"I'll just have tea. I don't enjoy eating in the morning."

"So I've noticed. You really should, you know. You are too thin, and eating earlier in the day is much better for you than eating bigger meals later."

"I really can't see where that concerns you," Spring replied. "Whether I'm thin or not is my business."

David chuckled. He did not want to get into it with her again. He really was going to try to get along with this girl. So he said, "Yes, you are right. You may eat whenever you wish."

Spring didn't want to argue either. She tried to soften her words. "I'm sorry I don't know my way around a kitchen. Mary has been showing me a few things, but I'm so slow at it, it's just easier if she does it herself."

"You learn only by doing, sweetheart," David replied, busily cracking eggs into a pan after removing a sausage and laying it on paper to drain. "But watching helps too."

Spring's heart skipped a beat when he called her sweetheart, but having looked hard at him after he'd said it, it seemed as though it was a term he would call anyone at all, so she relaxed and didn't take it seriously.

Actually, David could have bitten his tongue when the term of endearment slipped out, for that was exactly as he thought of her, as a sweetheart. He knew he was losing the battle of his attraction for Spring when it began to come out in the open like that.

Spring cleaned up the kitchen after he ate, and he sat at the dining table going over some of his accounts. He studied quietly, and she did not disturb him, pouring him an unsolicited cup of coffee and getting a nod of thanks for her consideration. Setting things in order gave her a feeling of wellbeing and belonging. She had not felt as though she belonged at the fort, for nothing there had been hers. Nothing here was hers either, and when Mary was here working, the kitchen was definitely not hers. But for the day, the house belonged to her. Her and David.

She drew in her breath sharply. Now where did that awful thought come from? She must remember that she did not like him and he did not like her. *He has never said that to you*, a little voice said to her. *No*, she answered it. But it made it easier to dislike him if she thought he returned the same feeling.

She sat in the smaller of the wing chairs on the braided rug in front of the fireplace, with one of the many books from the well-stocked bookcase to the right. She lit the lantern and opened the book of sonnets by Elizabeth Barrett Browning. On the flyleaf was a short inscription: "To my Darling, Isabel, my only love, Davey."

Spring almost felt as though she had just read someone's mail, so personal was the inscription to his wife. She hesitated over what to do next, but opted to go ahead and read the sonnets she so loved.

David entered carrying more wood for the fire, which he built up on the grate in a short time. Soon it was crackling merrily.

"What are you reading?" he asked, straightening up and sitting opposite her.

"*Sonnets from the Portuguese*," she answered. "I like Elizabeth Browning. She had a lot of the same feelings about things as I do."

"Really? What?"

"Oh, she did not like abuse of any kind, especially to children."

"I like some of her writings too," he said, leaning forward and taking the book from her hands. He thumbed through the pages, and his eyes lit upon the words he had written to Isabel four years earlier. His eyes met Spring's, and he saw the firelight reflected there, the lovely arched brows and the fringe of chestnut hair on her white forehead. The girl looked at him intently and then glanced away to gaze into the flames. Raindrops drummed noisily on the rooftop.

He shut the book slowly, and with that action, shut his thoughts and heart to Isabel Thornton Saunders for good. He had done his best, and that was all anyone could be expected to do. He suddenly felt unburdened and free and ready to go with his life.

Spring's words brought him back to the present. "I've been meaning to apologize for getting Joker killed. I hope you know that I would never do anything to hurt any animal ever, or a child, and in fact, would do my best to do otherwise. I was foolish to do what I did, and though it's no excuse, it was because of my own selfish motivations that I ran away, and therefore we were attacked by that cougar. I'm very sorry, and when I do leave here and get hold of my money, I hope you will let me pay you for him."

It was the longest speech Spring had ever made, and the sincerity in her eyes told him she meant what she said. He fingered the book he still held and gave her a small smile from under the dark moustache.

"I know you didn't mean to do any harm. I know you are not stupid. In fact, you are much more intelligent than many I've known, but out here, when you aren't used to a place, you must really stop to consider all the alternatives before taking any action."

"You are right," she conceded, and then added, "I should also thank you for—"

"For saving you, again?" He laughed aloud, throwing his head back, causing her to blush. Luckily, the room was sufficiently darkened so as not to cause that embarrassment, for he then said, "Dear Spring, I would have done that for anyone I came across in your position."

His words caused her to want to snap back that death was perhaps better than being here with him, but then the thought came to her that after all, he did not just happen to come across her. He had come after her. Now why did that give her pleasure?

A scratching sound came at the back door, and both David and Spring left their chairs to investigate. The rain was coming down so thickly as to obscure the view of the fences of the corral and around the barn and some of the further buildings as well.

Outside on the porch stood a soaking Suzie with her three roly-poly pups, shaking from the chill. Immediately, Spring's heart went out to them, and she opened the door, going out onto the wind and rain-swept porch.

"Get in here, will you, before you catch your death?" David spoke with exasperation.

"But we can't let them stay there," she began.

"Don't worry, we won't," he said, pulling her back through the door. "I'll get some rags to dry them off."

It reminded Spring of the constant rubbing she had done on the runt of Suzie's litter; only this time, she could feel the difference almost a week could make between their physical bodies. Sitting on the rug before the roaring fire, she rubbed their paws and their thick-furred backs and soft tummies and saw how strong they were. Their eyes were just opening, and the little creatures tumbled merrily over one another.

Suzie, dry now from David's ministrations, kept a watchful eye on her children and a trustful one on Spring.

Spring immensely enjoyed the wild antics, which gave way to her mirth, letting her bright laughter fill the room with a sound that, undetected by her, brought tears to David's eyes.

He had taken his chair again and took great pleasure in seeing Spring care, in her gentle, loving way, for Suzie's offspring.

"That's beautiful," he said to her.

As she gazed up at him from her place on the floor, the fire's glow cast its orange brilliance across her face and graceful neck as she inclined her head. He was reminded of an angel as her chestnut hair glistened about her small head in the firelight.

"What's beautiful'?" she questioned, unaware of the picture she made.

He moved to the floor to draw back one of the pups that had ventured too far and placed it next to the others by Suzie to nurse.

"You are, your laughter in this house. You are beautiful," he said softly, reaching over to her face to brush a loose tendril of hair away from her cheek.

She felt the brief touch on her face, and with that one touch, her heart began to pound in her chest so loudly she was sure he could hear it. Here they were, alone together. No one else was around and wouldn't come to help her if she needed them. She had to say or do something.

"I'm not beautiful," she said, trying to drag her eyes away from his penetrating gaze.

His hand rose to her cheek once more, softly touching it, and it crept around to the back of her head and under her hair, locking her in his grasp.

And then, horror of horrors, his face came closer and closer, and he whispered, "Yes, you are, Spring—the loveliest and most beautiful woman I've ever met."

She tried to pull back and was desperately frightened.

His lips were almost touching hers, and she gasped out the only thing she could think of to say. "I'm in love with John Granville, Mr. Saunders, and he's the only man I ever want in every way."

If she had thrown snow water on him, she couldn't have done a better job of dousing the fires he himself had been trying to smother. His hand dropped, and he leaned back, the blue of his eyes lightening; but his face, manner, and voice were calm, though hard and cold.

"Ah, yes, the ever-present but suspiciously absent young lieutenant. Forgive me, he's so nondescript I'd almost completely forgotten about him."

"Don't let's talk about him," she said shakily, moving away to sit in her chair. She picked up the book of sonnets resting on the side table and opened it.

"Fine with me," he replied, poking the logs to better places in the hearth. "He's not a subject I enjoy."

Spring did not answer, for she was staring at the place where the inscription to Isabel had been. The page had been torn out and was nowhere to be found in the book.

Chapter 10

"Are you almost through with that?" David asked, walking up to Spring as she bent to the clothes basket and took out another sweet-smelling damp shirt. She reached up to the line and pinned the shirt onto it.

"Just about. Why?"

"I thought I deserved a break since I got up at four thirty this morning and have been out overseeing the outbuildings and seeing what repairs needed to be done on them. I do that twice a year—get the supplies and then have the men work on them. But I'm tired, and it's getting on toward lunch, and I thought we could go for a walk down by the lake and have a picnic." He spoke nonchalantly, for when he did not want to show any kind of emotion, he was able to hide it.

Spring kept busy with the wash, but glanced at him out of the corner of her eye. Since he had almost kissed her several days ago, they had both stayed clear of each other, being polite but being strangers. Actually, though neither one really wanted to be attracted to the other, it was happening all the same. Well, she didn't suppose it would hurt to go to the lake with him. If she mentioned John once in a while, perhaps that would keep Mr. Saunders in his place.

She bent to retrieve the basket and said, "I'd like to go. How far is it?"

"About a forty-five-minute walk. I'm going to swim when we get there. It sure is a warm day."

"I hope you don't expect me to swim. I told you I was afraid of water." She went through the back door as he held it open for her.

"Well, it's really very easy, but no, I won't throw you in if that's what you are afraid of."

"Throw you in? What in the world are you up to now, Davey?" Mary looked up from baking pies at the cooking table.

"We're going down to the lake. Could you please throw us something together for a picnic lunch?" he asked.

"Sure, I can," she said, going to gather in a large checked cloth a hunk of bread and cheese wrapped in a brown cloth. When Spring was out of earshot, having gone to her room to brush her hair, Mary said to David, "Here, you might like this too. It may come in handy." She slipped into the bundle a bottle of white wine from a stock he kept in the supply room.

"Don't know why you think we'll need that," he said, giving her a frown. "We'll have plenty of water."

"I know that," she said in return. "However, you never know what you may or may not need."

"Mary, you are incorrigible." He leaned down and pecked her on the cheek. Then he called out, "Spring, are you coming?"

"Yes, here I am." She had tied her hair back with a green ribbon that matched her eyes. Little curls strayed about her face, and she did not even look her nineteen years.

They started off, David carrying the red-checked bundle, tall and muscle-corded, the material of his blue shirt stretching across his broad shoulders, his back tapering down to a slender waist. The blond head was covered by his gray hat with the Indian feathers sticking out from the band. Beside him strode Spring, barely reaching his shoulder, the red highlights of her hair glistening in the bright midmorning sun shining from the corn silk–blue sky. Her yellow-and-green skirt swept through the yellowing grasses, and she felt gay and happy for the first time in a long while. A soft, warm breeze ruffled the aspen leaves as they passed under. They made their way down the slope after the house and other close buildings disappeared from view.

Coming out on the hummock, they stopped, and David pointed to the crystal-blue lake below. There were birch and aspen trees along one side of the lake, but the other side was clear for a small distance, giving way to a white beach area.

"It's beautiful," Spring breathed in genuine pleasure.

She looked up at her companion and smiled.

"I love this place," he answered quietly. "I'm very fortunate to have it. Come along now. Right here is a little tough going, but after we get below these few big rocks, it'll be fairly easy to descend." He went on ahead, stopping every few minutes to see that she was following with no trouble of her own. Just as he reached the bottom, he turned to her.

Her soft-booted feet slipped on some loose pebbles, and she would have fallen at his feet if he hadn't reached out to grab her. He caught her around the waist with his arm and drew her to him. He was always surprised, when an occasion arose to touch her, at how fragile she felt in his hands; and yet she worked hard around the house doing a lot of the work Mary had done. She never complained if hurt. She was strong.

Spring felt the muscled arm pull her close, and she had to admit to herself that her heart had skipped a beat, not so much from nearly falling, but from being held next to him. He smelled good, clean and masculine. He quickly set her away from him, asking if she was all right.

"Oh yes, I just slipped on those pebbles. Sorry I ran into you."

"Well, it'll be all right now," he answered, and again he led the way down toward the lake with Spring following.

Arriving at the water's edge, Spring could hardly contain her feeling of complete abandonment. She stood close to where the ripples moved onto the gritty sand and held her arms out wide as if to embrace the whole world. She raised her face to the sun and let it bathe her inside and out, and she drank in the fresh air with a delicious feeling of wonder.

Wrapping her arms around herself, she turned to find David staring at her with unconcealed amazement in his eyes. His eyes were unexpectedly deep blue behind the dark fringe of lashes. She felt it more than she saw it.

"Venus," his voice was husky in his throat.

"Isn't she a goddess of some kind?" she asked, trying to shift his mind onto something other than herself.

"Yes, the Roman goddess of love and beauty. That's what you look like standing there in the sun."

"Mr. Saunders, I wish you wouldn't say things like that to me. Please remember I'm promised to someone else."

David didn't answer her but knelt down to spread the checked cloth and food on the sand. Then he went to stand by Spring by the rim of the cove where the water lapped gently. "The lake is fed by the same stream that comes down by the trees up by the house. It keeps running pretty well all year long from the winter snows, unlike some streams. So the lake stays full enough to have some fun during the year. We usually come down here on special occasions like the Fourth of July. We picnic and swim, build a campfire, and sometimes stay out all night. We do this even though Colorado isn't a member of the Union yet."

"The women come too?" she asked, glad he had dropped the subject of her looks.

"You bet. In fact, they are the ones who urge us to get going on the idea. Lorna comes, and Mary, and sometimes the men bring someone from the city."

"I'd like to meet Lorna sometime."

"Sure. I can show you the way, and you can walk there this week, if you like. It's in the opposite direction from the one we took today."

"Why can't I ride?"

"I think you know the answer to that one, my girl."

"I promised you, Mr. Saunders." Spring gazed across the diamond studded lake.

"Hmm. Well, we'll see. Oh!" he exclaimed suddenly. "Look up there!" He pointed with his finger into the sky above the trees on the opposite shore. Just above the tree line, a large bird rose and took to the heavens.

Spring had never seen such a large bird before and asked what kind it was. The bird soared and swooped, spreading its long, broad wings and gliding over the lake's surface until it landed on a thick branch of a fallen tree close to where David and Spring stood.

"It's a bald eagle," he said to her in a soft voice. "Do you see the little red string around the eagle's right leg?"

Spring looked at the bird's bright yellow legs and sharp-taloned feet. She nodded, holding her breath. She was surprised when David moved from her side, nearer the eagle, until the bird was next to him. He held out his arm to it, and the eagle jumped from the branch and onto the arm of David Saunders.

Spring thought for certain that the bird would claw David or peck his eyes with its long, strong break that was at least two and a half inches in length and over an inch from top to bottom. She saw that the eagle was not really bald but only had the appearance of baldness due to the smooth white feathers on its head.

David motioned to Spring to come closer, but slowly. She was afraid to move, for the bird now looked at her with its piercing black eyes. However, David was talking to the eagle and calling it Freedom. She came up behind him and peered at the bird perched on his arm.

"I found Freedom one day on the ground when I was down here. He'd fallen from his aerie—that is, his nest—and had broken his wing. He was just an eaglet, of course, about four weeks old."

"He's very beautiful," Spring whispered. "But he seems so powerful too."

"He is that. Right now, old boy, you are just too heavy for me to hold on my arm like this. Stand back, Spring."

She did as he asked. David bent his knees and lowered his arm, and then swung it up into the air. Freedom took off into the soft breezes and again became one with the universe. "He must weigh at least ten pounds now."

Spring turned back to the picnic on the sand and sat down. She slowly unwrapped the cheese and bread, asking for and receiving the knife David always carried with him. He sat beside her and opened the bottle of wine as she cut the cheese and tore off small pieces from the bread.

As she was thoughtful, David asked her, "What are you thinking of?"

"Oh, nothing."

"I know very well that something always goes on in your head, Spring. Your mind is always moving." He took a bite of the light lunch.

"It's just that I'm surprised you would let the eagle go after you had fixed its wing." She looked right at him, daring him almost to pick up on her message, which he refused to do.

"Well, of course I would. It deserves to be free. He needs to be free."

"Then I wish I was an eagle. I could be free then too." She did not raise her voice, but her meaning was very clear.

He sighed and took a drink from the bottle of wine. It was smooth and cool in his throat. What was he to say to her?

"You would be a beautiful eagle," he said, finally. "You could touch all the mountaintops, sail over the rivers and canyons. You would make a lovely sight."

"That's not what I meant, and you know it."

"My sweet Venus, I told you, you could leave sometime. I wish, though, that you could find something here that you liked, that you would want to stay."

"What, Mr. Saunders? Why do you wish that?"

He gazed at her intently, searching his own heart for the right answer, and then said, "I don't know, Spring. I wish I did know. Now, I'm going swimming. Do you want to try?"

"No, thank you. I'll just lie here in the sun and watch you." Realizing he was going to disrobe in order to swim, she blushed a deep red and walked down the shoreline until she heard him splashing in the water.

She turned and watched him as he headed out toward the middle of the lake, taking powerful strokes, moving swiftly. At times he disappeared from view, causing her to search frantically for him, but he always surfaced in a different spot from where she was looking. She went back to the picnic blanket and lay down. Soon the heat from the sun caused her eyes to droop, and before she knew it, she had fallen blissfully asleep on the thought that, after all, life wasn't so awful here in this paradise.

Slowly she came back to consciousness and realized her face was in shadow, and that shadow came from David's body.

He was sitting next to her and staring out over the lake. The sun had moved across the sky, and a few stray clouds had trekked their way after it.

Suddenly, David's hand touched her cheek. It was soft on her face, and she didn't move. "I think you got too much sun. You should wear a bonnet." Her skin did feel a little tight. She struggled to a sitting position. He smiled at her. "Have a nice nap?"

"Yes. I hope I can sleep tonight."

He sat clad only in his blue denim pants and boots. His back and chest were bare and brown and looked satiny. She felt herself wanting to reach out and touch him. She was astonished by her thoughts and knew no nice girl would think them, but she couldn't help herself. He was a handsome specimen, but she wished she was not here with her feelings almost out in the open.

"I suppose we must be getting back. Mary will worry."

Spring stood up and gathered up the food. The empty wine bottle sat by David's side. "Did you finish that whole thing?" she asked, incredulous.

"Yes. I'm sorry, did you want some?"

"No." She watched him pick it up.

"Do you mind that I drank it?" he asked.

"No, should I?"

"No, it's just that someone else—" he began as they started away from the lake.

"Someone else what?"

"Someone else did. Well, come along. The sun's heading down behind the mountains."

They had not walked more than fifty feet when Spring realized that she had left the remains of their lunch back by the lakeside. David went back to retrieve it, and she walked on, making her way through the tall grasses.

Presently, she came upon a small brown-and-white calf she knew must be only a few weeks old. Its legs were still not in their full strength, and it stood still looking at Spring with its big brown eyes. Always concerned for small animals, she approached the calf carefully, asking it where its mother was. Reaching it, she held out her hand and patted its head. Unexpectedly, she heard David shout across the open space between them, and she looked up, startled, into the angry protruding eyes of the animal who was the calf's mother. Spring backed away, still with her hand outstretched; and she saw the cow duck its head and paw the ground. Spring reeled around and fled across an open meadow, catching her feet and skirts in the roots of the grass. She tripped and almost fell when she glanced briefly over her shoulder to see what the cow was doing.

What she saw made her heart leap into her throat, and her mouth go dry. The huge animal was halfway across the open area, heading straight for Spring.

Abruptly, Spring was hit from behind, and it was a moment or two after she hit the ground that she realized it was David who had made contact. He wrapped his arms about her, and together they rolled away from where they fell into a stand of deeper grass, and there they lay motionless. David's heavy breathing told Spring he must have also run after her, but out of sight of the cow that was bearing down on her. He held her tightly and whispered to her not to make a sound. She was only too glad to obey.

After a few seconds went by, while they listened to the rooting of the mother searching for them, all was silent. David cautiously raised his head and saw the cow leading her young away to the southeast.

"They're going" he said. He looked down at the young and still-frightened Spring lying in his arms. Her eyes were closed, and her head was thrown back. The milky-white skin of her neck pulsed with her heightened heartbeat. "Are you all right?"

"Yes," she breathed. "You, to the rescue again."

He laughed lightly. He removed one of his arms from under her and smoothed back the hair from her forehead. "Yes, what would you do without me?"

He did not expect an answer and therefore was surprised when she said in a low voice, "I don't know."

She opened her eyes and saw his face was very close to hers. She did not move, but lay in his half embrace expectantly. When his lips touched hers, it was unlike anything she had ever experienced before.

David's lips were soft and warmly dry. The hairs from his moustache tickled her upper lip, and she could smell the sweet wine on his clean breath. The pressure of his mouth did not hurt, as John's had, and her own lips did not press into her teeth. He did not rob her of her dignity with that gentle pressure, did not slobber with the repulsive wetness of other kisses she had received in the past. When he raised his head, he touched her cheek with his own lightly roughened one, and then he kissed her temple.

"My beautiful Venus," he said shakily. She had not really kissed him back, but she had not pulled away or been repelled by him. He knew that. He was too afraid to love her. Love hurt too much. It was ridiculous to be afraid of a woman when he had been through all the hair-raising things he had.

There were not many men he feared, if any, but he did fear an involvement with Spring Ames. He did not want it, yet he could not help himself.

At last Spring moved and spoke. "Please, Mr. Saunders, I thank you for helping me out again. I will try not to bother you the rest of the time I am here." Then desperately, she said, "But please, you have . . . I have got to remember my promise to John Granville. I . . . I love him and am going to marry him."

David was silent, and he searched her face. He could see the telltale signs, the flash of her eyes, the upward tilt of her chin and nose. She would honor that promise because of her stubbornness, not because of her true feelings. She was going to show him she could be free.

David let her loose so suddenly that Spring felt totally alone when he stood up. A chill settled upon her as she too arose.

"I . . . I hope I didn't hurt your feelings," she said lamely.

"Who, me?" His hard laughter echoed off the surrounding hills. "I didn't think you thought I had any feelings." His voice was as cold as his now-whitened eyes. "No, my dear, you didn't hurt my feelings. Now, let's move it before it's completely dark out here."

They did not speak all the way to the house, immersed in their own thoughts. Spring was afraid of her feelings. She had felt absolutely at ease with them until that day her parasol had been torn unceremoniously from her grasp. Then David "Whip" Saunders had become like a thorn in her side. Everywhere she turned, he was there, saving her from some doom. He was always there being so right. He was always there taking over from people less competent. He was there dishing out punishments, and he was there with people sticking up for him and thinking he was so wonderful.

Well, went on the admonishing thoughts, she had made up her mind about him before, and though he was extremely attractive and kissed with a tenderness she hadn't known he possessed, he was still cruel and unjust. She would just have to make herself steer clear of him.

David was glad Spring had brought him rudely to his senses. What was wrong with him anyway! He planned that the next time he went to Denver, which would be in about three weeks, he would take her with him and be done with her once and for all.

So what had started out to be a fun adventure ended up at the same old stalemate. The strange thing was it did not make either of them happy.

Chapter 11

✕✕✕✕✕✕✕✕

"Mary, I'm going up to visit Lorna today," Spring said. "I enjoyed meeting her for those few moments the other day, and she invited me to come up. I'm caught up on all my work here, so . . ." Spring was standing by the kitchen door talking in a rush.

"Well, I'm sure it's fine with me if you go, honey. However, I don't think you should go when Davey isn't here to ask." Mary put down her rolling pin.

"I don't think I should have to wait around for His Royal Master to return. Who knows when that will be? He's already been gone for five days." Spring spoke sullenly, knowing full well he had left in a bad humor the day after their picnic and was probably using his absence as a punishment, for everyone was warned to stick around the place, and he had given her a particularly penetrating gaze. Of course, "warn" was the term Spring gave to his general instructions.

Mary placed her hands on her hips. "Your work is all up to date, Spring, but I'd sure give a pretty penny to know what happened out there on your picnic to make you and Davey in such a foul mood and him to ride off without a word as to where he was going or what he was doing."

Spring spoke now from exasperation and frustration. She had tried not to let everyone know she was upset, but Mary and Pap were quite attuned to the atmosphere in which they lived, especially when it concerned David Saunders. "If you must know, Mr. Saunders attacked me on the picnic. It was all I could do to get away from him." The minute the lie was out, Spring blushed with such shame as she had never known. How could she say such a thing? she wondered.

Mary's eyes opened wide, disbelievingly. "Why, that is really something. You are sure?"

"Of course, I'm sure," Spring mumbled, compounding the lie with more. "He . . . he . . . you know."

"He didn't rape you, did he?" Mary's voice rose to a high pitch.

"No! No, I got away from him in time. But that's why we weren't speaking when we got back here and why I don't want to be here if he comes in. I'm going, Mary, whether I have your permission or not."

"Well, all right, dear," she answered, with worry shaking her voice. "Better take some of this fresh-baked bread with you." She turned to wrap the loaf.

Taking it, Spring placed her hand on Mary's shoulder. "Please don't tell him I told you. I don't want to embarrass him."

Mary saw that Spring couldn't look her in the eye and assumed it was she who was embarrassed, so she promised.

Later, when she told Pap about it, he was as shocked by David's behavior as Mary had been. He wasn't sure he believed it. Oh, he thought Spring was blowing some pass made at her way out of proportion. Mary wasn't as confident. Davey was, after all, a hearty, virile man; and Spring was lovely, and they had been alone for all that time.

*   *   *

"I hope you don't mind me coming up here like this, without an invitation," Spring said to Lorna and Henry as she settled down to luncheon with them. "It's really lovely up here, and it was a very nice walk. Do you think Suzie will go back on her own?"

"Oh yes, she's got to feed her pups," Henry put in.

Spring seemed to be in a rush and appeared apprehensive. She gave a small laugh. "She just followed me. I tried to make her go back, but it was like she was guarding me." She bent her head to the soup in front of her. She did not realize that that was exactly what Suzie was doing. She looked up and saw that Lorna wasn't eating. "Are you feeling all right?"

"Oh, just a little nausea. I'm at the end of my third month." She smiled shyly and glanced at her husband.

Spring did not comment. In Boston, ladies didn't mention such things in front of men, even their husbands. It was a subject that was taboo, and the proceedings leading up to pregnancy were only whispered about, and in private at that.

"Where is Jacob?" she asked.

"He's sleeping. Being two years old does not always mean he sleeps through the night. He kept me awake for half of it," Lorna said.

"Then when he wakens, why don't you let me play with him or take him for a walk while you rest? I'm quite good with children, and I really like to do something for those I stay with," Spring spoke earnestly.

"That would be lovely. That way, Henry can get some of the fence work done." Lorna looked relieved.

"You know?" Spring's eyebrows raised, furrowing her forehead. "Why don't I just stay here a few days with you. That way, I can give you a hand."

Lorna looked at Henry, and he leaned back in his chair, folding his arms across his chest. He gazed at Spring. "What do you think Dave would say to that?"

"What difference does it make?" she asked. "He doesn't care about me or what I do, as long as I don't run away, and I promised him I wouldn't do that. Besides, he's not my owner." Her green eyes flashed with defiance.

"Well, it's fine with me if you stay, and I'm sure Lorna would appreciate the help you can give her," Henry replied, rising from the table, "but I won't do anything to antagonize the boss."

"Are you afraid of him?" Spring boldly asked.

The man smiled down at her upturned face. "No, Spring. He's a friend, and one is not afraid of friends. He's given me a life here, a good life for me and my family. He's a good man. I respect him for what he is, for what he's come from. I won't do anything to cause him trouble." With that, Henry turned, took his hat off the peg by the door, and left.

"Everyone thinks Mr. Saunders is so wonderful," Spring murmured, more to herself than to Lorna. "I think he's perfectly . . . perfectly . . ."

"Perfectly what?" Lorna asked.

"Perfectly hateful." After a moment, Spring said, "Tell me about him. Mr. Saunders, I mean."

Lorna smiled. "Davey is wonderful. I don't know that much about him. That is, no real details. But I do know his mother left him in his father's care when she couldn't take his father's drinking and physical abuse any longer. She was older when she had Davey. There were no other children. But his father treated Davey very cruelly, and he tried to run away on many occasions, only to be hunted down by Mr. Saunders's dogs. This was in Tennessee, and it wasn't until he was about fifteen that he got away for good, and he's been on his own ever since."

Spring listened with fascination and urged Lorna to go on with her story. "Well, before he left, he secretly learned how to use the whip. He swore that he would use it on the dogs the next time they attacked him. I don't know if he had to use it, but he got away. At any rate, he never went back to Tennessee."

So there had been a reason for the whip. It wasn't just to mete out punishment to men for the joy of it. Mr. Saunders used it for self-defense.

"And then he was captured by the Indians."

"By the Indians? How? Why?" Spring was appalled.

"Well, I'm not sure. As I said, I don't know all the details, but he was making his way across the country and had hooked up with a wagon train that was attacked. One of the Indians liked his hair so much that they couldn't bear to scalp him, so in a way, that saved his life. A little later, he was traded to the Arapahos for some horses."

"This is really hard to believe," Spring said in awe. She rose from the table to clear the dishes but couldn't keep from hearing the rest of the tale. She sat back down and asked Lorna to tell her more. "How old was he?"

"I think about eighteen. He lived with them for several years. One of the Chief's sons, Black Claw—"

"Black Claw? That's the one who took me!" Spring exclaimed.

"Yes, he is. That's one of the reasons Davey got you away so easily. Henry told me all this. You see, Davey would never brag over connections he has or accomplishments of his. Anyway, Black Claw and Davey never got along. Black Claw felt that Davey was going to, in some way, take over the tribe or anything that was rightfully his. One day, Black Claw brought in a white man who was almost dead. Davey persuaded the Chief not to let him die, and he cared for this man, along with the help of a young Indian maiden named White Feather. I think they fell in love, but never married, as Black Claw and the girl were promised to each other. I'm not sure if I understand all that part correctly. But she would never marry Black Claw, and—" Lorna blushed and ducked her head.

"What? What happened?" Spring leaned forward in anticipation.

"Well, I understand Davey and White Feather did have a child."

Flashes of memory stole their way into Spring's mind as she saw the beautiful young woman, perhaps a few years older than herself, run up to David with the young child that he cradled in his arms and kissed. And he had kissed the woman too. Only then did Spring realize that her hands were clasped so tightly together that her knuckles were white and her fingers hurt. She remembered too how light the child's hair had been and how angry Black Claw looked when he saw David and White Feather together.

"Was the child a boy?" Spring whispered.

"No, a little girl."

"I saw them at the camp. Why didn't Mr. Saunders marry her since they have a child?" Spring asked.

"Henry says that he felt White Feather should remain with her people and the child with her mother. She stays with the old Chief, but Black Claw still wants to marry her." Lorna saw by Spring's face that she was quite upset by all these revelations. "Well, I needn't go on."

"Oh, yes, please do," the younger girl begged. "I don't like Mr. Saunders, but I want to understand him."

"Are you trying to convince me or yourself?" Lorna asked.

"What do you mean?"

"Are you trying to convince yourself that you don't like Davey by saying it often enough?"

"No!" Spring exclaimed. "Besides, I'm promised to another."

"Where is he?"

"I don't know. But he'll find me. Please go on with your story."

"All right. The white man who had been brought into the Indian camp was Pap, and after Davey saved his life, they were like partners and have been together ever since. Pap worked for your father, and later, when they left the Arapahos, they went to the fort, where your father hired Davey. Every once in a while, Davey goes back to see the old Chief, who was kinder to him than his own father was. Then on a trip to Denver, one time, by some coincidence, Davey found his mother."

"How wonderful for him," Spring remarked, remembering the joy of being reunited with her father after so many years.

"Not totally wonderful. She was a madam in one of those houses."

"A madam? You mean like Molly?" Spring couldn't imagine that David's mother had been like Molly.

"Yes, there was no way to support herself, apparently, and she made a lot of money. At first, Davey wouldn't even talk to her, but she was quite old and failing fast. She begged for his forgiveness, and to prove she loved him, she left him Saunders's Haven. She'd won it in some high-stakes poker game."

Lorna was looking especially sleepy now, and the two women heard sounds of cooing and gurgling in the bedroom. "I hear Jake. Better change his diaper." She left to take care of her motherly duties, leaving Spring to ponder the strange life story of David "Whip" Saunders.

Before taking Jake outside, Spring asked to be told how Isabel fit into the picture, but Lorna refused to say anything about that. No one seemed to want to talk about that part of his life. Well, maybe she would never know that about him. He sure was a combination of a lot of experiences, she thought, watching Jake as he toddled along the ground. He was an enigma, to be sure.

Spring tied the note to a piece of string she had fastened around Suzie's neck. She knelt down by the dog and patted her, rubbing the soft fur about her throat.

"Now, I want you to go home and take that note, Suzie. Be a good girl and take that note to Mary or to Pap." She stood and said, again, "Go home, Suzie, go home." She placed one hand on her hip and the other pointed in the direction of the white house with the red trim.

Suzie took a few halting steps and then stopped, looking over her shoulder at Spring. "Go, girl," Spring repeated sternly. Again Suzie took a few steps, stopped, and then turned, whining in her throat. "Go, Suzie. Find Mary or Pap."

At last, Suzie headed in the proper direction, stopping once in a while to look back over her shoulder. Spring watched her until she was out of sight. She turned and went back to the house. Henry was washing his hands at the kitchen sink. Spring sat on the floor in front of the fireplace with the baby. He was having a marvelous time knocking down the blocks that Spring set atop each other. Each time she built up two or three, Jake's chubby hand came swinging across, scattering the blocks over the wooden floor. Then his baby giggles filled the room.

Henry came and sat down to watch them. It was very nice for Lorna to have a girl nearer her own age to converse with once in a while. It was too bad Spring wanted to leave.

"Jake has really taken to you," he commented. "Some babies won't have anything to do with a stranger."

"Oh, I think these little ones can tell when someone likes them. And I sure do like him." She picked up the tyke and planted kisses all over his face. "He's a lovely child."

"Why do you want to leave here, Spring?" Henry suddenly asked.

She was startled by the question and wondered why everyone asked her about that. "Well, I just can't stay here. Besides the fact that I'm engaged to John Granville, I can't stay with an unmarried man, and I'm unmarried. It's just not right. Also, there is nothing to keep me here. No future."

"What about Dave?"

"What about him? He does not like me, and the feeling is mutual. He's been married before, and from what I understand, she tried to get away, so something must be wrong with him."

"Why does something have to be wrong with him? Why couldn't something be wrong with someone else?" he asked.

"At the risk of seeming rude, Henry, I don't think you know him as well as you think. He must have done something to Isabel. Everyone thinks Mr. Saunders is so terrific, and yet, they won't talk about her. Maybe no one wants to admit there is a flaw in his character." Somewhere deep inside herself, she knew she was being unjust. But she had to stand strong against him in order to stand by her conviction to marry John.

"Everyone has flaws, Spring. As for Isabel—" He stopped and cocked his head. Hoof beats sounded from a distance, and he got up to go out on the porch to see who was approaching. Spring followed him, carrying Jake on her hip.

The rider was David, who jumped off Aphrodite even before she came to a halt. Henry reached for the baby, but not before David noticed how natural Spring looked holding the baby in that way.

"Hello, Henry. Mind if I have a few words with your guest?" He pushed his hat back onto his head, and Spring discerned anger in the whitening of his eyes. She sighed.

"Whatever you have to say can be said right here and now," she said, placing both hands on her hips. But when she looked to Henry, he gave her a half smile and disappeared into the house.

David strode over to her and grabbed her by the arm and dragged her off the steps, out into the yard. Without preamble, he started in. "Just what the hell do you think you are doing?"

"I'm not sure what you mean," she said. "But I'm visiting Lorna for a few days. She's not feeling well, and I'm going to help out."

"Mary told me you decided to come here on your own." He pulled his hat down over his eyes, watching Spring's face, but she would not look at him. "Now look at me when you talk to me."

"God, I'm sick of being treated like some idiotic child!" she exploded, turning away and looking out at the purpling sky to the west. "I can't breathe without you getting upset about it. Mr. Saunders, I appreciate the help you've given me, and I know I've caused you some problems, but for heaven's sake, please stop harping at me. You are smothering me! I need room to breathe." In anguish, she turned back around and saw with some astonishment that he was no longer mad at her. Instead, there was a look of sympathy on his face, and his mouth and his eyes had softened.

"You're right. I'm sorry. When you weren't at the house, I got worried. Don't look at me like that," he said sharply, for it seemed as though her eyes filled with pain.

Indeed, she was in pain, but not physically. It was unbelievable that he would admit to being wrong about something. She did not stop to realize that this was just the fairness of the man. The look of pain on her face was there because of the guilt she felt over the fact that here he was apologizing for his actions, and she had lied to Mary about his attack on her. It was not in her nature to lie or to hold grudges. What, perhaps, was the reason for her frustrations? She held everything against him, no matter who or what was at fault. She did not think of this now, however.

All she knew at the moment was that she lied to Mary about him, causing Mary to have doubts about him, and she couldn't let that go on.

She took two steps closer to him and stared up into his face. The hard lines of his face stood out boldly against the background of darkening skies, and she could see a muscle twitch beneath the stubble of five days' growth of beard.

"Mr. Saunders, I did a terrible thing today that I have to tell you." Her soft pink lips trembled, and her voice shook, for she was afraid of his reaction.

He reached out his hand and placed it on her shoulder, giving it a gentle squeeze. "What is it?"

"I lied to Mary about you." She lowered her head, looking down.

"Look at me, Spring." Her eyes reached his and held. "What did you tell her?"

"It was a horrible thing. I can barely tell you. It is so awful."

David's eyes crinkled around the corners, and the tips of his moustache turned up. "It can't be as bad as all that, my girl. I'm sure I have done every bad deed you can imagine I've done, even if not done to you. Now tell me what it is."

"Well, I told her I couldn't stay at the house, or rather didn't want to be there when you arrived back, because you . . . you . . ." She took a big breath. "Because you attacked me and . . . and tried to . . . you know." She gave up with a shrug of her shoulders and tried to move away.

David took her face in both hands and tilted it upward. "Well, that wasn't very nice, was it? If I am going to be accused of doing anything, I sure would like it if it had really taken place." He let a small low laugh escape when he saw she was startled by his statement. "However, you did pick the one thing that I've never experienced doing. I may be all manner of things, but I am not a rapist. It's much more fun and pleasing when both parties are in agreement."

Shocked, for she had never been spoken to in this manner, Spring jerked away. She believed he wasn't a rapist, but he said it so lightheartedly that she thought he didn't care at all what she said about him. Then he laughed aloud, the noise filling all the outdoors, and Aphrodite snorted and pawed the ground.

Spring stomped her foot on the hard-packed dirt. "Stop that," she demanded hotly. "Have you no manners? Look, I'm sorry I lied, and I will set it straight with Mary. Now, may I stay here a few days?"

David regained control of himself. He vaguely wondered if her made-up story was some wishful thinking on her part, and then thought it probably wasn't. He climbed atop his black mare.

"Yes, you may stay until day after tomorrow. I'll come and get you." He turned the horse around.

"No, I'll walk, thank you," she said, firmly.

He tipped his hat to her. "As you wish, Miss Ames."

He kneed the horse and rode off into the darkness, and it was several moments before Spring moved to enter the cabin. That man was getting under her skin. And that was more than a bit uncomfortable.

*   *   *

139

Spring stood at the top of the last rise before going down to the white house. Pap and Joe were out by the barn working on tack, and Mary was taking clothes off the line. She did not see David, who happened to be on the roof of the house with some new shingles. He had stopped work to wipe perspiration from his forehead and to gaze out in the direction from which Spring would come. He had been watching for her all afternoon, wondering if she would really come.

She had kept her word. He saw her look back from where she had been, and she raised her head to the sky before running lightly down the slope. She was slender, young, full of life.

She called to Mary and, reaching her, embraced the older woman. She began talking in words that escaped David's ears, except for one or two floating up to him. Words like *lie* and *sorry*. Her hands moved about in an agitated manner as she spoke, and then she hung her brown-red head like a small child.

Mary put her arm around her, and they walked into the house. David knew then that Spring had told Mary of her deception concerning his so-called attack on her.

His mind drifted back to the picnic and the kiss they had shared. He remembered the softness of her lips. Her inexperience was evident, but she had not pulled away as Isabel always had. Isabel. Would he ever be free of the belief that he was the cause of Isabel's frigidness? His thoughts went to White Feather and the joyfulness with which she always came to him and of the swiftness with which she had given him a daughter. Neither of their lives would have been satisfactory living with Black Claw around, and so David had taken his leave. He had great respect and affection for White Feather, but not love. He had loved Isabel, and she had killed that love.

So what did he feel for Spring? Why did he want her near him? It was an answer not easily found. He began hammering nails into the shingles with perhaps more effort than was needed, but at least it kept his mind off Spring.

Chapter 12

It was after the first week of June, and Spring had spent the whole morning in the garden weeding. She had never seen so many weeds, and it just seemed as if she had the job done only yesterday. The sun was reaching mid-sky, and it was very warm; the ground, moist and damp, sent up little puffs of mist. She brushed her hair back with the back of her hand and thought for the tenth time that morning how wonderful it would be if she knew how to swim. Then she could go down to the lake to cool off. Suddenly the idea struck her that she could go down anyway and just cool off. She finished off the row and washed her hands in the outside tub. She had no proper suit to wear for bathing, so she gathered another set of clothing and some food from the larder and went out the front door. Mary was just approaching with an armload of kindling.

"Hi, I'm going down to the lake for a swim. I won't be gone too long, so don't worry." Seeing the question on Mary's lips, she went on, "I don't think Mr. Saunders will mind. Since I was up at Lorna's, he seems to have been nicer about letting me go about where I want."

"Well, I don't know, honey . . ."

"I do. Don't worry." She set off, walking a little and then skipping in between. Mary, looking after her, thought that she had settled down now and was a lot happier. Spring and David didn't send barbs to each other all the time either.

Spring had no trouble getting down to the lake, though she kept an eye open for any stray steers. The lake was as clear and clean as it had been the last time. She rolled up her drawers and pulled her skirt up from the back between her shapely legs and tucked the hem into the front of her waistband.

Wading out into the water, she stood and ate the food she brought and scooped up handfuls of water to drink. Then she slowly sat in the water and let it close over her. The water came up to her shoulders, and it felt cold and delicious. She went out a little farther and tried to remember how David had looked floating on his back. She tried to emulate that too, but her bottom kept sinking while her feet protruded from the water. Soon she gave up and went to where it was shallow enough to just lie in the water without her old fear creeping in.

Later, she left the water and went behind a bush to take off her wet clothing and put on the dry ones she had brought along. Now she felt very refreshed. The sun was edging its way west, so Spring thought about heading back to the house.

She rolled her things in a bundle and meandered back to the open field.

She had not put her boots on, feeling utterly free, and was not surprised when she stepped on a sticker. She bent to pluck it out and then heard hoof beats close by. Raising her head, she saw David bearing down on her at a swift gallop. She was about to raise her hand in greeting when he wheeled the horse in and jumped down.

The look of pure rage on his face caused her to swallow hard and her legs to turn to jelly.

"Hi, I was—" she began to say around a closing throat.

"I don't want to hear any more of your lies, you little tramp." He seized her arm in a tight grip, viselike in its intensity. "I know you were running away again. I saw that you took extra clothes and food. Mary tried to tell me you came down here to swim, but you are afraid of water! Well, no more. This is it. I told you what would happen if you tried to desert me again."

All the while he was talking, he had pulled her over to Aphrodite. Mounting, he grabbed hold of her shirt, the blue lace one from Molly's, and pulled her up and over the saddle in front of him, tearing the collar and almost choking her. She was not able to get in one word—so furious was he.

On the way back to the house, she bounced up and down on her stomach, knocking the wind out of her, while he upbraided her for her deceitfulness, her lies, and her inconsideration for anyone else.

Spring did not know what he was going to do with her.

She was more frightened now than she had been when the Indians came to the fort and took her away. David's face had been ruddy with rage, and his eyes were so white as to be two chunks of ice. His lips had been in a hard, straight, uncompromising line.

When they arrived back at the house, all the hands, Pap, and Mary were standing out front waiting for their return. They had rarely seen David in such a state and did not know whether or not to interfere.

He pulled up short, slid off the horse, and yanked Spring off all in one motion. She was so weak she almost fell to the ground. Mary ran up to him to try to explain again what Spring had been doing, but when she snatched at his arm, he shook her off with such vehemence that she fell back against Pap.

"Stay out of this, goddamn it," he shouted at her. And then to the rest of them, "If you don't like what you see, you are all free to leave!" He dragged Spring over to a tree and shoved her roughly against it.

"Dave, think about what you're doing," Pap warned him.

"I mean it, Pap. If you interfere, you can . . ." He left the thought unfinished.

"What are you going to do? Honestly, I wasn't doing anything!" Spring managed to gasp out.

"Shut up," he commanded. "I told you before, if you tried any of your little tricks, I would teach you a lesson you'd never forget. Remember what deserters get? Ten lashes for a second offense. This is your second, but don't worry, I'll go easy on you. I'll only give you five."

He spoke to her between clenched teeth while tying her small, white hands together around the tree. The rough bark bit into her cheek, and she remembered those men begging for mercy and crying, and the sound of that whip. She hadn't seen or heard it since they had arrived at the Haven, but now she would. And now it was meant for her.

David stood behind her. The soft fragrance of lilacs arose from Spring's hair, but he shut his senses to it. He said in her ear, "I . . . I'm going to enjoy this very much."

He took hold of the neck of her blouse and jerked downward, tearing the material to the waist, taking the chemise material with it. Spring's breath caught in her throat, and she shut her eyes tightly.

"Davey, you can't do this," Mary wailed. "Please, she wasn't running away. Please. Spring, tell him."

But Spring knew it would do no good, and Mary's words fell on deaf ears. David turned and walked away from Spring, aware that all the eyes of his friends were on him. He shut his mind to them. Hell, he was the boss, and what he said went, whether they liked it or not.

Now he turned back to the object of his debilitating anger, and before him stood Spring, pressed against the dark wood. Her back was white and slender, and he imagined for an instant what it would be like to run his hands over this smoothness, down to the dimples where her spine converged with the beginning roundness of her hips. In his mind, he saw another, similar figure, and an emptiness and loneliness filled his being with such blind wrath against himself and what he was about to do that he hesitated for only one moment.

But then he saw Spring stand a little straighter, hugging the tree to herself, and he took it as a sign of defiance rather than the bracing of mind and body for the assault. He raised the whip in his right hand and let it fly to its mark.

Spring heard the lash whistle through the air and felt it tear across her back. For a brief time, there was no pain, but then the air hit it, and there was such a searing, burning sensation that she thought she would surely faint. Her legs sagged against the tree, and her face pressed into the wood, dragging across the bark. But she did not scream or let out the groan that was aching to escape her constricted throat.

David raised his hand again. He saw the bloody path that zigzagged across her delicate spine, and he was absolutely appalled by his perverse actions. He had never felt so debased as a human being than he did at that very moment. His arms went up once more before he realized it. However, this time, he checked his forward motion just in time, and the whistling whip landed at Spring's bare feet, lying unattended on the ground. She heard what sounded like an animal in terrible agony, and she managed to glance over her shoulder. David was staring up at the sky with deep intense suffering written on his face. The ugly, mournful, terrified cry was emanating from him. Suddenly he was astride Aphrodite, riding off toward Denver.

Spring did not remember how she got from the tree to her bed. Her first recollection of what had happened came when she felt a white-hot burning pain across her back; and when she opened her eyes, she was admonished by Pap to lie still. She had no time to be embarrassed, nor did she have the inclination; so great was her suffering. She was completely undressed from the waist up, and Pap was tending to the injury on her back.

Mary, with a tearstained face, knelt beside the bed, cleaning up the deep scratches the bark of the tree had made on her cheek.

"Oh, my darling girl. I'm sorry, so sorry. I've never seen Davey like that before. I don't know what came over him. It was almost as if he was crazy." Mary's voice trembled, and fresh tears began to course down her cheeks.

Spring lay in a kind of semi-sleep staring at Mary. She wanted to scream at her to be quiet and never to mention that man's name to her again. She never wanted to see or speak to him again. Inwardly, she cursed Mrs. Butler for making him promise to find her. It would have been much better if she had perished at the hands of Black Claw.

Pap worked diligently on her back. He had had much experience during the war between the States doctoring up wounds of one type or another. After cleaning her wound and press-packing a herb medication into it, he had Mary help him push the parted skin back together, and he placed tape closely all along the whip's pathway, hoping to leave as little scar as possible.

When he was through, he sent Mary out of the room, and then he built a fire in the fireplace. He pulled the quilt up over Spring's back and then dragged a chair up to the bed.

"Spring?"

Her eyes fluttered drowsily open. She didn't speak. "You've had a very traumatic experience. There was no excuse for what went on here this afternoon. Dave—"

"Pap," Spring croaked out, licking her lips. "I hate him. I never want to see him again. I don't want him near me. I was beginning to think maybe we'd reached an understanding, that we . . . that we could be sort of friends. But after today, God, you understand, don't you?"

"Yes, honey, I do understand you feel that way now." Unhappily, Pap ran his hand over his face. "I'll talk to Dave as soon as he returns about taking you to Denver or wherever you want to go. I think he's lost all right to an opinion where you are concerned." Gratefully, Spring thanked him and then closed her eyes. "Spring, I want you to remain on your stomach and try not to move about on the bed. I don't want you to pull the wound apart, all right?"

She nodded and then let herself slip into the blissful retreat of sleep and forgetfulness.

*　　*　　*

It was a wonder that Aphrodite made it to Denver without mishap. David Saunders, usually in complete control, arrived there in utter despair and heart-rending sorrow. What kind of bastard was he, anyway? Had he actually picked up his hated father's cruel traits after all?

In all his years of defending himself and fending for himself, he had never struck a woman or child or animal out of anger, or for any other reason. Yes, he had fulfilled his duty many times in giving out punishment for the army, and he had been in fights where he had hit men, and he had probably killed one or two along the way. But he had never purposefully set out to do bodily harm to anyone. And to do it to Spring, of all people. And he had also shoved Mary. God! He must have been a different person.

He rode up to Molly's and tied his horse to the post outside. It was very early in the morning, and hardly anyone stirred except

Ben the bartender, who was doing his morning chores. David walked into the saloon, up to the bar, and proceeded to drink himself into oblivion.

This behavior continued for four days, despite Molly's efforts to the contrary. She let him sleep in her bed, and that was exactly what he did do: sleep and drink for four days. Not one bit of food passed his lips. He didn't wash or shave. It was as if he wanted to become how he felt.

Some of the time, he talked in his sleep, and Molly received some of the story, but David always ended up sobbing uncontrollably. His words were mixed up within the sentences, and Molly didn't know who he was talking about half the time. Was it Spring or Isabel? She knew that Whip was a deeply troubled man, but burying himself in drink and sleep was not going to solve his problems.

By the fifth day, he was so weak from lack of food and so inebriated with alcohol that he couldn't even move. Molly and two of her girls stripped him of his clothes and got him into a tub of very hot water, David protesting the rough treatment in no uncertain terms. But he could not fight them off.

Washed and shaved, he felt better as he sat in front of the fire. On a small table was a bowl of soup, which Molly forced him to eat, for she said she would not bring him any clothes or whiskey until he ate.

Wrapped in a blanket, he felt warm; and now that his stomach was filled, he felt more like his old self, before he had gone crazy. That was exactly how he described himself to Molly, who lent a quiet but constant ear.

"I don't know," he said. "Something just snapped in me. When Mary told me Spring had gone swimming and some of her clothes and food were gone, I thought for sure she had run out on me again. It was the swimming thing, I guess. She's afraid of water, so I thought she had lied to Mary."

"Lots of people don't swim but say they're going to, Whip," Molly reminded him. "It just means they are going to get wet and cool off."

"I know that. And her hair was wet. And another thing I remember. Oh, God," he said with deep anguish. "When I rode up to her out by the lake, she didn't run, but she had been bending down, and when I had almost reached her, she looked up at me with such joy in her face, like she was glad to see me. But I would have none of it. I will never see that look in her eyes again. Never!" He stared into the fire.

"Don't be too sure, Whip. She's a smart girl, and I think a forgiving one too. And don't be so hard on yourself. You have reasons for feeling insecure. Good ones."

"I can't blame all this entirely on Isabel. She was weak, and I could not help her. But it is because of her that I've been distrustful of Spring. I wish there was some way I could make it up to her." He spoke wistfully, like a small child.

Molly leaned forward and touched the blanket-covered knee. David raised his blue eyes to her. She was a dear person to put up with him and his erratic behavior. He sighed.

"You love her, Whip, don't you?"

David stared at Molly for a full minute before he answered her. "I never thought I could love again, after what happened with Isabel. I knew I was never going to let myself. But then this fire-breathing, tempting Venus entered my life. A woman who is full of life and wants to live it to the fullest, who takes interest in things many women don't, a refined woman who's not afraid to work and get her hands dirty. An intelligent and sensitive, caring woman who has a willful mind of her own. A woman who stands up to me and says what she thinks."

"And you love her." Molly's statement loomed large in his mind.

"Yes, God help me, I do. But she will never love me. She's like Isabel in that way. And she wants to leave me, like Isabel did." He rose from his chair. "Well, now I've had my confession. Get me my clothes, will you? I promise you I won't drink anymore, at least not to excess, as long as I'm here."

David's conclusions about his love for Spring were welded in his mind that night when he took Molly to bed with him. It was the first failure he had ever had, and though he was a little embarrassed by the affair, or lack of it, Molly assured him that that was the ultimate proof of his love for Spring.

From then on, he slept in a small room in the back hallway. Alone.

He made arrangements for a wagon to be used for supplies on the eighth day he was in town. Most of each day was spent with friends he hadn't seen for many months and he hadn't seen the last time he had been in town. That had been on his ride to Saunders's Haven with Spring. He wondered if she would be there when he returned. He couldn't blame her if she wasn't. He also took care of several business ventures. He had many of that type of associations such as livestock, real estate, silver, and banking interests in Denver.

One whole morning he spent in the newspaper office going over accounts of the attack on the fort. A list of the dead was included, even that of civilians. The colonel's name appeared at the top. These had been confirmed by several eyewitnesses. There was no mention of John Granville or his few cohorts.

The account went on to say that upon investigation of a military team of experts looking into situations involving Indians, it appeared as though the Indians had had some inside help. There didn't seem to have been a guard on duty, or if there was, they were the ones who let the Indians into the fort. There was no forced entry. Also, many of the supplies had been pilfered, things that the Indians would have had to have been made aware of prior to the attack.

Visions of Lieutenant Granville and Black Claw in their private conversation came to David. Was it possible that Granville was really behind all this? What could his purpose have been? That could he have gotten out of any deal he made with Black Claw? Black Claw had been utterly evasive when David had spoken to him. He had not wanted to release Spring. Did she have something to do with it?

He gave the papers back to the clerk and went out into the afternoon sun and walked slowly along the sidewalk, glancing into the store windows as he went. He came to a ladies' apparel shop and saw a lovely, handcrafted shawl in soft colors of green, yellow, and a red-brown. He thought that would be perfect for Spring for the late evenings when the chill set in. She had been using an old one of Mary's. Lightheartedly, he entered and bought it for her and picked up a new apron for Mary, and some sachet for her more delicate clothing. He felt terribly guilty for having treated her so badly, and though he knew Mary would forgive him, his transgressions, he needed to make some visible atonement to her.

With his packages under his arm, he continued down the walkway. His stomach growled, and he realized it was past luncheon, so he made his way to the nearest restaurant. He was seated by the window with his back to a rather large, ostentatious fern. On the other side of this fern sat two gentlemen conversing in soft tones. There were no other occupants in the room.

After David ordered from the menu, he sat back in his chair and lit a thin cigar. It was not something he did often, but he did enjoy a good smoke once in a while. He felt relaxed and happy for the first time since he had ridden away from Spring up at Lorna's, resolving to let her have her freedom about the place. It would have been about now that he had planned to bring her to Denver to let her be on her own.

"Colonel Ames . . ." The voice floated over to David, and he was instantly alert.

"You mean that wasn't part of the plan?" came the other voice.

"Hell, no, but it would have all worked out to the good anyway." The man laughed. David recognized the voice of John Granville. He sat very still, not wanting to miss a word.

"You see, once his daughter found out her father was dead, and I was the one to rescue her, well, she would have fallen right into my arms. That would have shown Whip Saunders who the smart one was."

"I understand that Miss Ames is a real looker."

"Umm, yes, she sure is. I wish I knew where she is right now. I'm pretty sure that she would honor her commitment to me. But being from the East, with her Victorian attitudes, I'm sure I'd have to find my real pleasures elsewhere. It would do my ego real good to take her and make her mine." John chuckled deep in his throat.

"Well, who took her from the Indian camp?" came the unfamiliar voice.

"I couldn't get anything out of the old Chief. Black Claw, my contact, was not there when I got there. He was taking some of the group farther north. I think they all knew the answer, but were not talking for some reason. But I'll find out. I want that girl. She has lots of money, and I want that too."

There was silence for a few moments while the men ate. Meanwhile, David was also served his food, but all he could do was push it around on his plate. The thing he really wanted to do right then and there was to confront Granville and tear him to shreds. Granville's intentions toward Spring were not honorable at all, and yet she still professed to love him and wanted to marry him. At that moment, his plan to bring her into Denver changed. He could not, would not, subject her to this type of humiliation. Even if he had to move out of his own home to allow her to stay, he would try to keep her from this hurt. To marry a man who had set out purposefully to delude her and to plan an attack that led to her father's death and the death of many others would be an affront to her honor. And there seemed to be no remorse on his part.

However, years in the West doing the scouting jobs at the fort and working for or against certain kinds of men had taught David Saunders that you didn't just jump into a situation without thinking. He would just have to let it ride and see what developed. Chances were that Granville would never find Black Claw. Black Claw might not tell him who took Spring away, and even if he did, John might not be able to find Saunders's Haven. And by the time he did, well, there could just be a hell of a lot of water under the bridge by that time.

The voices came drifting over once more. "What if Miss Ames is married to someone else or she's not a virgin any longer?"

John laughed lustily. "Well, my friend, there's always her money. Perhaps I could sell her the information that, say, one Whip Saunders planned the whole thing. She'd believe me on that score. She can't stand him."

The two men rose and picked up their hats. David turned his head to the window by his side, but the two men were too engrossed in their conversation to notice anyone else. Outside, David saw that

John had a full beard and wore civilian clothes. Well, the pieces all fit now.

David felt an overwhelming need to protect Spring from this man, and then he laughed at himself. What Granville had said was true. Spring hated him, now more than ever. So where did he get off thinking that she would allow him to?

He threw some money on the table and started back to Molly's. Deep in thought, he did not notice the hustle and bustle of the growing city of Denver, comprised of all the modern buildings and the newest trappings to fill the stores. Finally, something caught his eye. In a storefront window, he saw an object he knew Spring would love, and without another thought, he went in and bought it, saying he would be picking it up at the end of the week when he had the wagon.

With the knowledge of John's major role in the Indian attack and his own true feelings revealed about Spring under his belt, along with his other purchases, he felt happy enough to whistle all the way back to Molly's.

At last he felt ready to return to his home.

Chapter 13

The two weeks that David was gone passed very slowly for Spring. Pap insisted she remain in bed for the first week, only allowing her to move for the necessities, and then back into bed. She did quite a bit of reading and mending of holes in shirts for the men and replacing buttons where needed.

By the beginning of the second week, she was grumpy, tired, and bored. She rose and dressed before anyone could stop her and presented herself at the breakfast table. She knew that the men had inquired after her, and it was time to make an appearance. She listened to Mary's protests and Pap's warning, and even submitted to further changes of the dressing; but she was firm in her resolve to get some sun and air. She was tired of being waited on.

She did, however, take it easy, for her back was still unbearably sore, and she did want it to heal properly. She walked about the immediate area the first days up, talking to the hands she came across.

They seemed anxious to let her know that they had not approved of the boss's actions, but he was the boss. Friends made mistakes and so on. Spring waited patiently until they finished and then would say briefly that that part of her life was over and she wished it to remain in her past, if they would be so kind. Also not to hold it against Mr. Saunders on her account.

They were definitely surprised to hear her speak so calmly about it, but she was like David in that way. She was very capable of handling her feelings on the outside. And this side she presented to the men.

Actually, Spring was just as surprised at her frame of mind. The immediate hatred she had felt toward Mr. Saunders and his actions with the whip had drained out of her over the days. She no longer hated him. She knew that much.

She had company on her sojourns about the place, and that was Suzie. The pups were now receiving more substantial food than just their mother's milk, so Suzie didn't need to spend as much time with them. So she tagged along after Spring.

Each day, Spring came back to the house with some item that caught her eye that day. It ranged from a crazily shaped branch from a fallen tree, to cat-o'-nine tails and bunches of wild mountain flowers of every shade and hue. She was relatively happy exploring, sometimes taking her lunch with her, which she shared with her companion. No matter where she went, she expected to see David riding his shiny black mare. Day after day went by, and he didn't come back.

She could not forget the horrified look on his handsome features when he stood looking into the darkening sky and that wild animal sound coming from deep within him. Whenever she thought of that, which was often, chills passed through her, and she knew how much he regretted his actions. He knew he had been wrong, not only to use the lash on her, but about her running away.

At the end of two weeks, Spring realized that Mary and Pap were worried about David. They talked about him, but if she entered the room, they fell silent. He had never gone off for so long without saying where he was going or when he would be back.

This occurred again one day as Spring entered the kitchen at lunchtime. Pap checked what he was about to say and asked instead what it was Mary was fixing. Spring knew they wanted to finish their conversation, so she turned and went out on the front porch. It was a gorgeous day, birds singing in the treetops, the purple-blue granite mountains surrounded by the yellowing hills of the valley.

Hearing a rattling of wheels, Spring's attention was drawn to the pathway that broke out of the mountainside to her left. From this distance, she did not recognize the driver of an approaching wagon, but then she saw Aphrodite tied to the rear of the vehicle. Three Indian feathers stuck out of the driver's hat band.

It was David. Her knees began to shake, and she couldn't swallow around the lump that appeared in her throat. She reached for the door handle behind her and managed to push it open.

She went swiftly to the kitchen and startled Mary and Pap with the news they had been hoping for. "He's back."

Turning on her heel, she fled to her room, shutting the door behind her. In the bathroom, she shut that door, knowing full well that those doors would not keep him out if he wanted to come in.

But he made no attempt to see her. After a while, she came out into the bedroom and sat in a chair by the window. She tried to read but couldn't. She was too nervous. Besides, there was too much bumping and scraping going on in the front room.

She was dying to see what it was all about, but she was afraid, so she remained where she was until she heard no more noise for about an hour. Her stomach grumbled from hunger, and at last, she could no longer stand the suspense.

She opened the door and quietly entered the room. She walked across it slowly, looking around, and saw nothing new or strange. Then she passed the larger of the two chairs in front of the fireplace. There by the wall, next to the edge of the fieldstones, was a beautiful wood-grained pianoforte. The finish was smooth and shiny; the keys white and glossy.

A small cushioned stool sat in front of it. On the top was a pile of books and other sheets of paper holding old and new tunes.

She stared at it in wonder and went up to it, running her hand lightly over the keys, but not striking them. Then her fingers trailed over the satiny wood. This was a heavenly instrument.

"Do you like it?"

Spring's hand clenched into a fist, and she turned shakily to David, who had come from the kitchen so quietly as to go unnoticed.

"Why is it here? Why did you bring it?" she asked in amazement.

"Didn't you say you wanted a piano?" he asked, knowing it would not make up for what he had done to her. He swung his hand out, gesturing to the piano. "I bought it for you."

The movement of his hand, extended out and in her direction, caused her to flinch against the big overstuffed chair, and she turned her head away, thinking he might strike her.

David comprehended immediately what went through her mind, and his hand dropped to his side. He said in a low voice, "Goddamn it to hell, I bought it for you. I thought you might like it." Then he turned and went outside, staying away and eating in the bunkhouse with the men.

It was while they were eating that the strains of a Strauss waltz mingled with the night air. It caused the men to stop their talk to listen to the sweet sounds emanating from the house.

Song upon song poured forth from Spring's soul that evening. Mary came in many times to just stand and listen to the accomplishments of this young woman. Spring didn't notice her; so involved was she with the music. She did not even notice the tears that welled up in her own eyes and fell from her cheeks onto the keys. Now, for a certainty, Spring felt at peace with herself in her feelings for David. Not only did she not hate him, she had forgiven him.

David could not eat after Spring began to play. He removed himself from the group of men. They had not reproached him for his deed, nor did he speak of it.

Now he sat on the back porch with his coffee cup, drinking in the night air and being soothed beyond measure by the notes and melodies filling the sky.

Soon Mary and Pap came out onto the porch and after asking how he was doing, said good night. David watched them walk arm in arm up the slight slope to their quarters.

The music stopped. The men were quiet in the bunkhouse.

Suzie came down to say good night and returned to the barn. All was silent. David knew what he had to do.

When he pushed open the bedroom door, he saw Spring standing in a white nightgown by the front window. Her hair was brushed, shining in the soft firelight and falling to her shoulders. One slim hand was raised to her throat.

She heard him enter, but did not move or speak. He went half-way across the room, standing on the braided rug, feeling the heat from the fire's flames.

"I want to see your back," he said.

"No, I will not show you my back." She turned completely away from him.

"You will show me your back, or I will come over there and tear that gown off of you." He said this quietly, almost as if he was having a nonchalant conversation with one of his hands. In reality, his heart was beating hard in his chest, and he knew that if she refused, he would not carry out his threat.

She, on the other hand, felt he was quite capable of doing just that. She did not want a scene or her gown torn, so she began to unbutton the small white buttons that ran halfway down the front of the gown. She then let the shoulders drop off to her elbows while gathering the front of the gown up about her breasts.

"Come over here, where I can see," he said. He watched her approach with bent head. When she reached him, he turned her around and stepped back so the firelight shone brightly on her scarred back.

"Spring." He spoke so softly and with such emotion that she could scarcely hear him. He took both her white shoulders in his hands and brought her to his chest. He buried his face in her lilac fragrant hair. "God, I'm sorry, I'm sorry. I have no right to ask your forgiveness and don't deserve it. I will never forgive myself, even if you would." His trembling voice broke, and he shuddered against her back.

Slowly, he brought her down onto the rug. She lay across his bent knees, and he traced the pink scar with a feathered touch of his finger.

"Pap did a good job on this, I think. Thank God it's no worse than this." He bent his head to the rude mark he had placed on her otherwise unblemished skin. She tingled all over as she felt his smooth lips caress the scar down its whole length. Spring knew she should stop him. But she had no strength tonight.

It wasn't only that, either. She didn't want to stop him. She had no one to love her. Everyone was gone, killed or absent, as in John's case. David had always been there for her every need and problem. Oh, she had balked at the idea of his seeming ever presence. To be honest, though, she had to admit to herself that she had needed him. And right now, without reasoning it out further, she needed another person to put their arms around her, to hold her, to comfort her, and so she did not stop him.

He turned her in his arms, cradling her. Her head was flung back on his left arm, exposing her delicately curved neck and throat. He bent and kissed the pulsing beat and whispered her name over and over.

Finally, she opened her eyes, gazing up at him. She reached up and touched his cheek. She smoothed her finger over the slightly crooked nose and said, "David."

It was the first time she had uttered his given name.

No one had ever called him David, and the way she said it gave him promise of a hope yet unfulfilled.

He gathered her in his arms and carried her to the bed. Soon he was next to her, and she began to shake uncontrollably.

"Don't, my Venus. Don't be afraid. I will never hurt you again."

"I've never been with a man before, David." She turned her head away. "I'm afraid . . . I don't know . . ."

"I know you are, my dearest heart. I said I wouldn't hurt you, but our coming together the first time may hurt some. After that, it . . . " He thought momentarily of Isabel and went on, "It should be good. I can promise you that, if you're willing. But I will stop now, if you want me to."

Spring turned to him and buried her head against his chest. The clean-smelling hairs brushed her cheek. "No, David, don't go. I need someone now. I'm so alone."

"You never need be lonely again, Spring. Never."

Later, lying in the crook of David's arm, Spring marveled at the past hour. She heard his heavy, regular breathing, and knew he was sleeping. The pain she had experienced had not been so bad. His touch had been sure and true and loving. He had known what he was doing, and it had brought out feelings inside her mentally, emotionally, and, most of all, physically that she did not know she possessed. She did not ever in her wildest dreams think she would urge a man to do the things and touch her in places that she had urged David to. And she had thrilled to his caresses and did not think there was a place on her body that had not been lovingly kissed and reverently touched. The funny thing was, she, Spring Ames, inexperienced, Eastern, and primly brought up, had pressed herself to him and asked for more.

David had laughed at her gently, and said she would have to wait a while, and that was when he had fallen asleep.

She supposed she should be ashamed for being a brazen hussy, but she could not bring herself to be. It felt good to be held by this strong man and protected by him. Yes, it felt good.

The chime clock on the living room mantle struck three. Spring had only dozed since David had fallen asleep. Now her ribs ached, and she needed to get up and move around. She moved from her place beside him and stretched her arms over her head. The dull ache receded. Wrapping her arms around herself, Spring went to the window.

Outside, the trees and the mountains cast dark shadows onto the land where the silvery moonlight struck. Everywhere was peaceful and quiet. She rubbed her ribs gently.

"Venus?"

She looked over to the bed and saw David raised on one elbow, gazing at her.

"Yes?"

"It must be chilly out there. Can you sleep?"

"I'm having some trouble. My ribs are hurting." She walked around the bed and crawled under the covers but did not come near him. He lay on his back, hands behind his head.

"Was I too heavy on you tonight?" he questioned.

"No," she answered truthfully. "They are bruised from when you carried me across Aphrodite's saddle. They are better, though, improving each day."

David reached under the covers and took her hand. "I saw a few scratches on your cheek. Did I do that too?"

"From the tree's bark," she replied simply.

He sighed deeply. "I hope someday you can forgive me, dear Spring. I'm a first-class heel and worse."

She turned to face him in the darkness. "David," she said, "if I hadn't already forgiven you, no matter how lonely I felt, I wouldn't have given you the only thing I have—myself."

He pulled her close against his hard body and stroked her hair tenderly. "A most precious gift, my girl," he whispered. After a moment, he said, "But I don't understand why you have forgiven me."

She thought a bit and then answered, "I know something awful happened inside of you because of Isabel. It may have started longer ago than that, your childhood maybe. Lorna told me a little about it, and I know it wasn't happy. Anyway, David, if I knew more, if you felt like telling me anything at all, perhaps I could understand better."

David lay still for so long that Spring thought he had fallen asleep once again. Suddenly, however, he said, "Why couldn't I have met you five years ago? Then maybe I wouldn't be like I am now."

She smiled in the darkness. "I'd have only been fourteen years old."

He grunted, giving her a hug.

"What did she do to you?" she urged him.

"Isabel was breathtakingly beautiful, like a crystal snowflake, all white and perfectly pure. On our wedding day, I was almost overcome by how blessed I thought I was in getting her for my wife. She was dressed in white. In fact, as I think about it, she always wore the palest of colors. Anyway, with her pale hair, lighter than mine, and white skin, she looked like an angel on a translucent cloud."

He fell silent, but the room seemed filled with her presence, brought there by David's memories. Spring wondered why David thought she, Spring, was so beautiful when he spoke so worshipfully about Isabel.

"Pap and I spent an entire year up here building the house and trying to make it a place that was comfortable, like she was used to. Of course, since she was from a rich family in silver, it didn't come nearly close enough. But it was no easy trick to haul all the things you call luxuries up here. You've been at Lorna's. She has none of these things."

Spring heard the bitterness creep into his voice. David always appeared above the hurts normal people had. He had seemed less than human to Spring from the moment she met him, but over the past weeks, it had become quite evident that he was very human indeed.

"I tried, Spring. I really tried to give her all I could. I bought her clothes, jewels, everything she asked for, and there was no end to her asking. Nothing pleased her. She found fault with everything, especially me. But I loved her despite all that. She repaid me with spitefulness."

Spring shivered under the warm covers. The clock chimed four times in the other room. David moved to his side, facing Spring, though he couldn't see her features well.

"How did she do that, David?" she asked softly, staring at the ceiling, not sure she really wanted to know.

"I've not ever told anyone this, Spring," he said. "It's something no real man would ever admit to another man, much less a woman. God knows she caused me to feel I was worth less than nothing at all."

Spring had no idea what David was leading up to. From their first meeting, he had epitomized "man" to her, in his every word, action, and movement. The only thing that was different than she expected of him, or that matter, any man, was the tender, loving way he had brought her to womanhood this night.

"What did she do to you?" she whispered.

David cleared his throat. "Well, to be blunt, our wedding night was a disaster. When I tried to make love to her, she screamed and scratched and hit at me. She said I was repulsive, and if I thought I was going to do those grotesque and dirty things to her, I was crazy.

At first I thought she was just frightened. I'd been with other women and so felt I wasn't being too clumsy."

"I know you weren't. Not if you treated her as you did me tonight," Spring put in, reaching over and touching his arm gently.

"Thank you for that," he said. "Well, to make a long story short, Isabel died as pure as she was the day she was born. I tried many times during our married life, but do you know, I never saw her without her clothes on? Soon I lost interest after being called all manner of names and told how ugly and repulsive I was."

"Oh, David," Spring breathed, putting her arm around him and drawing him close. "How awful for you. You aren't ugly or . . . or repulsive. I admit, I myself was a little startled by what you did . . . by what I did, but repulsive and ugly? Never, David. You are gentle and kind, and I'm grateful you were my first. I don't think it could have been a better experience, and probably a lot worse with someone else."

David pressed Spring to himself. His guardian angel was sure watching over him to at last bring him and Spring together against all odds. He kissed her eyelids, temples, and cheeks lightly. She shivered under his caring touch, and when he reached her mouth, her lips parted under his, and they kissed deeply, leaving both breathless, when he drew away.

"Spring, my goddess of love, what about John?"

Surprised, she lay still beneath him. To be honest, she hadn't thought about John seriously in many days. Now she remembered the wet kisses he had planted on her mouth, his roaming hands all over her. She had been repulsed by John. Did she still want that? She had never broken her word to anyone. What about her promise to marry him? Her mind was so confused.

"I don't know," she said at last. "I do know he's not here, I have no one to hold me when I'm lonely, and you've always been here to help me. I know I've said some horrible things to you and I meant them at the time. I can hardly think, David. Too much has happened. I just don't know. Just hold me and take me again. I want you. I know you don't love me, but pretend for now, all right? We can both pretend."

She entwined her arms around his neck and her fingers into the hair at the nape of his neck. He adored the wild abandon with which she gave herself to him again. He did make love to her, but he was not pretending. Not even a little.

Chapter 14

✕◇✕◇✕◇✕◇✕◇✕◇✕◇✕

In the light of day, Spring couldn't believe what had gone on the night before. She wondered if it had all been a dream, but there were definite signs on her body to tell her it had not been.

When she awoke, it was late. David told Mary to let her sleep, gave Mary several instructions and said he would be gone for several days to the lower elevations to check on the number of calves born and what the prospects were for the marketing of the steers. He had gone off whistling, with a happier countenance than Mary had ever seen.

Spring couldn't stand the sidelong glances Mary constantly gave her. Though Mary didn't ask any questions, she was dying to know what had happened the previous night. David was so happy, but Spring seemed nervous.

Finally, Spring couldn't take it in the kitchen with Mary, so she sat for several hours at the piano, playing especially boisterous tunes. In the afternoon, she went out to range the hills; so restless was she. She had her faithful companion with her, but she could not keep herself from looking for David. He was nowhere to be seen.

She reached a summit and sat down among the wildflowers, the sun bathing her head and shoulders. Suzie lay with her head on Spring's knee.

"You are a lovely girl, Suzie," Spring said, stroking the silky fur. "It must be nice to be a dog, though, with not a care in the world."

"You have cares'?" a male voice sounded behind her.

Glancing over her shoulder, she saw Hap climbing the last of the hill.

"Hi," she said brightly. "Have a chair." She indicated the ground beside her. Suzie lifted her head in greeting and then placed it back on Spring's knee. "What are you doing up here?"

"Oh, it's a slow day. Usually is, whenever Dave is gone, though we have our specific jobs to attend to." He sat back, resting on both arms.

"Gone?" Spring asked, surprised. "Where did he go?"

She didn't know whether to be relieved that she didn't have to see him, or upset that he would leave without saying anything to her. And the usual close-mouthed Mary never said a word to her about his having left. Why would he leave? Did last night mean nothing to him? Suddenly, her face flooded red with shame and embarrassment. She accepted him so readily, and he didn't think enough of her or what had transpired between them to say good-bye. No, she thought, he was too sincere when he'd told her about Isabel. He wouldn't have told her something so deeply personal if he was just using her to satisfy his own physical needs. Spring's head began to ache, and her mind was in a turmoil.

"Am I boring you?" Hap asked, with a laugh.

His words brought Spring back to the present. She laughed sheepishly. "No, I was just thinking of David checking the outlines." Luckily some of Hap's explanation of David's absence had penetrated her mixed-up thoughts.

"David, is it?"

Spring shrugged. "He's rescued me from so many things we thought we ought to be on a first-name basis."

"Ah, I see." He nodded, but Spring was uncomfortable.

Did Hap suspect anything? "Listen, I really enjoyed your concert last night. You play well."

"Thank you. I enjoy it."

"I play the guitar fairly well," he said.

"That's not an instrument often seen in Boston."

"No, I don't imagine. I'd like to learn to play piano, though." Hap pulled a piece of the tall grass from the earth and stuck the end in his mouth.

"Really? I'll bet with a few simple instructions and what you already know about chords, you could probably play by ear. Want a lesson?" she asked.

"Sure," he replied, jumping up and pulling her to her feet. "It would be great to have piano music to dance to during our parties."

They walked down the yellowing hill. "Mary told me about them. Why don't we plan one?"

"Do you think we ought to wait for Dave to come back?" he asked.

"Hmm. I don't know. One less man to cut in for the dances," she said, smiling mischievously.

Hap laughed aloud. "You're right about that. Ask Mary and see what she thinks. Say, are you planning to stay up here?"

"I don t think so," she answered. "Come on, Suzie. Stop digging around over there." Then she said, "I'm in kind of a limbo right now. My past is gone, my future disappeared. All I have is each day. It's a funny feeling. But I do plan to marry someone if I ever get to Denver, where I can inquire as to his whereabouts." Suzie ran up to Hap with a stick. He took it from her and threw it away. She bounded after it.

"You mean the army lieutenant?" he asked.

"Yes."

"You mean you'd marry him after what he's done?" he questioned, incredulous.

Spring raised her red-tinted brows as she watched Hap throw the stick for Suzie again. "What do you mean?"

Hap checked himself. Dave must not have told her what he'd learned in Denver about Lieutenant Granville. "Just mean that he disappeared."

"Well, I'm sure he had a reason. Here we are. How about your first lesson?"

They had eaten steaks over a campfire set up in the backyard, with large ears of corn dripping with butter. Lorna and Henry rode over and put Jacob to sleep on the one bed in the house. It was a gay group. The men were in good spirits, and indeed, spirits were being freely imbibed by them. A large bowl of corn had been popped and was sitting with the drinks on the table by the front window. Mary had also made a big chocolate frosted cake. The chairs and the table in front of the fireplace had been moved to the edge of the room, and the braided rug was rolled up, leaving a nice area empty for dancing.

There were enough for one set of square dancing, with Pap making the calls while Hap played the guitar. The extra men took turns taking the one ladies' part, but they didn't seem to mind. Spring had never square-danced, and they all had great fun at her expense when she made the wrong turn or move.

Their raucous laughter overflowed the walls of the white house and spilled out into the star-studded night.

After a while, Hap tried out his newly found expertise at the piano by playing the waltzes of the day. It was during one of these dances that Spring, held in a tight embrace by Joe, who breathed heavily in her ear, looked up to see David leaning casually against the wall by the piano. He was staring at her, a quizzical look on his face, a cigar held between his white, even teeth. Her step faltered, causing Joe's already shaky movements to lead into a stumble, and they bumped into Mary and Pap. At that moment, Hap saw David out of the corner of his eye, and he missed several notes. All movement halted as they turned to look at David, still lounging by the wall.

"Having a party, I see," he commented, lazily. "While the cat's away, the mice will play?" He spoke with a hint of concealed amusement.

Spring extricated herself from Joe's pawing grip and stepped forward. "It was my idea. I hope you don't mind."

"We all organized it," Mary put in.

He stood up straight. "It's fine," he said, removing his cigar. "I'm glad the piano is being put to good use. Continue." He moved away to the kitchen.

Everyone stood motionless for a few seconds, and then Pap said, "Why don't you play for us, Spring, before we all say good night. It is getting late, and Henry and Lorna have a little ride ahead of them."

"All right," she said, wiping her palms on her skirt.

David had certainly looked at her in an odd way. It was very disconcerting. She sat on the cushioned stool and leafed through one of the books David had brought her. She found some Stephen Foster and after everyone found a comfortable spot, she put her hands to the keys. The electricity that had filled the room at David's appearance quickly evaporated, and this was a good way to end the evening.

David didn't mind at all that his friends felt comfortable enough to use his home as theirs while he was away. What had caused his rather strange behavior was the sight of Spring in the arms of another man. He listened to the songs she played while he cleaned some of his gear. He remembered that no one had felt free to come to his home when Isabel was there, and now, because of Spring, the house was filled with life.

He had promised himself that he would never marry again, or ever love again. He had changed his mind on that part, however. But even if he wanted to ask Spring to marry him, he had drilled it into his head over the past few days that he must never ask her. He did not ever want to take her freedom from her again. If she asked tomorrow to leave, he would have to let her go. As to their lovemaking, he would have to put a stop to that too. He would not approach her. A pregnancy would only entrap her, and he just wouldn't do that to her. He might have to move out of the house, but if that would help keep her free of him, then so be it.

He went back into the front room and took a place on the floor across the room, leaning against the front door. Besides the firelight's flicker upon the upturned faces of "his" people, only a lantern on the piano shed any illumination in the room.

Spring turned a page in the book and saw Foster's tune "I Dream of Jeanie with the Light Brown Hair." She could feel David's eyes on her, and her fingers shook slightly. She straightened her back, a gesture David now recognized as a sign of courage, and her fingers began the last melody of the night.

She began to sing the words, her soft, clear soprano lending an aching sweetness to the already lovely tune. Her delicately rounded cheek was bathed in an orange glow; the tilt of her head and the arch of her graceful neck brought a feeling of incredible joy to David's heart. Even after she left, he would always be eternally grateful she had come into his life and shown him his life was still worth living.

She finished the piece, folded her hands in her lap, and bowed her head. The room was silent, except for the crackle of the flames. Everyone was relaxed, and it was in this subdued manner that they took their leave for the night.

Spring tossed and turned on the big bed. Why didn't he come to her? Was he really angry about the party? The chiming clock tolled off twelve, and yet sleep eluded her. How long had it been since she heard him thumping around upstairs? This was crazy! She had to go to him then.

She crawled out of bed. Surely, if she went to him, he would see how much she wanted and needed him. She would drop any idea of John if David asked her to marry him. Especially now since they had been together. Was that really why she would marry him?

No. She was coming to realize the real reason.

She climbed the extending ladder from the dining area to the large attic loft above. She had not been up here, and the only light guiding her was the silver white of the moon shining through the south window. The light spilled out onto the floor, and she saw David lying on his mattress.

Quietly, she made her way over to him and looked down. He was on his back, covered to his bare chest. One arm was behind his head, the other thrown across his stomach. His eyes were shadowed, so she couldn't tell if he was asleep or not.

He wasn't. He had heard her come up the ladder and appear like a white ghost out of the floor. Light on her bare feet, she seemed to float across the darkness; and when she stood there in the silvered moonlight, she resembled an ethereal, wraithlike fairy princess.

She stood motionless above him. He took his arm from his head and reached out to take her ankle in his hand.

"I'm sorry, did I wake you?" she asked.

"No. Is everything all right?"

"Not exactly. I mean . . . God, David, don't you want me anymore?"

Her tone was the closest to a cry he had ever heard her use, except for her private grief over her father, and his heart melted.

"I'd be out of my mind if I didn't," he answered softly.

"I missed you, David. You were gone for six days. You didn't even say good-bye." She was sounding like a nag, and hated herself for it.

David Saunders knew what he wanted to do, and it had nothing at all to do with what he should do. He took her other ankle in his warm hand and realized the ankle bracelet was missing. He wondered what that meant, if anything; and for lack of something better to say, he said, "Your feet are cold, sweetheart."

She didn't know what to reply to that or what to do next, and she remained silent. David's resolve was slowly ebbing. She did come to him, after all. This was what she wanted. But didn't he want it desperately too? He didn't know anything except that he wanted to love her. He released her foot.

"Take off your nightgown," he ordered.

She quickly slipped it off and stood with the luminous rays dripping off her shoulders, to her breasts, to her slender, smooth thighs and legs. She held her head high as he viewed her. She was a sight to behold. Venus. A creamy-white body that was not a statue or a mythical goddess, but flesh and blood. And so was he. His body hardened for her, and his loins ached with longing. He threw back the cover and held his hand up to her.

With a sob she managed to keep buried deep within, she came to him and pressed herself to him, feeling every hard-muscled curve of his frame along hers. Their kisses left them both breathless; and when, at last, he took her, he did so slowly, but with purpose, for he had the knowledge in his heart that he could not keep her any longer, and that this would have to be the last time for them.

Later, spent and utterly happy, Spring talked nonstop of her childhood, the day she almost drowned when ice skating because the ice had broken beneath her and she had gone under. Another had drowned. She spoke of how she loved teaching and hoped to do more, and of what her music meant to her.

Finally, David laid two fingers over her lips and then kissed her. "Spring, I want you to know that I plan to carry out my promise to you and take you to Denver."

She was shocked into silence and felt a chill steal over her. "When will that be?" she managed to ask in a normal voice.

"As soon as I can get a few things in order. Probably the end of July."

What are you saying? her mind cried. *How can you make love to me, how can you make me love you and then go on with your life, after you dump me?* The thoughts flew around in her head.

"I thought maybe . . . maybe you and I might get . . . married," she ventured.

He forced himself to laugh coldly. "Married! God, no, Spring. After all I went through with Isabel, I'll never marry again! Besides, what about Lieutenant Granville?"

She hesitated, feeling stoicism wrapping itself around her heart, and then replied, "Yes, I do love John, but I don't know if I'll ever see him again. And . . . and since we'd gotten along . . ."

He laughed again. "Well, I told you it was more pleasant when both parties willingly participated. Anyway, I saw John in Denver when I was there last."

Her mind reeling, Spring could not take in both thoughts at once. First, he sounded so cold and uncaring about their lovemaking, and then John was all right. And he had made love to her with that knowledge and took her most precious possession away when he knew.

Suddenly, she sat up, and on her knees, faced him. She was unaware that her hair tumbled seductively about her head and that her breasts swayed in full view of his gaze. She slapped him with an open palm and then pummeled his golden-haired chest with both small fists.

"God, you are unbelievable! You knew John was alive and well and came home and didn't tell me. You made me your whore with no regard for my feelings! That's worse than any whipping you could have given me." When she raked her nails across his midriff, he caught her wrists in a bone-crushing grip. She thought they would break.

"Stop it!" he commanded, though his heart ached with anguish for her. "Stop it right now." He didn't know whether to tell her about

John, but he didn't want her to think he thought of her as a whore, either. Never that.

She asked again when he didn't answer, she stated, "Well, I won't again. I won't be your mistress while I'm here. I won't!" Her voice lost its intensity, and she laid her hot forehead on his furry chest, the tears squeezing from her tightly closed lids, mixing with the sweat of his passionate endeavors.

"No," he said, calm covering the agony that reached to the depths of his very soul. He was glad that the moon was now hidden behind some clouds that had stolen their way across its pathway, for tears of his own caused his eyes to burn and stab at his eyelids. "You have always wanted to be free of me. I refuse to keep you just because we have become closer. This is all for us. We'll go to Denver at the end of July." He released her wrists, and she numbly rose to her feet. She stepped over him and picked up her nightgown. She slipped it over her head and then went away as quietly as she had come.

Chapter 15

Great preparations had been taking place for the Fourth of July celebration. However, Spring did not take part in them. In fact, she had no intention at all of participating. Mary and Pap had appealed to her better nature, and even Lorna had ridden over one morning to urge her presence, but to no avail.

Since the awful revelations of David's purposeful ruination of her character and reputation, after he knew of John's whereabouts, she took on a mechanical quality. She spoke and answered at the right moments and did her chores, even accomplishing more than usual. She ate little. She thought about killing herself, but knew that would probably just give David Saunders great satisfaction that he had finally destroyed her altogether.

She did not entertain the thought of running away, because with the end of July in sight, she did not want to go to the trouble. Spring avoided David at all costs, not realizing that he too was doing the same. Most nights she slept alone in the big house. The closeness each had experienced with the other had been new and precious to both. The sudden ending of it had been a vicious attack on their very souls. They each suffered, alone.

David and Spring were civil to each other when they did come across each other, but not communicating when it wasn't absolutely necessary. But when news reached his ears that Spring was refusing to accompany the others to the overnight stay at the lake, he left the house immediately in search of her.

He looked everywhere he could think of in the immediate area, but he couldn't find her. He wondered briefly if she had run off, but a quick check of her room showed nothing missing. Suzie was gone from the yard area, and having been told of Spring's wide-ranging walks with Suzie for company, he knew he must widen his searches.

He found fresh tracks leading off into the trees where the grasses were flattened, and he found a small piece of white material from Spring's petticoat caught on a berry bush. He held it in his fingers, feeling its softness and smelling the fragrance of lilacs on it, then placed it in his shirt pocket.

He came upon a clearing among the trees in which the sun filtered down through the leaves and branches, sending misty shafts of rays to the center. In the middle knelt Spring, a ray resting on her bent head. He walked softly over the moss-covered earth and knelt on one knee in front of her. Suzie lay at her side. She licked his hand as he scratched under her chin.

David said, "I hear you don't want to come to the lake with us."

The young girl shook the dizziness that had caused her to sink to the ground, from her head. She passed a small graceful hand over her eyes, but kept staring downward.

"No, I don't wish to go," she answered in a small voice.

"Look at me," he said.

She didn't move. He reached out his hand and tilted her chin up. "Look at me." Haltingly, she did so, and he saw a grayish pallor on her usually pink-cheeked face. He concealed his concern and asked, "Why not?"

"You know very well," Spring replied, moving her chin away from his fingertips but keeping her eyes on him.

"I think we are both adult enough to not let our differences get in the way of a good time. I'll even be on my best behavior toward you." His tanned face broke into one of his rare, endearing smiles, and Spring could scarcely look at him.

"If you think I'll run away, I won't. I can wait until July's end," she offered.

"I know you won't leave," he said softly. "But I don't want to leave you up here alone."

"I'll be all right, really. Besides, David, I've been getting these dizzy spells."

"Oh, come on," he urged, thinking she was using that as an excuse, "if you feel that badly, I'll put you on Aphrodite and lead you to the lake, like Joseph did for Mary, going to Bethlehem."

All of a sudden, a great fear clutched at Spring's heart.

Surely these dizzy spells didn't mean that. Looking closely at the muscled man kneeling in front of her, she saw that he had not made the same parallel from his lighthearted statement that she had. But it couldn't mean that. She was only ten days late.

"Spring Ames," he said, cutting into her thoughts, "you'll be going to the lake with us tomorrow. Is that understood?"

He stood and gazed down at the fired highlights of her bent brown-red head, brushed back and caught in a red ribbon.

She nodded mutely. Back to his old dictatorship, was her thought.

*   *   *

The camping area was all set up, with the tents set back from the water in a large semicircle around the campfire, where the women would cook the food.

BJ, Hap, Jack, and Joe had gone to town to bring back some female companionship. To everyone's surprise, BJ had returned married. Her name was Penny, a cheerful, applecheeked girl, buxom and blonde. Everyone was paired up.

Spring and David were conspicuously apart.

The weather was simply beautiful, the sky a marine blue with a few fluffy clouds wending their way across the heavens. The sparkling water rippled easily from the gentle warm breezes. As the sun rose higher in the sky, it became hotter and hotter.

Lorna and Henry took Jacob into the shallows to play. The women wore funny ruffled suits to go in the water, and the men just stripped to their underwear.

Spring did not know what had come over these usually dignified people. She guessed it was the lack of responsibility, for they all behaved uproariously, as if there was no tomorrow. Standing near the water's edge, she was not a little envious of their fun. Even David was in the water with the rest of them, like he hadn't a care in the world, throwing the women about and playing King of the River. Their shouts and laughter echoed off the mountainsides, coming again and again in waves. At last, Spring could no longer stand to watch their antics. So she turned to her small tent and crawled in to lie upon her bedroll.

She had felt well that morning when she'd risen; however, David had insisted she ride Aphrodite anyway, just to be on the safe side. But lying in the small, hot tent, she soon felt like she was suffocating in the heat-filled enclosure, and she had to crawl back out. She found the others returning, dripping from the lake.

Hap ran to his tent. "Hey, look what I got in town." All attention was focused on a brown oblong object with points at two ends that he held high over his head. "Bet you don't know what this is."

No one spoke.

"It's a football," Spring supplied. "I saw the first game ever played at Harvard."

"That's a smart gal," Penny said.

"What's a Harvard?" someone asked, amid general laughter.

"Do you know how to play?" Jack asked.

"Only barely, if I remember correctly," she answered. "There are two teams, each with a goal area." She picked up a stick and drew lines in the sand. "Then you either toss or kick the ball to someone on your team who runs to the goal. Of course, the other team tries to stop you. I think they call that . . . umm, I don't remember, but you grab that person. Anyway, they try to get the ball and take it to their own goal."

With a few made-up rules of their own, they formed two teams, and Spring found herself on a different team than David. Mostly the women just squealed when chased and were afraid to catch the ball. After thirty minutes of intensified play, Spring was thrown the ball by Hap. Miraculously, she caught it and turned to run, dodging Penny's outstretched hands. It looked as though she had a clear field ahead, so she slackened her pace, but then heard soft footfalls behind her. Glancing over her shoulder, she saw David rapidly closing the gap between them. She sped up, past the goal line and kept on running, the football under her arm.

"Spring," David called above the yells of jubilation from her team, "you can stop now."

She didn't know why, but she kept on going, dashing through the trees on the far left of the beach area. David started after her, and it wasn't long before his longer stride brought him to her heels. However, she didn't stop. They were out of sight of the others now, and David could not imagine why the object of his pursuit kept up her mad pace.

At last, he leaped at her, grasping her about the waist and bringing her gasping to the ground. Her heart pounded crazily, and the roar of blood in her ears was deafening. Dizziness swept over her, and she lay facedown, motionless, drinking in as much air as her aching lungs would allow.

David caught his breath and rolled her over on her back. "Are you all right?" he asked. She was very quiet and very still. The leaves cast shadows on her creamy skin, her lips were slightly parted, showing her white teeth.

He gazed at her, finding it such agony to love her. He put his hand tenderly on her throat and he laid his lips over hers, taking complete possession of them.

At first she responded to the sweet pressure, giving in to her need of him; and then like a bolt of lightning, she remembered his deception. She beat at him with her one free hand. He seized it, raising it above her head and taking it with his other hand. Then slowly he trailed his hand down the underside of her raised arm, to her ribs, and to the tightly stretched blouse over her breast. He caressed her, cupping it in his hand and rubbing his thumb over the nipple teasingly.

"David, don't. Please. I'll scream—"

"They won't come, Venus," He tried to kiss her again, but she turned her head away, fighting the yearnings that were slowly spreading through her body.

"You promised you'd behave. You are a miserable cad," she hissed through clenched teeth. He released her, and gave her a hand to get her on her feet. He bent to pick up the football. "Yes, my dear, I just wanted to remind you." He laughed, hating himself for his cruelty.

"You needn't. Just looking at you reminds me." She straightened her back and stalked off.

"Hey," he said, catching up to her, "I want to take you for a canoe ride."

"No, thanks." They reached the edge of trees and proceeded along the beach. They saw that the rest had given up on them returning to continue their game, and had started eating.

"Hungry?" he asked.

"No."

"Then we'll go canoeing. I see that it's been dragged out."

She turned to face him and squinted up to look at him. "I said no, damn you!"

He tossed the football up onto the beach and unexpectedly bent and swooped her off her feet and, despite her kicking all the way, dumped her in the canoe. She didn't want to jump out into the water, so she sat sullenly glaring at David.

"Pap, bring me that yellow thing in my tent," David requested. He walked to the man carrying a long yellow object and then waded into the water again to mid-thigh, and climbed into the canoe. It rocked from side to side, and Spring clung to the edges, averting her eyes.

"Here," he said, handing her the present. "To replace the one I broke."

Her eyes turned to and saw a folded ruffled parasol. Her clear, joyful laugh floated forth. "You are impossible," she murmured.

"Put it up and lean back against those cushions. And don't be worried," he said, noting her wary expression.

She obeyed him, holding the parasol in one hand and trailing her other in the cool water. David handled the paddle expertly, and soon the gentle lap of water, along with the warmth of the sun, made Spring relax and enjoy the moment.

David wore only his trousers. His tanned, muscle-corded arms strained with the exertion of moving the canoe. He watched her with interest. He took in every inch of her, every contour, every plane. He wanted to commit her to memory.

"Look"—Spring pointed—"there's Freedom." The eagle swept across the sky above them, swooped low, and then veered off. "He must have been saying hello to you."

When they were some distance out, David stopped rowing, leaning back on his pillows. "Like your parasol?"

"Yes." She laughed lightly. "Do you think if a big wind came up I could be carried off to freedom?"

"No doubt," he grunted. "Speaking of big winds, I want to talk to you about John Granville."

Spring was totally humiliated that he would bring that up to her. "No, David, I do not want to hear what you have to say. How dare you even think I'd deign to discuss my betrothed with you?" All her frustrations, dashed hopes, and despair came pouring out. "You ruined me, David Saunders. God, how could you?" A sob caught in her throat, and she looked away.

He did not want to, indeed could not discuss their feelings right now. He felt she should know what kind of a man John really was.

"You listen to me, little girl, and you listen good." And though she shook her head in flat denial throughout his story, he told of John's plan for the Indian attack, that he did it for Spring and her money, to get at him, that it was John's fault her father and Mrs. Butler were dead.

David went on and on in a steady drone, and at last Spring could bear it no longer. She sat forward and closed her parasol. She did not know where the horrid words sprang from or where she'd heard them before, but there they were, spilling from her mouth.

"You are a lying bastard. You are the cruelest son of a bitch alive. First you take the only thing left that's really mine, and now you try to take John away as well by making him seem bad and mean. You don't want me, why not let someone else have me?" She stood, sending the canoe rocking precariously.

David tried to steady the madly rocking canoe and demanded she sit down before they went into the water. Instead, she raised the parasol above her head and brought it down with all her might.

"Spring, the canoe will tip over!" He brought up his arm to ward off the blow.

"You lying bastard! Goddamn lying cheat! I hate you!" With each word, she brought the parasol down again and again until, as David had predicted, the canoe overturned, throwing them both into the lake.

The water closed over Spring's head. At first she didn't realize what had happened, and then for a moment, panic set in as she recalled falling through the ice ten years ago. She kicked frantically, only to get her legs entangled in her long skirts.

How easy it is to die, she thought, letting herself go limp and her mind go into utter darkness.

David didn't know how he managed to keep himself and Spring from drowning. The repeated blows from the parasol had broken two small bones in his right wrist, sending severe pain up his arm. However, when he surfaced, he dove under the water several times hunting for her, before he saw her floating about ten yards away.

Using his left arm to do most of the work, he swam to her and turned her, with great difficulty, to her back.

The party onshore had stopped eating when they heard snatches of Spring's yelling over the water. Then in fascinated horror, they watched as she stood, beating David with the yellow parasol, to send them careening into the blue, whitecapped lake.

Immediately, Hap, BJ, and Henry took to the water, swimming toward the diving David as quickly as possible. When they reached him, David had found Spring and had crooked his right elbow under her chin, and had begun his arduous way toward the shore. He asked Hap and BJ to retrieve the canoe and Henry to swim next to him to perhaps spell him if he needed it.

Spring was not a heavy woman by any means, and David was a strong swimmer, despite the handicap of his wrist wrenching with pain. However, she was unconscious and weighted down with a long skirt and petticoats, so his progress was vastly impeded.

David had met with many frightening experiences in his life, from being pursued as a young boy by his father's hunting dogs, to being captured by renegade Indians, to the awful knowledge of

Isabel's death. But he didn't think any of those incidences measured up to this horrible journey across the lake with a limp, seemingly lifeless Spring under his arm. He didn't even know if she was alive, and he begged God, if there was one, to let her be alive and well.

Finally, Henry had to take over while David floated on his back to shallow water. When he arrived up on the sand, the women were in a circle around Spring, who was stretched out on her face. Pap was astride her back, pushing on it, while Henry lifted her elbows above her head, every other time Pap pushed.

In quiet desolation, David watched, mesmerized, the water dripping from his hair and clothes. He didn't even notice when Hap and BJ came to stand beside him after hauling the canoe up onto the dry land.

What seemed an eternity passed, and nothing happened. Spring just lay there unmoving. Pap and Henry continued their ministrations. Suddenly, Spring let out a cough and a choking sound, and water gurgled from her mouth and nose. The men continued their work, and in a few minutes, it was over. Mary gathered her into her arms, tears coursing down her cheeks.

David retreated into the background. He walked away, holding his wrist, to the stand of trees where only recently he had held his love in his arms. He was violently sick, after which he cried uncontrollably. He didn't remember ever crying before, not even for Isabel.

When he was calm again, he returned to the beach where Pap snapped the bones back into place, splinted, and wrapped his wrist.

Spring was in her tent with Mary, he learned; and she had insisted everyone stay and not return home on her account.

"She apologized over and over for disrupting everyone's fun, that it was her fault the canoe overturned and that you'd warned her to sit down. Dave, what the hell was going on out there?"

David winced with pain as he inspected his bandaged wrist. Wasn't it just like Spring to keep the blame from him? He drew his knees up and rested his elbows on them, peering down at the sand between his arms and legs.

"I tried to tell her about John. Pap, she will be helpless against his ruthlessness, but she is bound and determined to be with him.

She called me a liar and a few other choice words I didn't think she knew. I think she wants more than ever now to be with him. And I can barely stand the idea of her with that man!" He looked up in anguish at the older man.

Pap placed an arm around David's damp shoulders. "Or any man?" he asked dryly.

"Or any man," he admitted quietly. "God help me, Pap, I love her."

"What's the problem, then?"

"She hates me. Well, I don't think she really hates me. I do think she cares for me in some ways, but she has this incredible sense of honor and keeping true to her word and promises. Pap, I did a terrible thing to her, worse maybe than taking that damned whip to her . . . I took her to my bed." His words came out in a groan.

"No wonder you two are at each other's throats. You didn't r—?"

"No. That's what's so strange. She says she loves John Granville, yet she allowed me to make love to her and accepted me very readily. I've got to let her go, let her be free to live her own life. That's all that girl has ever asked of me from the moment I met her." David's attention was drawn to Spring's tent, and he saw Mary come out. He got up and walked over to it.

Mary stood with arms folded across her chest, guarding the entrance. "You stay away from that girl, you hear me, Davey?"

"Mary!" Pap interrupted. "Hold your tongue!"

"I mean it, Pap. Anyway, you yourself said you would keep him away from her after that whipping. He has no right—"

"I know what I said, and I was wrong. He has every right, Mary," Pap said, urging her away from the tent. "Remember who you are talking to."

Mary took a breath and got herself under control. Pap was right, of course. She looked up into David's face, surprised not to see the angry signs he wore when he was not pleased. Instead, she saw incredible pain and sorrow.

He placed a hand on her shoulder. "It's all right, Mary. I fully understand how you feel. I just want to talk to her, to see if she is all right."

"Well, she's very sleepy, but awake. Davey," she said as he was about to duck into the tent, "I'm sorry . . . I said . . ."

When he crawled inside, he found Spring turned to the wall. Covering her shoulders was the bright new shawl David had bought her in Denver. The brown-red yarn in it matched her hair perfectly. He sat cross-legged behind her.

"I'm sorry," he said. "Why didn't you yell so I could find you out there?"

"I didn't want to be found," she mumbled against her arm. "I wanted to die, David. Sorry to disappoint you." She felt empty, cold, and alone.

Such rage filled his being that his whole body shook, and he thought he would explode. It was all he could do to remain calm and in control. He reached out and took her shoulder in his left hand and pulled her to her back. She stared at him with vacant eyes. The usually brilliant jade-green eyes were dull and almost lifeless.

She saw a muscle twitch in his cheek and his mouth in a hard line, and she saw his bandaged wrist.

"What happened to your arm?"

"You broke it with that damned parasol," he answered in a hardened voice. "What do you mean you wanted to die?"

"That's it. Plain and simple. When I first hit the water, I started to kick, but then I thought how nice and quiet and soft it was under the water, and so I just closed my eyes . . ."

"Shut up!" he commanded roughly.

"You asked."

"I would not have been happy if you had died."

"Why? It would have solved all our problems, wouldn't it?" she asked. "But no, you had to play conquering hero again and save me from a watery grave."

Her calm words, so simply said, caused David's stomach to wrench into knots, and he thought he might be sick again. He didn't know if he could go on talking to her. He took her hand in his, limp though it was, and held it against his cheek.

"Spring, I want you to promise me that you will never think of letting yourself die like that again. It wouldn't have solved anything, believe me. You are so full of life, not only in your words, but in your actions. You've brought me so much joy, to all of us here. Your music soothes us and makes us happy. Whenever we see you dancing in the fields with Suzie at your heels, carrying wildflowers in your arms, you make us feel glad that we are alive. Spring, no matter what you may think, I . . . I do care about you and what happens to you, so please promise me that you won't do anything foolish."

"Are you speaking for yourself?" she asked, half hopefully.

"Yes, but also for all of us."

She looked away, disappointment consuming her. She felt him kiss the palm of her hand, his lips warm and soft upon it. She sighed. "Yes, I promise, David. The water was just there over me, so I thought I'd take advantage of it while I had the chance."

"Oh, Spring, you talk such nonsense." The next words he spoke came out nonchalantly, but belied everything he really wanted to say. "I want to be your friend. Can't we at least be that?"

Friends! God, what did he want from her? Didn't he have any idea at all what he meant to her, that what they had shared wasn't just to pass the time for her?

She swallowed hard. She supposed she could be friends with him, but she wanted him to love her. Well, she guessed that wasn't possible. She removed her hand from his and rolled back over.

"Yes, I'll be your friend, David, if that's what you want."

He gazed at her, curled up, defenseless, and small; and his heart ached. She had promised him, and she did keep her promises. He had to be satisfied with that.

Spring slept all afternoon while the others played cards or read, or took short naps themselves. David's wrist pained him some, but now that it was set, he was able to move about quite well and fairly uninhibited.

For dinner, they had roasted potatoes, bread with thick chunks of butter, lemonade, and chicken turned on a spit over the fire. To top it all off, there was a large layer cake made by Mary, and Lorna brought two apple pies.

Twilight was just beginning when Spring emerged from the tent. Her shawl was wrapped around her against the cooling air. They did not notice her until she was almost upon them. Then they all stared up at her in what she thought was wonderment.

"Please don't look at me like that," she said, laughing. "You look as though you'd seen a ghost."

"Hi, darlin'," Pap put in. "Are you hungry? We've got plenty left over to eat."

"Yes, you have enough for an army," she replied. "But no, I'm not really hungry. Did anyone happen to bring my tea?"

"Of course I did." Mary searched for the tea brought by David from his Denver trip. "Did you think I'd forget you?"

"No, I didn't," Spring said, giving Mary a hug.

The firelight shone in the faces of the rest of the group. They seemed to be paired off, but all together at the same time, like one happy family.

"Listen, everyone," Spring started, sitting in the circle between Mary and Lorna. "I hope I didn't ruin your day by my silly antics. I didn't think the canoe would turn over, even though David warned me." She laughed gaily. "And to think I actually broke his wrist with that flimsy old parasol. You know, David and I and parasols don't get along." She proceeded to tell them about the way they had met, casting an amusing slant to the story instead of the way she really remembered it.

David listened with bewilderment. To think that a few hours ago she was almost dead, and had talked about not wanting to live. And now, she was so alive and joyful.

"I can't get over how happy and gay you are, Spring," Penny said, from across the circle. "You almost left us this morning."

"That's why her name is Spring," David spoke for the first time. "You know how after a long cold winter everything is stark and empty? Then you see new life growing up out of nothing, and soon a whole mountainside is filled with all colors of wildflowers. Everything is alive, new, and fresh. That's how Spring is. She bounces back from tragedy and unhappy events."

They all looked from him to her sitting opposite each other. He had spoken quietly, without undue emotion, as if reciting facts about a good friend that everyone should know.

Spring smiled. "Either that or I'm a great actress, right?" The group laughed.

Spring didn't realize the truth of her words or the fact that David, too, was acting out a part of his own. Both did an exceptional job of hiding their real feelings—not only from themselves, but from the others as well.

"Well," Spring went on, "I'm glad I didn't spoil the day for you. I plan to behave myself and stay clear of the water."

"Yes, and Dave had better stay clear of you," Hap said. "The way you were beating on him with that little parasol, it's amazing he's around to talk of it." That sent everyone laughing once more and the mood of the afternoon that had been heavy with near tragedy was lifted. It was because of Spring.

Chapter 16

✕⋄✕⋄✕⋄✕⋄✕⋄✕⋄✕

By the end of July, Spring felt for certain that she was pregnant with David's child. She was really in a turmoil as to what she should do. She knew she couldn't stay here. Plans were made for her departure to Denver at the end of the week. But she didn't think for one moment that John would welcome her along with a child, especially David's. No self-respecting woman would appear in polite society pregnant and unmarried. She would be completely ostracized from the community.

Every day, when she arose, she had to spend some time in the bathroom, bending over the tub being sick. She was always late getting to her chores, and she tired quite easily, wanting to nap in the afternoons. No one asked her why she was always late, or even appeared suspicious, so she felt safe from having to say anything—at least not yet. She really didn't know what the signs for being pregnant were, but since she was extremely tired and nauseous, and her breasts were unbelievably sore, she could discern no other reason for her malady. There was also the unglaring fact that her monthly time had not come the last time, and she never missed.

She was glad that Penny and BJ had not accepted her offer of giving up her room to them while their little cabin was being built. She felt miserable enough to want the comfort of David's bed at night. Instead, they slept upstairs while David took BJ's place out with the unmarried men in the bunkhouse. Sometimes Spring had to put pillows over her head to keep out the sounds that came from above, for though they were not directly overhead, she knew exactly what they were doing, and it made her miss David all the more.

She and he were getting along fairly well since the overnight. They were friendly, as he wanted them to be. Most of the time, however, they did not run across each other until the evening when it was time to eat. He still took his meals in the house, though for now, they, Pap, and Mary, were joined by the newlyweds.

One late afternoon, after the men had quit work for the day on the new house, which was up over the hill in back of the white one, Spring went into the barn in search of Hap.

Since they had the piano and music in general in common, they had become good friends. This time she had a favor to ask of him.

When she entered, she saw him at the end of the stalls grooming his horse. Suzie perked up from her bed and trotted alongside her. She did not see David bent in the first stall working on some gear.

"Hi, Hap. Done for the day?" she asked with a smile. Hap turned to her. Her hair was pulled up on her head, her face clear and fresh. She had bloomed recently, it seemed to him.

"Yes. Do you need something?"

"Yes, I do need a favor. You know I'm leaving at the end of the week for Denver and—"

"I sure hate to see you go, Spring. I'm really going to miss you." Hap reached out and touched her delicate pink cheek with a rough finger.

"Thank you, Hap. I'll miss you too. All of you have been wonderful to me. But I'm a little apprehensive, you know, to be in a big, unfamiliar place, and I'd sure like to know how to use a gun. Do you think you can teach me enough in the time I have left?"

"Sure, that's no problem—"

"No, you will not teach her how to use a gun, Hap."

David's voice sounded ominous behind them. They turned to him. "Why not?" Spring asked. "I think I should know how to use one. It'll come in handy."

"I said no, and that's final." He stepped closer, and she saw that the blue eyes, which hadn't taken on this quality for such a long time, were turning to ice.

"It won't be a problem, Dave," Hap put in. "I'll do it in my spare time."

"Damn it, Hap, don't you listen? I said no!"

Spring was embarrassed to have gotten Hap into trouble on her account. She snapped at David. "For heaven's sake, you don't have to be so mean about a simple request. All I asked for was—"

"Spring!" His voice was low and deadly calm. "I said absolutely not, and I wasn't kidding."

"All right," she burst out. "All right. Forget I asked!" She gathered her blue skirt in her hand and stepped around him. "You are the most unreasonable man. I'm sorry, Hap."

"That's all right, Spring." And in puzzlement, he watched her walk away, and then he turned his attention to David. His handsome features were working to keep control.

"Remember what I said, Hap. I think you know why, don't you? No guns for Spring."

"Yes, sir," he answered and turned back to his horse.

After leaving the barn, Spring walked up the hill and stood outlined against the purpling, azure sky. A brisk wind whipped her skirt around her legs and pulled some tendrils of hair out of her bun. She took some deep breaths trying to calm herself. She didn't try to figure out what was eating at David this time. It didn't matter anymore. She would be gone in a few days anyway, and though she still felt she needed some kind of protection when she got to the city, she thought she could find out how to use a gun from someone, even if she had to hire someone to teach her.

She also had another plan, and that was to get rid of the baby. God knew that David didn't want it. He had a little girl by White Feather that he didn't want responsibility for. If he didn't want her, then he wouldn't want another by Spring. She wasn't sure how she was going to go about it as yet, but she hadn't spent all those years in a girls' boarding school for nothing. When the lights were out and the girls gathered in their tight little circles and talked girl talk, some rather sketchy information as to how to end a pregnancy had come forth.

It wasn't that Spring would have done such a thing if she and David were to always be together, or if he even loved her a little. But she just had no choices in the matter. She could not survive in

Denver as an unwed mother. If she had someone to go to, to help her, she would. There was Molly, of course.

Spring thought, sure, she'd help, but she was too good a friend of David's, and he must never know about this. Not that he would care; it was just better if he never knew.

The sun began to hit the mountain peaks in the west, and suddenly, she felt a presence beside her. It was David.

"Hush," he said. "I want you to hear the sun go down."

"The sun go down?" she questioned, forgetting for the moment that she was angry with him.

"Yes, now listen." They stood still, two dark silhouettes against the sky. The big yellow ball turned a pale shade of orange, and it seemed to spread and become larger as it went lower behind the mountain. David took Spring's hand in his, and suddenly the wind picked up, and there seemed to be a very distant dull *whish* of a sound, and the sun was gone. He squeezed her hand. "There. Did you hear it?"

"Yes, I did. I didn't know it made a sound like that when it sank. That's marvelous. Thank you for showing it to me."

He looked down at her hand and dropped it. "I wanted to explain to you about the gun."

"You don't have to. You do run things around here."

She couldn't help but bait him a little. "That's not the point. The night we were first together—no, now don't turn away. I'm not going to talk about that part. It was about Isabel we talked. I never told you how she died. Did anyone else tell you?"

"No, but it isn't important, is it?"

"It's important for me to tell you. Will you listen?"

Spring sighed. The more she knew of this man, the harder it would be for her to leave him, but she capitulated and waited for him to tell her about Isabel's death.

He raked his fingers though his hair and then caught her eyes with his own intense ones. "I told you about her, how she hated me and this place. But I didn't realize just how much, and I really never understood just how much. That doesn't really matter. What matters is that she did. Anyway, Isabel was like you in one way. She did not want to stay here and said so almost every day, it seemed. She always threatened she would leave but never was resourceful like you were in the beginning. She never did any of your tricks and actually try to get away."

He did not speak with any anger; in fact, there was a touch of amusement in his deep voice, so, not taking any offense at his words, she remained silent.

"Well, at first, it really bothered me that she said she would leave, and as it turned out, I should have let her go, given her a divorce, but I wouldn't. I'd beg and beg her to stay and try to work things out between us. She'd say things like, one day I'd wake up and she'd just be gone and I'd never find her."

He glanced away, suffering written on his face from reliving the past, and Spring yearned to put her arms around him to offer comfort. Instead, she hugged herself.

"One day, that's about what happened. It had snowed, and it was late afternoon. I'd been out to the barn to feed the horses, and when I returned to the house, she wasn't there. I looked and looked, and finally I found a trail in the snow that led down by the hummock. I found her. She had taken my revolver sometime during the day and blown her head off."

Spring drew back, shuddering in the darkening night air.

It was all she could do to keep her arms wrapped around herself instead of throwing them around him in sympathy. His voice went on in a far-off manner.

"There was blood all over the snow, and she was wearing white, and she was gone. She'd left me, like she said she would, like my mother did, like you want to. That's why I have to let you go and be free. I care too much about you to keep you here when you want to be somewhere else, with someone else. I realized that the day I took the whip to you. The instant I heard it crack against you, something gave way in me. I no longer grieved over Isabel. I no longer felt responsible for her or her death, because I knew I'd done my best for her, and there was something hidden inside of her that would make her do such a horrible thing as to take her own life. That's what frightened me so much when you said you wanted to die. She was never full of life as you are, so vital and always new. I can hardly believe my eyes every time I see you. I will always be sorry, but grateful that you were the instrument it took for me to purge myself of Isabel and to realize I must let you have your freedom. Thank you." His deep voice shook with intense emotion, and Spring didn't know what to say. She shivered.

"Let's go down to the house," she said, turning to begin her way. He stepped in beside her and placed an arm about her shoulders to give her some warmth, and they walked all the way back in silence. At the steps, she went up to the top and then turned. Now they were eye level. She smiled at him and caressed his cheek with her hand.

"What?" he asked.

"Dear David, I'm sorry you had to go through so many years of uncertainty and pain. I'm glad that I helped even though in the way it was." Now she lied to him and was glad for the darkness so he couldn't see her features well. "I'll be happy in Denver, and if I ever need help, I'll call my knight in shining armor. I love John, and I know he'll make me happy." She kissed his cheek, and then went in to the house.

"Hi, we were beginning to worry about you two. Where have you been?" Mary asked, placing food on the table.

"Up on the hill," Spring answered.

"We were discussing giving her some shooting lessons," David said, washing his hands under the pump in the sink. "She may need to protect herself in town. We'll start the lessons tomorrow, Spring."

She stared at him in astonishment. She didn't realize that her words to him about being with John had changed his mind about her needing to learn to use a weapon. With John, she would need every chance she had. "All right," she said, taking her place at the table.

Suddenly Mary giggled. "Pap, I can't keep still any longer. May I tell them our little secret?"

"Of course, dear. Women! They can't keep anything to themselves," he teased.

"What is it?" Penny asked.

"Pap and I are getting married. I guess you and BJ put the bug in our ear," Mary said, grinning.

"Sorry about that, Pap," BJ said, getting an elbow in the ribs from Penny, and then a long kiss.

"Mary," Spring said, getting up to put her arms around her dear friend and giving her a kiss. "Congratulations. And to you too, Pap. Mary's wonderful."

"I know that. I've known that for years. I don't know for the life of me why I waited to take the big step."

"What do you think, Davey?" Mary asked. She watched him butter a slice of bread slowly.

"Well, I think you two are meant for each other. When is this event going to take place?"

"We really don't want to wait any longer," Pap began.

"No, now that I've got him where I want him," Mary interrupted, "I don't want him changing his mind."

"We thought we'd go into Denver about August second," Pap stated, beginning to eat and glancing at Mary out of the corner of his eye. Spring realized the implications of this right away but said nothing. She waited for David's response, and it came almost immediately.

"Spring? If we allow them to marry on August second, I cannot take you to Denver at the end of the week like we planned. Remember, I need to be the one to get your money at the bank set up and all that."

Spring glanced from Pap to Mary and then to David.

Could she stick around here any longer than planned? "When will you be back?"

"We wanted to stay a week, but if that ruins your plans too much . . ." Mary managed to sound wistful.

"No," Spring hastened to say, "that's fine. I couldn't stand in the way of your getting married. And when you come back on the ninth, I'll have a little reception for you. I'll try to make a cake. That is, if I don't blow up the kitchen."

This met with laughter, and Spring began to eat. She could feel David's eyes on her and wondered what he was thinking.

But his facial expression was blank, though he stared hard at Pap for a moment before continuing with his meal.

*　　*　　*

Spring waved a last good-bye as Pap and Mary disappeared around the granite cliff. She returned to the house. It seemed deathly quiet. Penny and BJ had removed themselves to Pap and Mary's, and David was going to remain in the bunkhouse. Spring felt selfish having the whole house to herself.

She puttered around, picking up a book or two, only to replace them on the shelves. She struck a few notes on the piano, but they bounced off the walls eerily. In the kitchen, Mary had left things spotless and had gone so far as to have left the afternoon meal on the stove, ready to heat.

Spring wandered outside. It was so warm. The bright sun blinded her eyes, but after becoming used to it, she swept the porches on all four sides of the house. Then she watered the flowers in the window boxes. There were quite a few things to do, but she was too restless to do them. If Pap and Mary had not decided to marry, she would be in Denver right now, embarked on a new life.

She was anxious for this to happen, but now that it was postponed for another week, she would set her plans for the present in motion. Being of a young age and gently raised, Spring was unaware of the seamier aspects of life. Since she had come to the west, she had come across some things she had been protected from before, such as Molly and her house, the female companions the men had brought to the campout. What she'd read and heard about these type women had all been bad, but it hadn't been so in reality. And anyone who lived with a man while unmarried, why, heaven forbid! But look at Mary. She was a dear, sweet friend.

Then there was herself. She had slept with David and did not think of herself as being bad, because she loved him.

However, what everyone had ever said about that was true. You got into trouble if you were with a man and not married. And under cover of darkness, Spring remembered hearing that when a girl got into trouble and had to get out of it, there was only one way. Well, there was no doctor up here, but it shouldn't be too hard to do what she had heard had to be done. She would get rid of it the day Pap

194

and Mary returned, when the evening came. Then the next day, she could leave with no regrets and be able to function normally in town.

Spring never thought of the life inside her as a living human, or that it belonged to David, or that it was conceived in love, at least on her part. If she did think of it in those terms, she knew she couldn't go through with it, and then she would be lost for good. It was an *it* and nothing else.

Spring went back into the house and went to the bedroom. Her simple exertions had tired her, and she felt nauseated. She undressed to her drawers and chemise and lay down upon the vivid quilt. It was quiet, warm, and no breeze stirred. Before she left, she thought, she would clean the house from top to bottom, things that Mary wasn't able to do every day. With this in mind, she drifted off to sleep.

*   *   *

David fit the door on its hinges and hammered the pins into place to secure it. Then he moved it to and fro and saw he had done a good job.

His stomach growled with hunger, and glancing to the sky, he saw it was afternoon. He told the others he would return after eating and set out for his own place. Topping the hill, he looked down upon his domicile, and all seemed peaceful. Too peaceful? There was no smoke coming from any of the chimneys, which told him Spring must not have his dinner waiting. She was becoming fairly adept in the kitchen, being a quick learner. He passed the barn and corral at a quickened pace and jumped up to the porch. No, no food was cooking, and no one was about. Now he was becoming alarmed.

"Spring?" he called, setting his hat on the table. Then he heard a cry from the bedroom, and he strode in that direction. Thrusting open the door, he saw Spring drenched with perspiration, tossing on the bed, her face contorted in fear and tears streaming from her eyes, and yet she was asleep.

He crossed to the bed, sat down, and took hold of her shoulders, soft and slender in his hands. He pulled her up, calling her name over and over as he held her tightly against his chest.

"Spring, my dearest girl. It's all right. Everything is all right. I'm here. Honey, it's all right." He tried to calm her uncontrollable shaking and sobbing tears that soaked his right shoulder. She clung to him desperately, digging her fingers into his arms and pressing herself ever closer to him. He rocked her gently, kissing the top of her head, smelling the sweet fragrance that was only her.

When at last her sobs turned to hiccups and small shudderings, she relaxed against him with great exhaustion, and then he laid her back on her pillows. Her face was red and swollen, her eyelashes clung together wetly. David brushed the hair away from her face, taking his handkerchief to wipe her cheeks.

"Feeling better?"

"It was awful, David. I've been having some rather ridiculous dreams lately, but this one was the absolute worst."

"Do you want to tell me about it?" he asked, taking in her lack of dress and how alluring she was despite her dishevelment.

She did not see his passing gaze for her eyes were shut.

Then the luminous, jeweled eyes stared up at him. "Well, it began as many of them. I am an eagle. It's me, except that I have huge black-and-white-feathered wings, and I can fly all over. It's fun to look down and see everything smaller, you know? Anyway, I flew here from the lake and saw Mary hanging clothes, you breaking that wild horse, everyone working. You all looked up and waved. Well, suddenly, everyone was gone, and I flew all over searching. No one to be seen." Spring's face furrowed in a frown, and she stared up at the ceiling. "So I flew to Fort Frontier. It was empty. The front doors hung open and . . . and inside, I saw my father hanging on . . . on the flagpole." Her eyes closed and then flew open again. "Mrs. Butler and Aunt Emma were there, dead too. I left, flying back to the lake, passing over here first, and still no one was here. When I got to the lake, I felt peaceful and glided about. It was nice to be free, though I was alone, but then,"—her hands fisted, and she held them tightly to her sides—"as I floated above the water, my wings fell off, and I fell headfirst in the water. It was so dark and cold, and then I saw something white, and when I came to it, oh God, David . . ." She dragged her frightened eyes to his. "It was Isabel without her head and blood gushing all over in the water, surrounding me and . . . and then the head floated by, and it laughed and laughed and laughed . . .”

Spring's eyes were wild, and David took her hand and stroked it. “It's all right, my sweet girl. It's only a dream, and though alarming, it won't hurt you. I too had many dreams about finding Isabel, but they eventually stopped. I shouldn't have told you how she died.”

“No, I'm glad you told me,” she assured him and, seeing the distress in his face, tried to calm him down.

He knew dreams had some significance but was not in any position to interpret them. To dream about people she had known or heard about, who were now dead, was no surprise. To dream about drowning in the lake when it had almost been a reality was no surprise, either. And to dream of being an eagle that could fly anywhere, anytime only confirmed in his mind that she still yearned to be free.

“You've been having lots of crazy dreams?” he asked.

“Yes, but not like this one.”

“Do you want me to sleep in the house tonight, in case?”

Yes, her mind begged to say. *Not just in the house, but in my bed.* Instead, she said, “No, I'm sure I'll be fine.”

“If you change your mind . . .”

She shook her head.

“Well, how about eating?”

“Ugh. It's too hot to eat.”

He raked her body with his eyes. “Really, Spring. You're much too thin. You're wasting away to nothing.”

She realized then that she was in her underclothes and blushed. She sat up to reach for her skirt and blouse, but he stayed her hand.

“Surely, you can't be embarrassed by your attire.” He grinned at her. “You may remember, I've seen you with less. Besides, as you said, it's much too hot, and honestly, I cannot see a thing through the material.” He stood and went to the door.

Spring imagined he was right. “I'll go wash my face,” she said, “and then have some tea and some bread. And, David”—she paused as he turned to look at her softly—“thank you . . . again.”

He winked a clear, blue eye at her and went to stoke up the stove.

Chapter 17

◇◇◇◇◇◇◇◇

It had been a tiring week, what with all her cleaning.

She not only washed all the curtains at every window, but she painstakingly washed each pane of glass until it shone with new glossiness. She washed and polished all the hardwood floors. She took every book off the shelves and dusted each one. She carried the rugs outside to beat them. David reprimanded her sternly for doing so much, but she was almost through and did not want to stop in the middle of her cleaning.

The day before Mary and Pap were to return, all that was left to do was the upstairs loft. She hadn't been up there since her one night with David and so had not seen it in the daylight. She was surprised at how little was up there. Just David's empty mattress lay where she remembered the loving, tender moments they last had shared in the closest way two humans could. She brushed those thoughts quickly away glancing about. A few odds and ends of furniture, which she dusted, and some cobwebs, which she swept down with the broom were about all that filled the loft. That is, except in the far corner was a trunk, three boxes, and a dressmaker's form. She dusted these as well.

Curiosity finally got to her, and before she swept the floor, she opened the boxes to find some small items of women's apparel, hats, gloves, shoes—all of the finest quality.

Much finer than any Spring had owned in her rather well-to-do life. When she opened the trunk, she found some patterns on top, and then beneath, wrapped in tissue, were the loveliest dresses she had ever seen. All were either white or the palest of colors, and she knew these had belonged to Isabel.

There was also a silver comb that matched the silver-handled brush she had been using all the while she was here.

Wrapped in other tissue was a wedding picture of an incredibly beautiful woman, one that appeared to be made from cold marble, standing next to a very well-built man sitting on a chair, one that was perfectly dressed in the latest-styled suit of the day—a young expectant, happy face. It was a younger David, without a moustache, but undeniably handsome all the same.

This picture was in a gold frame, and the look on the faces held hope, and yes, there was love in her face as well as his. How could Isabel have loved David and treated him so shabbily?

She set the picture aside and began taking out the dresses.

They were filmy and cool to the touch. One white dress caught Spring's eyes in particular, for it had silver and gold threads interwoven in the sheer satin material. Spring held it up to her own body and saw it was too long for her, so she knew that Isabel must have been taller. She knew she shouldn't be going through these things, but they were so lovely. But none of it was her business, and as she thought about putting them away, she smoothed her hand down the front of the dress and heard a crackle under her right hand. She reached into the pocket and pulled out a small slip of paper with "Davey" scrawled across the outside. Spring put the dress over the trunk lid and unfolded the paper, and what she read brought tears to her green eyes, and she sank to the floor.

Darling Davey,

I cannot go on like this. You will not believe me when I say how much I love you. I always have, even when you wanted to do those awful things. I just cannot. Please forgive me. I set you free of me.

Isabel

Spring read the note over and over and was startled when she heard David's voice behind her. "What are you doing?"

She rose to her feet shakily. "I'm sorry . . . I shouldn't have gone into the trunk . . . It was none of my business . . . Here, I found this, and I think you should read it." She held the note out to him, her hand trembling.

He frowned at her, saying nothing but taking the paper and walking over to the window. He read the note, his heart setting up a hammering in his chest and tears smarting his eyes. He turned to Spring and did not bother to hide them.

He cleared his throat and said gruffly, "Will you please put everything back?"

"Yes, right away." She watched him walk away and comprehended from his reaction that he still loved Isabel deep in his heart, and always would.

Later, when she went back upstairs to retrieve the broom she had left there, all the boxes and the trunk were gone from the corner of the large room. She did not know who had removed them, though she thought it was David, and she did not ask him why they were gone.

The next morning, Spring was up early, for she had much to do. She began by baking the cake for the reception of the newly married couple. She had watched Mary several times baking cakes, and so for her first effort, the white cake with white frosting came out quite well. Spring spread the dining table with a lovely French lace tablecloth from the well-stocked linen closet off the supply room. Spring imagined that all the fine-woven flax had been handpicked by Isabel and, because of their lustrous finish, must have cost quite a bit. Spring also found a full set of bone china, creamy white with a gold border, the initials *DMS* also scrolled in gold in the center of each plate. There was a lot more finery in the large closet, but Spring did not want to take the time to look, nor, after seeing David yesterday with such grief in his eyes over his one love, did she want to see more of the expensive gifts he had given to her. All that and this only made her resolve firmer by the day. .

After giving David his breakfast, which she set on the table for him, she went to the bathroom and bathed with lilac-scented water and washed her hair. She smoothed on some body oil Mary had given to her to keep her skin from drying out.

She began with her arms and legs, and when she reached her breasts, they seemed to be a little fuller than she noticed last, and was there even a slight bulge below too? She was not sure how far along she was, but she thought she felt a little hard knot there. No, she could not stop and think of that! For later in the day, she wouldn't be far along at all. There wouldn't be anything left.

She entered the room and dressed in the printed yellow skirt and the pale-green blouse. Everything was fresh and clean smelling from the mountain air. She brushed and brushed her lengthening hair until it was dry and shining like copper, and she tied it back with a yellow ribbon.

She then packed in a small bundle, her little amount of belongings, leaving the silver-handled brush where she first found it. She also put back on the ankle bracelet from John that she had removed the morning after she and David had first been together. That, in her mind, was the beginning of the final break from David. Getting rid of it would be the last.

Turning from the room, she went back to the kitchen and placed plates, napkins, crystal goblets, and silverware on the table in a buffet style. In the middle, she put a large bouquet of wildflowers in a low vase. On one side, she put the cake, and on the other, a large punch bowl reserved for the lemonade she would make when she was through with the final deed for release from David Saunders.

Stepping outside in the noonday sun, she set off to the north where the hills were high and rocky. She knew she had plenty of time, for David had taken his lunch with him. She passed by the barn, and unfortunately, so Spring thought, attracted Suzie, who attached herself to Spring. No amount of urging would persuade the dog to go back home.

Sighing, Spring shrugged her shoulders and walked on for quite some time until she came to a summit of outcropped gray rocks. She sat in the shade to one side. She drew from her pocket a kitchen knife, and began to whittle the stick she had picked up along the way. She shaped one end of the stick to a fine point and rubbed the skinned wood with her hand to smooth off any splinters. At last she was ready.

Spring did not really know what she was doing, nor did she realize the magnitude of the action she was taking. She just knew that she was alone in the world, and when she reached Denver, she would only have herself to depend on. She told herself she did not love David and was doing this for John, as well as for herself. Since no one would ever know, what harm was there? She had, weeks ago, shut her heart and mind to "it" and now, mechanically in spirit and action, put her plan into action.

The sky above was so blue it almost hurt to look at it. The air was clean and sweet, smelling of wildflowers, and yet Spring did not allow herself to think about it.

Instead, she pulled up her skirt and pulled off her drawers. Feeling very removed from herself, as if she were watching someone else perform this hideous act, she knelt on the grass by the rock and inserted the sharp, pointed stick into the birth canal and shoved with all the courage she could muster. A pain so severe shot through her whole body that she imagined for a moment that she might have used a knife instead of the honed stick. And then, blessedly, blackness clouded her brain, and she fainted into the shade beside the boulder.

Suzie jumped up from where she had been resting, idly watching her beloved Spring. She slinked over and sniffed about Spring's face and then licked her cheek. Spring did not move. Suzie barked two quick yaps. She whined deep in her throat. She nudged the young prostrate woman with her black velvet nose, and when Spring did not stir, the dog became frantic. Suzie circled Spring, barking in short, rapid sounds.

Sniffing, she came across the bloodied stick, and Suzie picked it up in her mouth and ran down the hill. Once or twice, she stopped and turned to see if Spring had gotten up, but she had not.

Suzie sailed over the grasses and rocks, through the trees, and to the white house with red trim. She ran up to the back door, dropping the stick, barking at the door, and scratching on it. No one answered her plea.

She picked up the offending weapon once more and went to the barn. No David. Then she began sniffing the ground, finally picked up his scent, and, legs flying, found her way to the little cabin the men had been working on for BJ and Penny. David was bent over, working on the front steps. Suzie raced up to him and dropped the stick at his feet, barking until her throat was dry and rasping, her voice hoarse.

"Go away, Suzie. I'm not going to play with you now. I don't have time to throw this stick to you." He hammered another nail into the wood, his right wrist having healed.

"What's that dog doing?" BJ asked from the edge of the roof. "She's never done that before."

"Oh, she just wants to play." David pushed the dog away.

Suzie ran a few steps back and barked again. Then she went and picked up the stick, dropping it between David's legs. "Oh, all right," he said, picking up the piece of wood. He raised his hand, holding the stick. "Only one time now." He drew his arm back and then felt that the stick was sticky, and he brought it down to inspect it. The end he was holding was covered with blood, and his hand now was as well.

"Oh my God," he muttered to himself. Suzie was causing such a ruckus now that David couldn't even think clearly.

"BJ, I think something has happened to Spring. I'm going with Suzie. You and Penny go down to the house to wait for us. Everyone else stay away. You hear?"

"Yes, I hear you." But David was gone, following Suzie as fast as he could run. Sometimes the dog disappeared from view, but always came back to show him the way.

David saw Suzie run up a rock-studded hill and turn at the top and bark, her voice barely audible. He climbed the hill, still clutching the bloodied wood, sick at heart at what he might find. His breathing came in ragged snatches, and he thought his lungs would burst. When he reached the top, he saw Spring's legs sticking out from behind the large rock, and coming closer, he saw her skirt was up around her hips, and there was blood on her inner thighs.

Stopping to catch his breath, he heaved the pointed weapon as far as he could throw it and hurried over to the still-unconscious woman. He did not look at her to examine her, but rolled her on her back, drawing her skirt down around her legs. He saw her drawers on the ground in front of her and picked them up in one hand. He thought he probably shouldn't move her, but he had to get her to the house, so he swept her up in his arms. He did not let his mind think but concentrated on his footing all the long way to the house.

Penny had already drawn the covers down on the bed when he arrived there. David's face told BJ not to ask any questions. He laid her gently down, seeing that there was some color in her face. Hearing horses coming across the front yard, he went to the window and saw Pap and Mary.

He turned to BJ and said roughly, "Tell Pap to get the hell in here right away." He could no longer look at Spring. She had tried to kill their child, and he was more shocked by this than anything else that had come into his life. Never in a million years did he ever think she could do such a thing.

What seemed an hour, but was actually minutes, passed before Pap came through the door. "What's the matter, Dave?" Then his eyes flew to Spring on the bed and the blood on David's hand. "What has happened?"

Mary entered and stood beside Pap. She covered her mouth with both hands, and Penny let out a little scream when David said, "I think she tried to abort our child. I don't know if she succeeded. And," he went on, glancing at the two women, "I don't want this to go any farther than this room. This is not a subject open to speculation or discussion among any of us. The business is mine and Spring's. No one else's."

He turned his attention to Pap, who was leaning over Spring, giving her face little slaps. "Mary, we need some smelling salts. Everyone else may leave."

David did not follow the others. "I want to know if she succeeded."

"I'll have to examine her, Dave." Pap took the salts from Mary and held them under Spring's small nose. She turned her head and moaned before her eyes fluttered open.

Her vision was blurred, and then she focused on David, and she knew that he knew what she had done. She felt great sorrow and despair and closed her jeweled eyes to the hard look on his face.

"Spring," Pap's voice broke into her empty mind, "what have you done? What made you do such a thing?" He gently examined her, pressing on the inside and outside of her. She drew up her legs in distress as her stomach cramped. "Okay, honey, that's all for now. I'll have Mary come in here and clean you up." He got up and took David by the arm, guiding him out into the living room.

David sat in his chair, his head buried in his hands. "Well, what do you think?"

"Not being a professional, mind you—"

"Don't beat around the bush, damn it. Just tell me!" David looked up, anguish tormenting his features.

"I still feel the fetus in the womb. It's not very far along, about six weeks or so. She did injure herself, if internally, however, but it may just be superficially. There is some cramping, which doesn't look good. But if she stays on her back for a while, the baby might make it. Spring will be all right, I'm fairly sure. I don't believe she tore up the womb, but she did cut up the mouth a bit."

"Thank God she's all right!" he exclaimed softly. "What about the baby? Apparently, she didn't want it."

"Do you?" Pap asked quietly.

David sat back. He brushed his hand through his white-blond hair, and he looked up at the ceiling, blinking back unshed tears.

"Yes, Pap, I do want her child, more than anything, except for her to be all right and happy. I guess she doesn't want my child, though."

"Oh, I don't know, Dave," Pap said, getting up. "Think about it. Perhaps she didn't think she had any other choice. I'm going to give her some laudanum to help her sleep and relax. That's what she needs now more than anything, no upset." Pap left David to sit and stare into the dead fireplace. That's the way he felt right at that moment—dead.

David did not go to visit Spring for several days. Though David had warned those present not to say a word about Spring and what she had attempted, everyone at Saunders's Haven learned, as if by osmosis, that she had tried to abort David's child.

Once everyone knew, they went by David's order not to discuss it.

All came to see her, but she preferred to lie abed and be alone, for unexpectedly, tears would descend on her. When Mary told her she was not to move for any reason, she cried mournfully. When told that if she refused David would personally tie her to the bed, she sobbed uncontrollably.

David sometimes heard her in her sorrow, but he couldn't find it in himself to go talk to her.

One late afternoon, Mary caught him in the barn grooming Aphrodite. She stood with arms akimbo, staring at him. Finally, he looked up and said, "What do you want, woman?"

"I want you to get yourself into that girl and talk this out."

"Why? She's got plenty of company trailing in there. She doesn't need me."

"Davey, you are all she asks about. What are you doing? Have you left, do you hate her, are you angry, do you really know what she did? I can't, I won't answer those questions. Now I suggest you get down off your pride and get in to that house and talk to her!"

David stared at her, the cold, hard look coming to his face. "Perhaps you'd like to take your disloyalty elsewhere, madam?"

Mary put her hand on his arm. "You don't scare me, David Michael Saunders. I'm telling you this for your sake as well as hers. I love you both." And with that, Mary left him.

He knew he would have to talk to Spring sometime. Now might be as good a time as any. He finished up with Aphrodite and went to the kitchen to wash up. Mary shoved Spring's supper tray into his hands.

Pressing his lips into a hard line, he went to her room. She lay on her back, seeming almost to sink into the bed. She was so small and fragile and so dear.

He kicked the door shut with his foot, and her eyes flickered open. In silence, she pushed herself up, and he put the tray within easy reach. He turned and lit the fireplace as the afternoon was cooling off. Then he went and stared out the window. Hell! What was he to say to her?

Spring didn't know how to react to his presence now that he had at last come to her. He looked distant, and his stance bespoke an uncompromising and hard way about him. She drank down her tea, burning her throat.

"Why did you do it, Spring?" he lashed out suddenly, causing her to jump. His face showed fear as well as anger.

"You tell me how I was to manage—an unmarried mother in an unknown place. You no longer wanted me. Just a cheap thrill, a . . . what do you men call it, a roll in the hay?" Her eyes flashed in defiance.

"Hold it," he said. "I don't recall ever saying I didn't want you. As a matter of fact, it was I who wanted you to stay. You always wanted to leave, be free."

"But you said you'd take me to Denver the end of July right after . . . right after we—"

"Yes, I did. However, I didn't say I wanted to take you. I just said I would."

"You and your semantics," she bit out. "Just how the hell do you feel about me?"

He stared at her through hard eyes and saw hers were shimmering like two bright emeralds. "How do you feel about John?" he demanded, loathing to say the man's name.

"What about Isabel?" she snapped back.

"Isabel? For God's sake, what does she have to do with anything?"

"What happened to that inscription to your 'Darling Isabel' in the front of the book of sonnets? And I saw your face when you read her note. You still love her, don't you?"

He looked at her in amazement and laughed into the still air. "You are so naïve. I just can't believe—"

"Stop laughing at me!" Her shaking voice rose to a high pitch, and he looked at her anxiously.

He dragged a chair to her bedside. "I tore that page out of the book and threw it in the fireplace. As for that note, I was surprised to read what she had written. She may have, in some perverse way, thought she loved me, but I wouldn't call it that. No, Spring, the feelings I had at the time I read the note were ones of great sadness for Isabel and pity for her, for her inability to accept life and live it. There was a lot of precious time and effort wasted during those years. But no, I do not love her. It did teach me, however, not to trap anyone here, again, in any manner, including marriage. That is one state I never want to be in again."

Her eyes wide, Spring nervously played with the sheet's edge. She took a shaky breath and said in a low voice, "Well, then, you have your answer about the baby. You know as well as I do I couldn't exist in the city with the child, and I knew you didn't care enough about me."—she held up her hand to stop him from interrupting—"to marry me and . . . and there is John to consider. I really have planned to marry him all along. I don't believe what you said about him. He always treated me well. So having the child would trap you, I thought. What I did wasn't against the baby or you. I thought I could get rid of it," she went on, seeing David wince, "and no one would even know. You've said yourself that a lot of what it takes to live out here is sheer survival. Well, David, I was surviving."

"You damn near killed yourself!" he exclaimed, pointing his finger at her. "Don't you realize how many women die during an abortion, even in the hands of a physician? It was an utterly stupid thing to do, Spring!"

"I don't have anyone to care for me," she bristled. "I had to do something."

"I care about you, Spring. I care for you. Me"—he tapped his chest—"you, and the baby could have a home here, if you wanted."

"Yes, you care about me like you care about your horse," she returned, thrusting up her chin. "And how could I live here any longer under these circumstances? Could you promise to leave me alone forever? What if I wanted to marry one of your men? What would we tell the child about you?"

"There's no use talking to you," he snapped, though he saw the logic of her questions. He rose and moved toward the door. "I want this child, and you will take care of yourself so it comes to term. Do you hear me?"

"You already have a child by White Feather. You tossed them off, didn't you?" she cried angrily.

"Who told you about them?" David strode back into the room.

"Lorna. But you forget. I saw them at the Indian camp."

He gazed at her through half-closed eyes. "That's a situation quite different from this. She loved me enough to have my child, though she knew I wouldn't marry her. I provide for Lily and see her two or three times a year. White Feather understands why we can't be together. Now, are you going to do as I ask?"

"You mean as you demand," Spring corrected. "You are so hateful, Mr. Saunders."

"Ah, my dear, we are no longer strangers. I don't think we need to go back to the Mr. thing."

She balled up her hands and hit them on the bed in exasperation. "If we remained strangers, I wouldn't be in this mess!" she yelled. She reached over and picked up her empty teacup and hurled it at him.

He ducked at the last moment, and the cup splintered against the wardrobe, missing David. "God, you have a rotten temper," he said. "It must be the red hair."

"I don't have red hair!" she hissed.

"Well," he answered before leaving the room, "it's close enough." And he heard her burst into frustrated tears behind him.

Chapter 18

It was mid-September before Spring was allowed up for the entire day. That is to say, she was up until afternoon, when David and Pap insisted she nap until about three.

She had been bored to stay abed for so long, even though she had experienced discomfort and bleeding for many days. These had subsided finally, as well as her nausea, and Pap assured David, after another examination during which Spring had shut her eyes in embarrassment, that she was still pregnant.

David had visited twice a day, but only to inquire after her health. He did not stay to talk. It was a relief to her not to have to keep defending her actions to him.

Strangely enough, he understood perfectly why she had attempted such a foolish thing. But he had been hurt by it, none-theless. Keeping the hurt inside, he put on a tough front, making everyone think she was a senseless child.

One morning, as Spring stood looking out the kitchen window viewing the beginnings of autumn, Mary asked, "Want to help me bake a cake for Davey's birthday today?"

"How old is the old grouch?" Spring asked absently.

"Thirty," he said in his deep voice behind her.

She grimaced but didn't turn around. "Sorry, I didn't know you were there."

"Obviously," he said in her ear, for he stood quite close to her, and he slipped his arms around her middle and felt her slightly pro-truding stomach through her skirt. He pulled her snuggly against him. "It's nice to see you up."

"Don't," she said, her body rigid. "Mary . . ."

"Mary left the room."

"Permit me to do the same," Spring responded, wanting, loving, yet not wanting his arms around her.

"I've decided we'll have a truce, my Venus," he answered, resting his lips on her chestnut head.

"I'm not your anything." She squirmed, and he released her. "I don't belong to you. I'm only here because of one rash act on my part."

"I believe there were three," he said, dryly. "And I remember every lovely moment of each one." He poured himself a cup of coffee.

"Don't remind me," she answered, also remembering each heavenly moment. "I shudder to think of even one of those times, much less of any of the moments." She tried to brush by him, but he stood in her way.

"Take a walk with me this afternoon when it's a little cooler," he suggested.

"Is this another command performance?" she asked, straightening her back and raising her chin to look at him. She saw he had some wrinkles around his eyes and they looked tired.

"No," he answered. "Just a request." He raised an eyebrow at her, sipping from his cup, and her reserve melted as he gazed at her tenderly.

"Well," she replied, glancing away from him," in that case, I will. About four, if you'll be through working by then."

"That will be fine." He reached out and caressed her soft cheek with his fingertips. "Until four." He set his cup down and was gone.

The late afternoon was warm, and azure skied, and golden hilled from the summer heat and the sun. David and Spring walked, she a half step ahead, twisting a lace-edged handkerchief nervously in her fingers. She almost felt as if she was being courted, passing banal trivialities between them, like she and John had done at the fort. John. She couldn't even conjure up his face anymore.

They walked over the back hill to the trees, and when they had reached the mountain stream that was the main source of the lake, they stopped to rest. Because she had had such little exercise in the past weeks, she wasn't able to get about without becoming tired.

The water rippled over the rocks in its path and gurgled in and around its obstacles. Birds chirped in the trees above.

David bent and picked up a few stones and tossed them into a deep pool overhung by trees and a great boulder.

"You have a way of disturbing sleeping things, David," she said into the quiet peacefulness as she watched the rings of water widen.

He made no comment, but he took her hand. "Come," he invited. He led her carefully over some protruding rocks in the flowing stream to a large flat rock in the middle. There they sat, stretching their legs in front of them. He stuck a thin cigar between his teeth and lit it. The smoke trailed lazily skyward.

"It's nice here," Spring offered.

"Yes. Despite everything, I'm grateful my mother left all this to me." He waved his browned hand in an all-encompassing gesture.

"Lorna told me your mother had a . . . a house. It was in Denver?"

"It seems Lorna talks too much."

"I asked her."

"Hmm. Yes, Molly's house," he went on, leaving the subject of Lorna behind. "Actually, my house."

"Yours?" Spring's gaze swept around to his. "You own that kind of house?"

"It was Mother's. Molly runs it. I give my share of the profits to the orphanage there." He spoke matter-of-factly, not to receive praise.

"Well, maybe, since you and Molly have a business arrangement," Spring said, half seriously, "you could get me a job there after the baby comes."

"What would you do there, clean rooms?"

"No, I'd be one of the girls."

Shocked, he bit out, "Don't ever say that again, much less think it, even in gest."

"I wasn't joking, and why not? I need a job, a way to raise the baby. I do have a little experience, don't I? After all, I've been your whore."

He threw his cigar, hissing, into the water and grabbed her shoulders angrily. Pulling her around, he took her in his arms and pushed her back to rest on his one bent knee. "Damn, you have a sharp tongue in your head. You are not a whore, nor could you ever abide being one. Ten men in a night. God, whatever makes you say such things?"

"To hurt you, David, but I doubt I could ever hurt you as you have hurt me. Look at what you've done to me." She took his hand and laid it on her belly. He felt the hard place again as he had that morning.

"It is my fault you are pregnant," he told her. "I realize you didn't know about so many things. Things women should know about their own bodies but don't. But I never meant to hurt you. God, Spring, believe me. Not ever. From the very first moment I knew you were pregnant—"

"You knew all along?" She was incredulous.

"It is my home. I know everything that goes on." His blue eyes penetrated her own, and the sincerity with which he spoke was evident. She dragged hers away and tried to swallow the lump that arose in her throat.

"Then explain to me how I got this way," she urged. "I don't mean physically. I mean, why did you . . . why did we?"

"You must know the act itself is purely physical. It doesn't take much for it to happen. It's when love is added to it that it becomes special and meaningful." Just talking to her about it made him want her. "When you respect that person and care for them, all that and more makes the difference between being a whore and being a loved and cherished woman."

"But you don't love me," Spring protested.

"Ah," he said, "but I do."

"What?"

"I do love you, Spring. I didn't intend to do that either, but it happened anyway."

"But you can't. You don't want to marry me," she burst out.

"I can love you without marrying you," he said, following the shape of her face with a finger. She grabbed at it angrily.

"I won't be your mistress, David. I . . . I admit I gave in to your advances because I was lonesome, and now I'm paying for my indiscretions." In her young and inexperienced mind, she could not separate the two thoughts that love and marriage could be separate. To her, they naturally went together. Because of that and her deeply ingrained pride, she kept the words of her love of him silent.

"You know I could take you whenever I choose to," he stated simply.

"No, please," she begged.

"Oh, my Venus," he said softly, pulling her against him and stroking her hair. "I will never harm you, for I love you. You are to be my child's mother. If we are ever to be together in that way, it will have to be your choice. I do that because you are free of me. I can wait until you want me, if you ever do."

A million thoughts rushed about Spring's head as she nestled next to him. He loved her! Yet he didn't want to marry her. He had known she was pregnant but hadn't said anything to her. It would have made so much difference in her actions if she had only known. Even though she loved him, she could never bring herself to live with him, as Mary had done with Pap for those years. At least they could have a truce until she left with the baby, for she knew she would be safest here for the birth than anywhere else. She would still have the problem of being an unwed mother, but at least the birth would be over.

"As I once told you, we can be friends. We are getting more and more in common all the time."

David laughed heartily and hugged her. Then he sat her up and faced her, but holding her hands. How smooth and soft they felt in his.

"The end of the month, we'll be having all my hands up for the annual 'Thank, God we got the steer off to market' party. Everyone comes and sleeps over. Most of the men stay up in the loft. I hope that won't disturb you."

"No, that sounds like fun. But what will they think when they see me?"

"Well," David shrugged, "they'll think I was very lucky to be the one to put you in the shape you are in now."

"Oh, you are awful to keep reminding me," she said, drawing her hands away. "I'm serious."

"So am I," he replied earnestly.

"John may not want me after he knows I'm not pure any longer," she mused.

"That would be his loss, sweetheart. I'd give anything to see his face when you tell him I had you first." He thought this aloud, not realizing he had actually uttered them.

Horrified, she drew back. What did he mean by that? Her tawny eyes blazed, shooting off sparks of indignation. "Is that all it meant to you, as a contest of which one of you got to me first?"

"No, no, I didn't mean that. I'm sorry. It's just that he . . . that—" He didn't want to go into what kind of man he was again. "It's just that he hates me. It would make him angry, is all," he finished lamely.

"He has reason to hate you," she muttered. "You have always made him feel less than he is."

He looked at her a long moment. Things were usually so clear to him, but he had no idea what would become of them.

He didn't think she knew either, that her mind was as confused as his was.

"October will be everyone's last trip to Denver before the winter sets in. We go to shows, plays, or whatever's going on." He thought he should just drop the previous subject and try to steer clear of topics that irritated them both. "You will need to get some new clothes anyway. I don't know how you've gotten along with so little."

"You mean I'll get to go too?" she asked in surprise. "Yes," he answered, glad to see the pleasure portrayed in her face."

"But I would like you to come back here to have the baby."

"Oh, that will be all right. I want to have the baby here, with Mary and Pap to help."

"What about me? I'd like to see my child born."

Her face flushed. "No, no, I couldn't."

"Well, we'll talk about that another time. It's getting late, and I better not miss my birthday dinner, or Mary will be upset." He helped her to her feet. Stepping up to her, he cupped her face in his warm palms, and said, "I love you, Venus, and I set you free."

With that, he helped her over the rocks to the bank. She really didn't understand what he'd meant by that, especially when she felt more trapped than ever.

The women put on a feast for the party, the likes of which Spring had never seen. There was barbecued meat of beef and chicken, breads and rolls, ears of butter-dipped corn, tomatoes, cucumbers, pickles, and peppers from their garden, big bowls of potato salad, and many kinds of pies and cakes.

Spring had to spend the rest of the day in bed so that she could participate in the festivities of the evening. David's orders. She felt guilty because she hadn't been able to do much in the way of preparations.

The backyard was strung with lanterns for the dancing and out-door cooking. Everyone was in a jovial mood and appreciative of all the preparations and their results.

No one made any outward comment over Spring's more obvious condition when she was introduced to all the men, some of whom had wives who worked for David. They were agreeably pleased by her attractiveness and quick wit, and she made them all feel at ease in and about the house.

Most were surprised at how homelike everything was since they had last been at Saunders's Haven and when Isabel had been there. If she had not been pregnant or David's eyes did not follow her wher-ever she went, some might have made themselves quite available to her. As it was, they took pleasure in Spring's graceful manner and joy-lit face.

After supper, they all gathered on and around the porch.

The piano had been moved outside, and Spring performed clas-sical to spiritual to popular songs of the day. Some songs she sang to, while others she invited them to sing along to.

Her pregnancy had brought an added bloom to her face and a sparkle to her eye. Because her skirt bands were getting too snug to wear normally, she had to hitch her petticoats and skirt up higher. It made her thickening shape all the more pronounced. None of this, however, hampered the men from asking her to dance the waltzes Hap played or stopped her feet from stepping out to the calls Pap made for the square dances.

Spring watched while David danced with all the women there. She was unaware of the covert way he also watched her. Because the outline men had brought their wives or girlfriends, there were plenty of females to dance with.

The unattached ones were blatantly flirtatious, and David seemed to wallow in it. Spring did not feel unattached by any means, but David felt she enjoyed herself much too much for a woman in her condition.

She danced every dance, with the exception of a few she played on the piano; and so it was little wonder that as the evening wore on, she became extremely weary. She did not want to go to bed, for she was having a lot of fun and was just glad to be able to be up and around after spending six weeks in bed.

Long about midnight, Hap began a waltz on the ivory keys, and Spring was startled when David asked her to dance. She accepted, thinking that it was perhaps the first time he had made any public physical contact with her in any romantic fashion. He took her firmly in his arms, and where he had danced at arm's length with the other women, he pulled her closely to his hard body, bending his head to rest his chin against the top of her soft hair.

David was oblivious to all around him once he had Spring in his arms. Her hand was small, soft, and yet a little worn in his, her body not so changed yet as to still feel slender and fragile, the lilac fragrance of her hair wafting to his nostrils gave him a sense of love-filled contentment he had never known before.

Spring felt secure encircled in his arm, her hand held lightly by his warm large one. He was light on his feet, his shoulder against her temple offered her comfort and solidity, and the smell of him was clean and fresh from the outdoors, with a faint odor of the wine she had seen him consume at dinner. She moved her left hand across his hard-muscled back. She felt so protected that it was with complete surprise when she unexpectedly felt lightheaded and wobbly-legged. Her stomach felt funny, and without a warning to David, she sagged against him.

David stopped immediately when Spring's leaden weight fell on him, and he looked down at her with alarm. His arm tightened about her, and he picked her up, her head falling back on his shoulder.

"Pap! Come with me," he demanded.

"What's the matter?" Mary asked with concern.

"I don't know. She just fainted." With that, he disappeared into the house with his precious bundle. Pap was right behind him with the smelling salts, waving them under her nose. Spring's eyes fluttered open in the firelit room.

Suddenly, she smiled a brilliant smile of wonderment.

Her eyes sought David, who was standing anxiously behind the kneeling Pap.

"Don't look so worried, you two," she chided gently. "Really, I'm all right. Pap, go on out and let everyone know I'm fine." She waved him away and then patted the bed beside her, indicating David was to sit beside her. When he did, she took his hand.

"Dearest, are you all right?" A frown of anxiety remained between his eyes.

"Yes, David, my sweet protector. In fact, something wonderful happened tonight. Oh, there it is again . . ." Quickly, she unbuttoned her skirt and slipped it, along with her petticoats, down over her hips, leaving her drawers exposed.

She took his hand and placed it over where the baby was growing. Through the thin material, she could feel his warm hand, and he felt small flutterings beneath it. "It's our baby moving, David. It's the first time I've felt it. David?"

He drew his gaze from his hand to her tear-glistening eyes. There was a look of almost-reverent worship on his face.

"Can you feel it, David?"

The flutterings continued, and he could only nod.

"David, I'm so glad I did not kill your child. It's real to me for the first time tonight. It's alive, and I'm so grateful for that."

A lump filled David's throat, and he laid his head on her breasts, gathering her in his arms. It was one of the closest moments they had shared together.

Chapter 19

The trip to Denver at the end of October was uneventful. Spring rode on one of the horses, because the wagon would have been too bumpy. Mary, Penny, and Pap rode in the wagon. When it came time to cross the Platte River outside of Denver, even though the river was not as full as it was last spring, when she had been going in the opposite direction, Spring rode up on Aphrodite with David.

Since the night of the steer-gone-to-market party, the two of them had developed a special closeness. There were no harsh words between them, and there was joking and wholesome conversation. She did not invite him into her bed, and he did not ask. Nor was there familiar touching, other than some hand holding when they took walks together. They had both become comfortable with each other. Sitting atop Aphrodite was the closest Spring had been to David since he had danced with her, and she had to acknowledge to herself that it was very nice indeed to have his protection as the water came up around them. But she had no real fear, for David was there. The trees were a gorgeous array of color against the autumn sky. The air was crisp and clear, and Spring was extremely content.

David installed her in a large room at the Palace Hotel.

She knew immediately that he was thought of as a very important man when they arrived, for the bellmen and maids quickly came on the scene to help her get settled with the least amount of trouble.

The room was draped with satin and velvet curtains of deep blue and gold, and the bed across the room boasted silk sheets and a brocade spread with real gold thread shot through it.

Sheer lace curtains hung from the bed's canopy. A roaring fire was already burning in the hearth, and Spring was in complete awe of the luxury in which she had been thrust. Mary and Pap were in a room down the hall, but it was not of such magnificence as this one. David's suitcases were not brought in to the room with the few belongings of Spring's, and she did not inquire where he was going to stay.

She did not have a chance to ask him, anyway, or how he could possibly afford to keep her here, for once they had arrived, he went right away to attend to some business, telling Spring he expected her to get right into bed to rest after being on a horse all day.

The fact that he ordered her to do this did not bother her, for it was not done with the arrogance he once had with her. Oh, he used it with others upon occasion, she knew, but not with her. She complied with his wishes and was happy just to have him come in during suppertime to eat with her.

He explained to her more fully that his holdings were much larger than what his circumstances up in Saunders's Haven would lead anyone to believe. Not only did he have revenue from Molly's house, which he didn't use for his benefit, but he had wide vested interests in some silver mines, and he owned a bank in Denver. And of course, there was the land and cattle.

There were a million questions she could have asked him about why, then, did he work at the fort like he did, or live up in the mountains without all the amenities, but realized that that would make him not the man he was. He was not pretentious in any way, though he knew who he was, exuding confidence in all he did to all he came in contact with. Very few people knew him as well as she did, if they knew him that well, or what things he had gone through in his life. Well, that was all right.

After eating, they sat and talked about their activities for the next day. He informed her that he had made appointments for her at several of the more prestigious establishments for the purchasing of new clothing for herself—dresses, lingerie, coats, and so on, and for the baby, though he suggested she may just want to buy material to make things over the long winter months. She was also to see a doctor that specialized just in delivering babies and female patients. She protested against that, but he soon made her realize that it was best, for Pap would accompany her and find out the latest things he needed to know, so he could be of the best help to her at the time of delivery.

Neither spoke of John or the chance that they might run into him. David was living day by day, taking what pleasure he could in Spring's company. It had been several months since he saw John in town, and he felt fairly sure he was no longer there. Spring did not want to see him now that she was swelling with another man's child. She wanted to remain with David at this time in her life.

"Well, I'll leave you now to go to sleep. We'll have lunch together tomorrow at Delaney's after you've done some of your shopping." He bent over the bed and touched her cheek. "Sweet dreams, Spring."

He looked tall and attractive standing over her in his well-cut suit of gray wool.

"Are you staying here in the hotel?" she couldn't keep from asking.

"Do you want me to?" he asked, eyes lighting up with hope.

"I . . . I just wanted to know," she answered vaguely, seeing the disappointment creep into his face before he could control it.

"No, I have other accommodations." He straightened and adjusted the suit over his white silk shirt. She remembered one other time she'd seen him look so debonair, and that had been at the fort. She remembered viewing him critically and had not found his looks wanting.

"May I ask where?" she asked timidly.

He smiled secretly at her. He winked when he said, "Sure, you may ask, but I may not tell."

She knew then that he was going to Molly's, but she didn't know that, again, he was going to take the back room and sleep alone. She stared at him, neatened her pillows behind her, and then turned away from him. "Good night," she murmured.

"I love you, Spring," he said quietly to her back. But she said nothing, and he pulled the silk sheet up over her slender shoulder and squeezed it. Then he turned on his heel and left the room silently.

David gave Spring carte blanche when it came to purchasing her clothes. She felt a little funny about it, but with Mary's urgings, she bought lovely attire in the latest style. These were mostly amenable to her condition, for they were with an empire waistline that gathered under her full breasts and fell sweepingly to the floor. Only two of the dresses were such that would be worn for very special occasions, such as the concert and the play they would be attending at the end of the week. The others were more practical for use back at the Haven. David approved of all the purchases.

She also bought a few little items for the baby, and the rest were in the way of materials of the softest, finest quality to touch a newborn's skin. She was quite excited to get to that particular project.

The second evening, David came to her room and gave her a little velvet box.

"What is this for?" she asked.

"I hope you won't take offense at it. I just thought it might make it a little easier tomorrow night when we attend dinner and the theater, with those highfalutin friends of mine and their stuffy wives. Open it up."

Nestled inside on a bed of more velvet was a ring of gold holding an emerald. On each side were two diamonds. She raised her eyes to him, and her face was pink with humiliation.

"What is this supposed to represent?"

"To me, it represents a small token of my esteem and love for you, the mother of my child, and I hope you will accept it as such. For them, they may take it as a wedding ring."

Spring turned away, walking over to one of the tall windows. The streetlamps were now lit, and music was coming from the saloon across the street. She did not know what to do.

Why should she pretend to something that he didn't want? She supposed it would be easier to let them think she and David were married, but what about later, if she saw these people? What would she say to them?

She faced him and squared her shoulders and tilted her chin at him. "David, I won't lie to you. It hurts me to take this ring under false pretenses from you. You may respect me, or even love me, I don't know. But it's not enough to make this ring represent the real thing. I'll wear it, but it's only to get through any uncomfortable situations this week that I do. When we get back to the mountains, you will have to take it back."

Looking at her, he knew without a doubt that he had offended her to the depths and was sorry for it. He reminded her, "Spring, ask yourself why you would marry me if I asked you. You don't love me. You came to me out of loneliness. You want to marry John. So just ask yourself, and I know it would be because of the baby and not for the right reasons. I'll see you tomorrow."

She stared into the empty room after he had gone and knew with certainty what her answer would have been. She would have shouted yes! to the heavens if he would have asked her, for she loved him with all her heart and mind, and yes, her body too. That was the real reason she had gone to him in the first place, not just for loneliness, though she may not have realized it at the time. She slipped the ring on her finger, and it looked very nice there. It looked like it belonged there. She wished it did.

It was their last night before the trip back to the mountains. They were going to attend a concert of classical music in the Denver City Music Hall. Spring was waiting for David to pick her up for dinner. When he arrived, he gave her a more-than-approving look.

Her hair had been styled that afternoon by a hairdresser who worked for several of the wealthiest ladies in town. The chestnut hair was pulled straight back from her face with the exception of little curls in front of her small ears and caught up in ringlets all about the crown of her head and down the back. The style made her profile all the more delicately pronounced.

Her satin dress was low cut, showing a deep cleavage that her normal shape would not have had. It was off the shoulders in little puffed sleeves and caught up under her breasts in the empire waistline. Its skirt swept to the floor in graceful, flowing waves and swept out in a train behind her. It was emerald green, making the color of her eyes appear jewellike. The hairdresser had also made up her face perfectly.

When David saw her, his breath was literally taken away. Walking over to her, he gave her an oblong box.

"More gifts?" she asked, arching her red-tinted brows.

"I could not make you any more beautiful than you are already," he answered solemnly, "but I would like very much if you would wear these." He watched her as she opened the box and looked inside.

"These are lovely," she whispered, taking out the emerald earrings encircled with diamonds and the simply hung emerald teardrop pendant on a gold chain. She went to the gilt mirror over the dressing table and snapped the earrings into place. She turned her head from side to side to view her reflection.

Walking back over to him, she handed him the pendant and turned her back to him. He clasped it behind her neck and then lightly placed his fingers on her bare shoulders.

"Spring," was all he said, but it said everything. Well, almost. It did not say he wanted her forever to be his and no one else's.

She stepped away, feeling the electricity in the air, to pick up her fur wrap. "Shall we go?"

They met Pap, Mary, Henry, and Lorna down in the hotel lobby and then entered an enclosed carriage that conveyed them through the noisy streets to the Chrystal Restaurant, where they were shown to one of the lavishly set tables by a fireplace. Spring was in a position where she could see all that was going on, from the small orchestra in a small gazebo off to one side, to the impeccable waiters performing their jobs to the nth degree.

Halfway through her meal, Spring became aware of a gentleman who kept staring at her. He was sitting at a table next to theirs, but he was facing her. Her passing gaze met his, and he seemed a trifle familiar to her, but she didn't think she had ever seen him before. She shook off the feeling, but every time she glanced up from eating or away from one of the others of her company, she was again caught by his eye.

She became uncomfortable under his scrutiny, not only because he was staring at her in such an intimate way, but because his gaze was so intent. Finally she could stand it no longer, and she excused herself from the table and went to the powder room.

The man's appraisal of Spring did not go unnoticed by either Pap or David who had been sitting on either side of her throughout dinner. The man, however, did not realize that he, too, had been under careful observation. So when he left the dining room, he did not know that he would be meeting these two gentlemen later that evening.

When Spring returned, she was relieved to see that the man had finished his meal and had gone on his way. She dismissed the incident from her mind and enjoyed the rest of the last night in Denver.

The party left after dessert and continued on to the Music Hall where they had box seats above the general audience. Many of David's acquaintances were also there, some who had already met Spring. These quickly dispelled the rumors flying about concerning the beautiful woman he was with. They told the acquaintances she was his wife.

Spring enjoyed the concert immensely for there was a piano concerto played by a very accomplished artist. She leaned forward in her velvet, cushioned chair, catching every note and delighted in the bird's eye view she had from her seat.

After intermission, she again felt eyes on her, and her attention wandered out over the audience; and there below, looking at her through a pair of opera glasses, was the same man who had been staring at her during dinner. She sat back in her seat, trying to make herself appear as small as possible.

Lorna leaned over to her. "You are attracting some attention," she said with a smile.

"I know. This same man did this to me at dinner. I don't like it at all."

"Tell Davey."

"No," Spring whispered. "There's no need for that. I don't want to bother him over something that will be all over when we leave."

At the close of the concert, they again boarded their carriage and headed back to the hotel. It was brightly lit, and many people were about.

"How do you feel, Spring?" David asked. "We do have a day's ride ahead of us tomorrow."

"It's been a full day," she replied. "I think I'll go on up to bed."

"Why don't you go with her, Mary," Pap suggested, giving her a nod.

"Sure, I'll get her all tucked in," Mary said.

"Good night, everyone," Spring said, turning with Mary to mount the stairs.

Henry and Lorna went up to their room, for they had left Jacob with a maid for the evening. Pap and David went back into the night and sauntered up and down the street in front of the hotel and opposite it, until they saw the man whom they suspected would show up near Spring again.

They shadowed him unobtrusively as the man walked about the area, and when he came to the dark alleyway beside the hotel, they suddenly crowded in on him and hustled him down the narrow, dark passageway.

They backed him against the wooden structure by the garbage cans.

"What . . . what do you want?" the man asked, flattening himself to the wall and blinking in the blackness.

Without warning, David lit a match and slowly lit a thin cigar. The flicker of the flame gave the man time to recognize Whip Saunders, but he did not know the man with him, other than they had eaten dinner together. He pretended ignorance of David's identity and said, "If it's money you want . . ." He reached into his breast pocket.

"We don't want your money," David's cold voice broke in.

"He wants to know your name and why you've been following us around all evening."

"I haven't been following you." This met with a rough hand grabbing his coat lapel and a shove against the building.

"Listen," David said through his teeth. "I don't have time to play your silly games. I want to know right now, if not before, why you have been following my lady friend."

The man was about to utter something about not even knowing what David was talking about when David took the cigar out of his mouth and held it close to the man's cheek.

"You seem familiar to me," David said casually. "What's your name?"

The stranger cleared his throat nervously. "I . . . I . . . that is to say . . ."

A hard fist landed in his midsection, forcing him to double over. Then he was jerked upright, and he grunted loudly. "Okay, okay. I was a private at Fort Frontier. Drake. Kenneth Drake. We never came into contact, you and me."

"Ah." David paused and grinned. "Now we are getting somewhere. You must work for John Granville."

"No . . . no, I . . . uh . . . I mean . . ." Another strike to the stomach brought Drake up off his feet.

"Listen, man," David urged through his clenched teeth and standing close to the frightened Drake, for he had seen Whip in action before and remembered how those eyes glassed over into chips of ice when provoked. "I have no real quarrel with you, other than the fact that you made my friend extremely uncomfortable tonight, and I didn't like that. Now, I want the truth, and this is the last chance I'll give you to tell it to me before I shove this cigar right up your nose."

"All right." David let loose of him and stood back while Drake adjusted his cheap suit. "I work for John Granville, and he's been looking for a young girl named Spring Ames. He's supposed to marry her. I'm sure you remember her from the fort. Her father was the colonel there. Anyway, John went north to find the Indians who abducted her and told me to stay here in case she turned up. That is her, isn't it? The girl you were with?"

David took a breath. He felt Pap beside him willing him to keep his mouth shut, but remembered how much Spring had enjoyed her time in Denver. He saw in his mind how beautiful she was in fine clothes and could feel again in his hand how rough hers had felt the night they danced. Did he want to subject her to a life in the mountains, take her finery away, and make a work woman out of her? Should he let her take her chances with John? God, what a thought! But then he also remembered how many times she had said she wanted to be with John, that she loved him. She had never denied that to him.

She never had uttered those longed-for words of love to him.

He decided to take the halfway track, to sit on the fence and see what happened. He stuck the cigar back in his mouth.

"Yes," he said, "that's Miss Ames."

"You married to her?" Drake asked.

Pap let out an exasperated breath. David went on, "If Granville can find her and she still wants to go with him, she's free to go. But tell your boss, or whatever he is, that she is staying with me for now. If he can find me, he'll have found Miss Ames. Tell him that."

David then turned on his heel and left the alley, with Pap a step behind him.

"Dave, you are a fool. Do you realize what you just did?"

"Probably not, Pap. Probably not."

Spring brushed out her ringlets at the dressing table. She did not hear David enter but only knew he was there when he appeared in her mirror. Her nightgown clung to her body, showing every desirable curve, which she did not attempt to hide. The filmy, pale-gold material blended with her creamy skin, and the red-brown hair cascaded to her shoulders in soft waves.

"Hello, I didn't think I'd see you until tomorrow," she said, standing up to move to the fireplace. He watched her slow movement across the room. The bed was turned down, and the shadowy room made his blood burn in his veins.

"Just wanted to see how you were."

"I'm fine, as you can see." There was a smile on her lips, but there was a sadness in her yellow-specked emerald-green eyes. The gown draped her slender frame, gathered under her breasts, and fell softly over her swelling abdomen. She had never appealed to him more than she did at that moment.

"Yes, I see. Well, good night." At the door, he heard her whisper goodnight.

Later, after many shots of whiskey had passed his lips, David stood out in the chilly night air in front of a saloon before making his way to Molly's. He didn't know whether he could take her harping, good-natured though it was, to go stay with Spring instead of staying alone in the small room at her place. He knew he had promised Spring he wouldn't approach her, but would it hurt to take what pleasure he could from her presence, and not just sexually, while he had the chance? After all, after tonight, John Granville might come riding up to the Haven at any time to carry her off for good.

He stumbled over some feet stretched out on the boardwalk, and he cursed loudly. What a shambles everything was. Deliberately, he made his way into the hotel and up the stairs. It was quiet now, and not many people were about. What person in their right mind would be up at three in the morning when they had to be in the saddle all the next day?

David staggered into Spring's room after unlocking the door clumsily. All was quiet and peaceful. The fire burned low in the grate. As he made his way across the soft carpet, he shed his clothing, leaving a trail behind him. At last, he stood by the bed. He saw her curled up in a ball under the silk sheets, one small hand cradling her cheek, her mouth closed in a little smile. Her dark lashes brushed her cheeks in a thick fringe. He pulled the sheet back and crawled into bed beside the woman he loved. But he did not touch her. The bouncing of his body jarred Spring to drowsy wakefulness. At first, she was startled, and then knew it was David.

"Hello, again." Her voice was sleepily soft.

"Sorry to wake you," he mumbled. And then his mind cleared when he felt her move over beside him and stretch her body along his and put her arms around him.

"Welcome, David," she whispered.

Instantly, his desire for her was evident, but he had never made love to a pregnant woman before, and he wasn't sure if he should. His kissed her open mouth and caressed her full breasts, slipping the thin straps down over her shoulders.

His lips trailed down her throat to the plenary breasts. He cupped them in his hands and kissed each one tenderly.

"David?" she asked.

"Yes, my dearest?"

"Please, now. I don't want to wait any longer."

With a cry of emotion barely restricted in his throat, he pulled up her gown. "Are you sure it's all right? I don't want to hurt you or the baby."

"Yes, it's fine. I asked the doctor when I saw him."

"You asked him?"

"Yes, darling. Please hurry."

David did as she bid, but did not hurry, going as slowly as possible for someone who had been starved for so long and wanting it to last. When through, he was not satiated; and it wasn't until morning came and it was time to begin their journey home, that he realized he hadn't slept at all once in bed with her. It wasn't until then that he was replete with regained knowledge of her, and she of him.

Chapter 20

It was perfect timing to arrive back at Saunders's Haven when they did, for the first winter storm hit that night, sending a foot of snow over the hills of the valley where the house was and covering the mountain peaks with a thick white blanket. Misty clouds hung between the hills and on top of granite rocks; and the air was damp with the promise of other storms to come.

Thus began a quiet solitude that Spring was not sure she ever wanted broken. On the bad weather days, Mary and Pap remained in their own cabin, and sometimes it was several days before Spring saw anyone other than David.

He moved back into the house from the bunkhouse after their return, and not only that, but into his own bedroom with her. Their days were spent peacefully and in friendly camaraderie. Mornings, David went out to work with the animals and to feed the chickens, while Spring worked in the kitchen baking bread, using the recipes Mary taught her. She spent a great deal of time working on baby clothes, making little nightgowns, hemming the soft white linen fabric she bought for diapers, and knitting little sweaters and bonnets out of green and yellow yarns. She realized just how much she owed Mary when it came right down to running a house. For she had not known the first things about cooking or sewing until she had come here, except for a little needlepoint she had done at women's social gatherings.

Sometimes they played cards, which Spring had never had the opportunity to learn and took great pleasure in winning a hand or two. But David wasn't the kind to let her win just to make her feel good, and that made the winning all the more sweet. It didn't bother him when she won, either, for it just proved to him all over again what a capable person she was, one who could think for herself, in more than one way. That was part of what he loved about her. She did not wear the ring he gave her in Denver now that they were back home. That seemed to be the only barrier between them, what each thought was the reason for not being married. Spring did not think she would ever understand how he could love her so desperately in all ways and yet not want to commit himself to her by marriage. He did not understand how she could accept him every time he came to her and still love John and want to marry him. So these things they did not speak of.

In the early evenings, she played the piano for him, sometimes singing as he lay on the floor by Suzie in front of the roaring fire-place. Or on occasion, they read to each other from the many books lining the shelves. They found they had much in common.

On bright, sunlit days, David and Spring would go for walks, but not far, for one never knew when a storm would blow and dump more snow upon them. It seemed that no sooner would everything clear up than another storm would come.

One day in December, Spring decided she wanted to walk to Lorna's. She dressed in a wool skirt and a linsey-woolsey shirt, long wool stockings, and thick-furred boots.

When David came in from feeding the animals and chopping wood that would last them several days, she told him of her plans.

"No, I don't want you to go there," he said firmly, warming his hands around a steaming cup of coffee.

"It's a gorgeous day," she answered calmly. "I'm tired of sitting around here and need to get out. I need the exercise. Besides"—she looked up at him sweetly—"I'm getting as big as a house." She patted her enlarged belly.

"It's too far for you to walk in your condition. I'll take you on Aphrodite."

"David, please, let me go alone. I need to . . . to stretch myself."

"This freedom thing again, huh?" he asked, his eyes slitting. "I'd hoped you'd forgotten all that."

"I have," she protested.

"It doesn't sound like it to me." He turned around angrily and knew he was being unreasonable. But he never knew when John would come and take her away. He didn't know how much time they had left. Caustically, he said over his shoulder, "All right, then, go. Get the hell out of here. I don't care what you do."

She stared disbelievingly at his back, and tears sprang to her eyes. Then she straightened up and pulled her coat on over her arms. She gathered up the bread she'd baked that morning and went to the door.

"I'll see you later," she said.

He said nothing, and she slammed the door purposefully behind her.

The moment David heard the door slam, he was filled with remorse for his tone and hard words, but he did not go after her. Instead, he watched her trudge up the back hill from the window, her scarf blowing back over her shoulder and Suzie prancing along beside her. He put on his coat and went out to the barn. There were some loose boards that needed fixing, and he began that chore working for several hours before heading back to the house long after lunch.

Glancing up at the sky, he saw it was no longer blue and clear, but filled with dark, angry clouds. The winds had whipped up, whistling through the passes between the mountains and hills.

David knew Spring had reached the Samuels' place long ago. He was certain that if there had been a problem, Suzie would've come for help. Nevertheless, his gaze swept the sky before he entered the house, and for the next hour, as he prepared and ate a couple of sandwiches, he stood by the window watching for Spring.

As the minutes ticked by in the quiet house, David's worry gave way to anger. Anger at Spring for keeping John between them, anger for her wanting to be free, anger for her not wanting to spend the better part of the day with him, and anger because she didn't have the sense to come home before the storm hit. He was also angry at Henry for not seeing she got home safely before now.

Soon, however, his anger became foreboding; and as the clock struck four, he donned his coat and hat and went out to saddle Aphrodite.

*   *   *

"Henry, I don't know what to do," Spring said, clutching his arm. "You can't leave me here with her." Her eyes frantically searched the worried man's face as he glanced anxiously at Lorna lying on the bed, hands clenched at her sides.

"Spring, I understand this is new to you, that you've only seen Suzie give birth. But believe me, the baby won't come for quite a while. There's a storm heading his way, and I've got to get Pap or Dave while there's still time. Now, you can do this, Spring, I know it." And with those words, he was gone.

The cabin was quiet inside, but the wind howled around its corners. Jacob was sleeping sweetly in his little bed.

"Spring," came Lorna's voice. "Don't worry, it'll be all right. I've done this before."

Spring walked over to the bed. Lorna's sand-colored hair was plaited in two neat braids, and her skin had a misty layer of perspiration on it. Suddenly, she grabbed her enormous stomach, her eyes shut tight, and a deep groan escaped her lips. Spring remembered the agonies of Suzie last spring, and this seemed thousands of times worse.

She looked down at herself, and a great fear clutched her heart. In three months, she would have to endure the same thing.

"It'll be all right for you, Spring, really. It's worth it," Lorna tried to assure her. She again twisted on the bed, and Spring couldn't bear to watch her.

"What can I do to help you?" Spring asked.

"Just be here. Everything else will take its natural course."

Spring straightened the covers and was startled when the front door burst open, sending cold air into the little bedroom.

"Henry, I'm so glad—" She stopped in the doorway, seeing David shake snow from his gray hat. "I thought it was Henry coming back."

"I passed him on the way to get Pap. I don't know how long he'll be. Pap rode out to see what the feed situation was for the steer. How's Lorna doing?"

"I don't know. She has bad pains."

"It'll be all right, honey." He passed Spring and went in to Lorna. Spring stood in the doorway, watching him talk to her quietly. Then when another contraction began, he let her grab his hands, her knuckles turning white until it was over.

Jacob cried from his bed, and Spring was glad there was something for her to do. She changed his diaper, trying to ignore the now unrestrained moans from the other bed. When she stood holding Jacob against her, she saw the covers had been thrown back, and while Lorna went through another bout of pain, David rubbed the big mound with his hands.

She averted her eyes and left the room with Jacob, setting him in his high chair. She gave him a crust of bread to chew on while she fixed him a bowl of oatmeal. Her attention kept being drawn to the next room as Lorna's distress mounted.

While she was feeding the baby, the front door flew open, and amid swirling snow, Henry and Pap entered. Shucking their coats, they immediately went to Lorna.

Several minutes later, David came out and went outside to put the horses out of the wintry elements. Spring cleaned up the kitchen area, keeping an eye on Jacob as he toddled about. He held up his blocks to her, and they sat on the rug playing his favorite game of build and topple.

David returned with some wood to build the fire. The frame of the cabin shook from the force of the wind, day became night, and the hours went by.

Spring was glad for the wind because it helped to drown out the awful sound of Lorna's suffering. David did not talk to her, for which she was also glad, since they had parted on bad terms that morning.

She fed the baby again about eight, realizing Lorna had been in labor now about seven hours.

She did not know how a woman could endure such lengthy, forceful pain. Yet Lorna was going through it for the second time.

Henry called through the door for David to come and get some blankets ready and hot water for sterilization. Spring sat in the rocker, moving back and forth slowly as Jacob went to sleep.

When David returned, he sat in the chair opposite. He saw a haunted look of fear in Spring's lovely face. Lorna was holding nothing back now. Spring wanted to run out into the storm with her hands covering her ears. She wanted to scream at Lorna to shut up, that it couldn't possibly be that bad.

David saw all this on her face and did not know what to say to make the situation any better.

"I'm sorry about this morning," he offered.

"What?" she asked vaguely.

"Nothing," he answered. "It'll be over soon. Look, I'm sure it's not that bad."

She gave him a look of disdain. "And I'm sure you know nothing about it." She glanced down at Jacob's cherubic face and then up in terrified alarm as Lorna screamed in the other room. Her jeweled eyes opened wide with unveiled fear. The baby stirred uneasily, sensing her great torment.

David took Jacob from her, cradling him against his chest and patting his back. The cabin gave a jolt that sent Spring out of her seat to pace back and forth in front of the door.

Lorna screamed every few seconds, drowning out any assurance Henry or Pap gave her.

David kept watching Spring. Whenever Lorna cried out, Spring's hands went over her ears and in between times, she ran her hands over her own growing child. It was moving about more than usual, kicking and elbowing her insides, as if it was trying to make an early entry into the world.

Suddenly, all was still. The wind stopped howling, Lorna stopped sobbing, and then a new sound filled the cabin. The new arrival began to announce its life in no uncertain terms.

Later, with Jacob installed once again in his own bed and Lorna asleep with the little pink girl in a box next to her bed, Henry, Pap, and David toasted the new one with several drinks as they sat around the kitchen table.

Spring watched them with disgust from her seat by the fireplace. The men laughed and joked as they passed the bottle around. Then Pap went off to sleep in the storeroom in back of the kitchen, and Henry went in with Lorna, shutting the door. Spring remained quiet as David fixed a makeshift bed on the rug. When he was through, he sat in the middle, taking off his boots. He looked up at Spring with a glint in his eye.

"Come on to bed, honey." He held out his hand.

"No."

"Oh, come on. I told you I was sorry about this morning. You need to sleep. Come on," he urged.

"No. You disgust me."

Incredulously, he stared at her. "I beg your pardon," he said, the liquor making him very polite.

"I said you disgust me. All three of you men. Sitting over there drinking and congratulating yourselves on a job well done when you didn't do any of the work. All Henry did was have the pleasure of putting the baby inside. Then when it . . . it got big, then Lorna had to get it out."

"Spring, honey, you're just upset and tired. Come to bed." He threw back the covers and crawled over to remove her boots. She suffered this but refused again to lie down.

"I don't want to be with you," she said. Before she could say anything else, he had her around the waist and onto the floor. She struggled against him, but to no avail.

"Spring," he said gently, "I see how you are feeling. It's different for everyone. You may have a very easy time."

"Don't try to placate me," she replied stiffly.

He gave a little laugh and took her chin in his hand, forcing her to look at him. "You know, I've had a lot more experience with birthing than you have."

"Good, then you have the baby." She pulled away, rolling to her side away from him, staring into the fire. She heard him sigh and lie back after he pulled the covers up over them.

"Good night," he said softly, patting her shoulder. She did not return his wish, lying sleepless long after his deep, even breathing indicated he was sleeping. Until today, she had been happy with the idea of giving birth to David's child. Now she knew she was frightened to death.

Chapter 21

The next morning, David was already up, dressed, and drinking a cup of coffee when Spring awoke. She stretched and sat up. Her body was stiff and sore, and her head throbbed mournfully.

"Good morning, sunshine," David said cheerfully.

"What's good about it?" she mumbled back.

"The sky is blue, the sun is out," he answered, ignoring her glum behavior. "Let's hurry now so we can start back home."

"I'm staying here to help Lorna."

"No need. Pap already left to get Mary to come up. I'm leaving in a half hour. You're coming with me." His tone had a no-nonsense quality, and though she bristled under it, she felt too exhausted and achy to argue.

After good-byes were said, she and David went outside.

There were about six inches of very dry snow on the ground covering remnants of the last storm that had left icy patches everywhere. The air was chilly, and puffs of smoke emanated from Aphrodite's nostrils as she snorted, pawing the ground, anxious to be on her way.

David made to lift Spring onto the horse's back, but she pushed him away. "No, I'll walk," she said. She couldn't pinpoint the reason for her foul mood. She only knew she wanted to be left alone.

"I don't want to fight with you anymore," he said, tiredly. "You look exhausted, and the walk will be much harder through the snow."

Spring buried her face in her mittened hands. At first, he thought she might be crying; but when she looked up, her eyes were blazing. She snapped, "For heaven's sake, stop running my life. You may be older than I am and more experienced, God only knows, but

I do have a brain that needs to be exercised once in a while by letting it think for itself. If you have any regard for my happiness, I can tell you right now, I'll be a lot happier down here walking than up there next to you!" She turned and started away. She had seen the change in his eyes and felt their chill much deeper than the one blowing her scarf around.

He fell into step beside her as she strode along, hands stuffed into her pockets. She usually bounced right back from a crisis, large or small, but she wasn't doing that this time, so David tried to calm his anger. He pulled his coat up closer around his throat.

"I'm going to have to get a nice, warm scarf someday to keep the wind from blowing down my neck," he commented.

Silently, she walked on, only yelling at Suzie to stop prancing around her feet, which sent the faithful dog skulking away sorrowfully.

The longer she walked, the harder it became. The wind blew hard, buffeting their bodies, but with her extra encumbrance, it was difficult to keep her balance, and her breathing became labored.

At last they reached the top of the rise leading down to the house. All was encased in white, and the red-and-white house with smoke curling from its chimney looked warm and inviting.

"Spring, let me put you on Aphrodite now. You look as though you're on your last leg." He reached out his gloved hand to take her arms. She jerked away roughly, stepping backward. Her foot sank through the dry powder of snow and slipped on an icy patch beneath. Her hands came out of the coat pockets, and her arms flailed as she fell over backward in the snow. The slope of the hill did not hamper but helped her rapid descent. She tumbled over and over, gathering snow beneath her; but it wasn't until she had almost reached the bottom that she stopped, sprawled out in the snow.

Suzie reached the prone Spring before David did. He had run behind her, calling her name, almost as soon as she began to fall. But he didn't catch up to her until she stopped. He knelt beside her, overcome with remorse and fear. When would he learn not to crowd her?

"Spring, dearest girl," he said, taking off his glove and brushing her disarrayed hair back from her face. "Honey, are you all right?"

She lay so deathly still, her face about as white as the snow under her, her shiny hair stark against the pearly wintry stuff. He cupped her chin and shook her head gently.

Her eyelids fluttered open.

"Are you all right?" he asked again. "Can you move? Is anything broken?"

Dazed, she shook her head and tried to sit up. He put a supporting arm around her shoulders and helped her stand. Her legs collapsed, and he picked her up and carried her into the house.

It was early evening. David had put her to bed immediately after he had gotten her clothes off, and she had slept the better part of the day. But she had lain awake for two hours, staring into space.

David tried to talk to her, but she never responded to him. She wouldn't eat either. It was as though she was in a little cocoon, not really part of life, but there.

When the clock struck eight, David entered the room again to stoke up the fire. Then he came to sit on the edge of the bed. He took her hand, but it lay limp in his. "How are you feeling now?"

Nothing. Silence.

"Goddamn it!" he finally lashed out. "Talk to me. I know that fall didn't break your tongue."

She looked at him intently. "The baby hasn't moved since this morning. I . . . I felt it just before I fell. There's been nothing since."

David's eyes closed, and then he pulled back the covers and pulled up her gown. He put his hand on the enlarged mound, feeling all around, and then he put his ear to it, listening. But he felt and heard nothing.

"You were asleep. Maybe it moved then," he slowly suggested, readjusting the blankets.

"I always awaken when it moves in the night."

David lurched from the bedside, and then without warning, he turned on Spring maliciously. "Well, I suppose it makes you very happy. I mean, after all, you tried to get rid of it!"

"David, don't . . ." Tears filled her eyes, and she held out her hand to him.

He ignored it, his eyes narrowing and his jaw clenching. "You don't want my child, you wanted to die drowning because you must have suspected you were pregnant. Well, okay, so you've finally got your way." He crossed to the wardrobe and began pulling clothes out. He stuffed them into a bedroll.

"What are you doing? Where are you going?"

"I'm getting the hell out of here. It's obvious you care more about yourself than the baby or . . . or me. But then you never cared about me, did you? Well, I can find comfort elsewhere, Miss Ames. It'll be Christmas soon, and I'm going to try to see Lily."

"And White Feather?"

"Yes, and White Feather. At least she'll be glad to see me."

"David," implored Spring, "please don't go. The weather's too bad. I did want . . . I do want the baby. Really. And I do care about you. I thought you knew that."

"Yes, you almost had me fooled. Quite the little actress, aren't you? But no more, Spring, no more." He was about to go out the door when she cried out to him.

"You're wrong, David!"

He turned back and said, "I'll tell Hap I'm leaving, and he'll tell Pap. You better let him know what happened. I'm sure he'll help you when"—his voice broke—"when you miscarry." Then he was gone.

Several moments later, she saw David, black against the moonlit snow, ride away on Aphrodite as she stood by the bedroom window. It was then that the rested baby began to kick and move about. Such relief filled her, but sorrow too, that David had gone without knowing she would still give him his child.

Day after day went by, until one week, then two had passed. The weather was crystal clear and cold beyond words. Hap kept Spring supplied with firewood and some company. But most of the time, she preferred quiet solitude.

She occupied part of her time by knitting David a soft blue-and-white scarf for Christmas. She dared not think he wouldn't come home for that holiday, and she made preparations for it with his return in mind. She baked fancy cookies and cinnamon breads, and fruit cake, using canned fruit she dried in the oven. She decorated the house with greenery and made a wreath with red ribbons for each of the doors.

Every evening, she lit a candle in each window, in case he came home in the dark. Every night they burned, throwing out their welcome into the empty blackness.

Two days before Christmas, Mary and Pap and Hap brought a little fir tree into the house, which they set up by the front-room window. They popped corn and strung it, along with cranberries, on the tree. Candles were put on the branches to be lit Christmas Eve. But still David did not come home. He had been gone for three weeks.

Christmas Eve afternoon, the clouds stole over the mountains. Mist hung between the passes, and fog swirled drippily through the trees. It began to snow about five o'clock. Mary and Pap ate at the house for dinner. Hap had also been invited, but he went up to BJ and Penny's. The other men, Joe and Jack, went to the outline to help the men there.

Spring would've staked her life on the idea that David would have returned by now. Yet there was no sign of him.

He had been furious with her when he left. She had no idea his fury was not only directed at her but at himself as well, that it was he who felt responsible for what he thought was the death of their baby. There had been no further doubt in her mind it was alive, for not a day had passed since it had lain so still for all those hours that it didn't make its presence known. Now, he was spending all this time with White Feather and their little girl. White Feather loved him. Spring's only show of love for him had been her willingness to give her body.

By ten o'clock, she blew out the candles on the tree and in each window. Pap and Mary had wanted to stay with her, but she insisted on being alone, that she would be fine. The house was so still and dark she could hear the snow falling to the ground as she lay in the snug, lonely bed."

The baby kicked and jabbed, and Spring tossed and turned.

She could not sleep. She imagined David in the smooth, slender arms of White Feather, the giving and the taking of body and soul, and she felt sick to her stomach.

"Stop it!" she scolded herself.

Suzie, sleeping on the rug by the bed, suddenly raised her head and whined, and then jumped to her feet to run to the window. Placing her front paws on the sill, she looked out. Her loud barking brought Spring to the window.

The snow had stopped falling. All was pearly white, frosting covered, and the clouds were breaking up, allowing the moon to intermittently shine through.

Suzie was very agitated, whimpering and barking, looking pleadingly at Spring with her trusting brown eyes. She unexpectedly howled, sending shivers down Spring's spine. The scar on her back tingled as she watched the dog run around the room in a circle. It was then that Spring saw a lone, shadowed rider coming across the white yard. She didn't know who it was, for he was slumped in the saddle, head down. As he rode in front of the window, he took his hat off and brushed his hair back, which shone blond as the moon lent light through the clouds.

"David!" she whispered, shutting her eyes in relief and thanking God for his safe return. Suzie dashed through the house and was scratching furiously at the door by the time Spring reached it. She had difficulty opening the sliding bolt in the darkness, but when it was open, Suzie raced across the snow to the barn. Without thinking of anything but to greet him and tell him of their baby, she followed, the coldness of the icy air through her nightgown and snow on her bare feet not penetrating until halfway to the barn. Nevertheless, she continued on her way, pausing in the double doors of the barn. A lantern burned low in Aphrodite's stall, where David was quickly bedding her down.

Lightly, Spring ran across the hay-covered floor and, standing behind David, she wrapped her arms around him.

"Oh, David, I'm so glad you're home," she said, hugging him close. She felt his gloved hands gently pull her arms away. Then he went into such a fit of coughing he had to lean against Aphrodite for support. "Are you ill?" she asked, touching his arm.

He didn't turn around but croaked through a hoarse throat, "Go inside. I'll be in, in a minute." Spring gazed at him, realizing he seemed thinner, even with his coat on, and he wasn't able to stand tall and straight.

"All right," she said and ran back to the house. When he finally came in, she had eggs, toast, and coffee ready for him; but he was too ill to eat it. His face was flushed, his blue eyes were glazed, and his head pounded. His buzzing brain wouldn't let him concentrate on who was aiding him, but he was glad to let Spring minister to him. He was soon in the big bed and asleep without conversation or protestation. That in itself told Spring how ill he was.

Once he was asleep, she saw how exhausted he was. Even the blessed relief of sleep did not smooth the fevered brow or the small wrinkles around his eyes. Besides the moustache, the usually smooth face was covered with many days' beard stubble.

Toward morning, the chills began, causing his teeth to chatter and his body to shake uncontrollably. Spring piled more blankets on him, but to no avail. So she crawled in beside him and held him next to her, offering him her own warmth.

Right before the fever broke, David became delirious and incoherent. He thrashed about to such an extent that Spring had to remove herself to avoid injury. Then the words and tears started. Spring listened with distress in her heart.

"No, Father, Father, don't beat Mother again. He won't make me cry. I don't care how much it hurts . . . oh God, the dogs . . . I've got to get away!" He breathed rapidly, as if he was running, and then he called out, "Mother, don't leave! Mother?"

For a few moments, he lay quietly. And then he smiled. "White Feather, so beautiful . . . thank you for Lily . . . Lily . . . God, no!" David shook his head from side to side, the tears falling from his cheeks to the hot pillow under his head. Suddenly his face twisted, and he asked, "Isabel, why?" His hand flew up to his nose, and then he drew his hand away, staring at it. "Isabel, you broke it. You broke my nose. I just want to love you. Don't leave me, please . . . Lily, don't leave me."

Spring shook David, trying to waken from his feverish nightmare. He suddenly grabbed her shoulders, and he pulled her down to him. His breath was hot on her face. His eyes, coldly hard and uncaring, opened wide to look at her. But she knew he really didn't see her. "All right, you may as well leave too," he said calmly, but with a hoarse, shaking voice. "They all have left me. The baby is dead. It's your turn to go. You can leave. I don't want you here!" His grasp loosened, and his eyes shut, and he slept peacefully.

He rested for two days, not waking for more than a few moments at a time; and when he did fully, he was confused as to how he had gotten there. He looked about the room and saw Spring curled up asleep in the overstuffed chair that had been drawn up by the bed's edge.

Feeling someone staring at her, Spring slowly opened her eyes to him, and relief flooded over her. She gave him a timid smile.

"Hello," he said. "How'd I get here?"

She knew he remembered nothing of the past few days. She explained to him about his arrival and ill condition. Then she asked, "Are you hungry? I have some broth ready."

"Yes," he answered. "I could use something." He watched as she stood up from the chair and shock registered on his face. "You haven't miscarried yet?"

Spring smoothed her hands lovingly over the child she was nurturing and answered, "No, David, and I won't be. The baby began moving again just as you rode away. There wasn't time to tell you."

His face closed in on itself. "Oh," was all he said.

If she had expected him to be overjoyed by the news, she was wrong. However, she didn't question him and went to the kitchen instead to bring back his soup.

*   *   *

That night, David was feeling well enough to bathe and shave, while Spring put fresh linens on the bed. After he returned to bed, she regenerated the fire and put the house to final rights for the night. He watched her as she readied herself for bed.

"Where have you been sleeping?" he asked her.

Brushing her hair, she answered from the bathroom. "I've slept in the bed with you. Rather, I lay there." She chuckled, bringing the lantern over and setting it on the side table. "I didn't sleep much. I slept more in the chair, I guess."

"Hap been taking care of things around here?"

"Yes, he's been a great help. It's been snowing almost constantly since Christmas morning. Pap's been down once to see how you are doing. He and Mary came back from Henry's right before Christmas, but everyone and everything are moving pretty slowly around here."

"It does in winter. Well, I'm going to sleep now." He rolled over, pulling the covers over his shoulders.

Spring felt shut out. She stood there for a moment, and since there was nowhere else to go, she slipped into the other side.

The next night, however, when they were in bed, she moved over to him, putting her arms around him, planting kisses all over his bare back. She pressed herself as close as the baby would allow. David lay still, unresponsive. As he had done the night in the barn, he gently removed her arms.

"No, Spring, I'm . . . I'm too tired."

"How could you be too tired, silly? You've been in bed for four days now, sleeping most of the time."

"Hell, I'm not in the mood, then." He tried to keep the irritation out of his voice.

"I could get you in the mood," she said sensually, moving her hand down his back and over his hip.

"Damn it! I said no!" He took her hand and squeezed it none too gently.

"Why, David? Why don't you want me?"

"My desire for you is gone, Spring. We have no future."

"What about the baby?" she cried out.

"You finally convinced me, it wasn't worth it. No involvement with anyone is worth it, Spring. Life and people only hurt you."

"I do want the baby. I love—"

"Don't lie. You've done everything else but that. Don't start now," he said tiredly.

"What happened while you were away, David? Something awful must have happened."

"Go away," he said softly. "Leave me alone."

Spring moved away, shivering in the warm bed. Her heart ached for this man beside her, and she didn't blame him for his rejection of her. But it hurt. Oh, it hurt.

As she lay, sleep escaping her, she thought of their relationship. He had been brutally honest with her throughout, even at their first meeting; and she had despised him for it and taken every opportunity to let him know. But he had never turned away from her, had always been there to help her out of every scrape, to give her encouragement. Sure, he had been arrogant, seeming always to get his way, but hadn't his arrogance been a cover for his feelings, and hadn't his righteousness come from his acute knowledge of the best way to do things? He had foiled her every attempt to do foolish things, and she had repaid him with anger and hurtful words.

Yet she had loved him, though keeping the knowledge of it to herself, being willing to bear his child. She was now frightened after little Abigail's birth. He hadn't understood that, but now, he didn't seem to even care about the baby, much less her. She had almost told him she loved him this night, but he had turned away.

The next morning, she arose and fixed breakfast, having it ready when he got up for his first full day. He appeared thin and haggard, but ate with a hearty appetite. Then he put on his coat to go tend the animals. The snow had stopped and was quite deep, the sky cold and gray.

Before he opened the door, Spring thrust a small package into his hand. He turned it over slowly. "What's this?"

"Nothing much," she answered, going into the kitchen to wash the dishes. "I made it for you for Christmas."

"I see." Carefully, he unwrapped it and took out the knitted blue-and-white scarf. He stared at it a long time, feeling its warm softness. Then, "Thank you."

She watched him trudge through the snow to the barn, with a heavy heart. Halfway there, he took the scarf and wrapped it around his neck. The rest of the winter months, he was not seen outside without it, but he never mentioned it again to Spring.

Chapter 22

It didn't snow again throughout January and part of February. The weather was unseasonably warm, and David spent every waking hour out of doors, seeing to the needs of Lorna and Henry, BJ and Penny, who were expecting their first child the first part of May. He hunted and trapped, and sometimes was gone days at a time.

He moved and spoke and went through each day doing the normal deeds, but he was changed. There was no emotion, no smiles or laughs, no eyes glittering in icy anger or twinkling with mirth. There were no heated embraces or passionate interludes in the night. There were no self-revealing conversations during the quiet moments in front of the roaring fireplace.

Spring's body grew larger and larger, and she had difficulty moving about, especially sitting or rising from bed or a chair. She was tired much of the time and found it hard to breathe. Sometimes she didn't know if the difficulty she had breathing was due to being so lonely or the fact that her increasing girth impeded that normal process. She did not know how much bigger she could stretch. Her back ached most of the time, but she never complained; and she tried to complete as much physical work each day as always, from washing floors, windows, and clothes to cooking sumptuous meals for David. Her pile of baby clothes and linens was completed and waiting. David noticed none of these things. Or at least he made no comment.

*   *   *

One bright day in mid-February, Spring was straightening up the supply room when David came in. She was surprised by this, as he did not search her out anymore.

"Would you come out front, please?" he asked.

She grabbed the shawl he had bought her and wrapped it around her ample figure, and followed David out onto the porch. Two men were standing by their horses, looking out over the snow-laden mountains. Three others were astride their mounts several yards away.

"Here she is," David said as he leaned against one of the posts supporting the roof and resting his leg on the railing. He stuck one of his thin cigars in his mouth and lit it. He looked calm, but if anyone cared to take a closer look, David had become quite pale beneath the outdoor color that tinted his face.

The two men turned around, and Spring recognized the man she had seen in Denver in October. The other, bearded, wore a hat pulled low over his eyes.

Without warning, the latter turned on the other and exclaimed, "You didn't tell me she was pregnant!"

Drake looked sheepish and shrugged his shoulders. "Sorry, I didn't know. She was sitting most of the time."

"Goddamn fool!" the man muttered. Then he took off his hat and peered at Spring. She grabbed the doorsill for support.

"John?" she asked. "Is that you?"

"Yes, Spring. I've finally found you. I've been hunting all over since the Indian attack. Get your stuff together."

Spring's mind was in turmoil, and her heart pounded in her chest. Things were moving too quickly for her to think. She glanced at David.

His eyes were half closed, and he spoke calmly. "She's not leaving."

"What do you mean, Saunders?" John asked through his teeth. "You told Drake—"

"I'm well aware of what I told your lackey." He drew on the cigar and let the smoke out slowly. "If Spring wants to go with you after the baby is born, she may. Until then, she stays here."

"She comes now," John said heatedly, taking a few steps forward and up two steps.

David stood up, and for the first time in weeks, Spring saw an emotion come into his face. There was the familiar ice forming in his eyes. But his voice remained calm and unruffled. "You forget, Granville, you are out of your territory here. This is my place and what I say goes." He indicated Pap, BJ, and Hap, who had presented themselves around the corner of the porch. David smiled a cold, calculating smile. It did not reach his eyes.

John's face reddened, and he turned to Spring. "When is the baby due?"

"Next month."

John relaxed somewhat, and his eyes shifted back and forth. Looking at David, he asked, "Do you think you are the father of this baby?"

"No doubt."

"Are you sure? Spring and I—"

He was totally unprepared for the laughter that met his ears.

"Oh, I'm sure. Spring was a sweet innocent before I got to her. Let's not pretend otherwise. Believe me, the child is mine."

John advanced up the stairs in a rage. "You swine! You must have raped her then!"

David checked his men with a staying hand. However, the chilling look he gave John stopped him. "As you can see, I'm sure Spring was at a slight disadvantage. She had no choice."

"David!" exclaimed Spring, shocked by the lie.

"So," he went on, "if you still want to marry her, soiled as she is by me, through no fault of her own, mind you, and if she still wants to marry you, then I'll be glad to be rid of her. She's been nothing but trouble."

John looked at Spring, whose appalled gaze he mistook for pleading, and asked, "Do you still want to marry me?"

Willing a silent David to now step in and make his lies into truths, to tell her again that he didn't want her to leave as he had done so often months ago, willing him to just give her once more that look of intense, desperate love instead of the gaze of cool estrangement he gave to her now, she took a deep breath, feeling as though her whole body was sinking into quicksand, and she was just too tired physically and spiritually to pull herself out. She dragged her eyes from David.

"Yes," she whispered.

David spoke again. "Better give her a chance to recuperate. Come back the end of April."

John nodded and, taking a step forward, took Spring in his arms, kissing her bruisingly. Then he turned, went to his horse, and mounted. "Until April's end, Spring." The five men rode off.

Spring walked woodenly into the house. David followed her and began packing his bedroll.

"I'm going up to the Rim cabin to hunt for a couple of weeks. Pap's coming with me. I'll send Mary down to help out."

"Why should you?" Spring lashed out, the quiet reserve of the past weeks falling away. "You don't care!"

Gathering his things, he stepped over to her, tilting up her chin in the old way. But he said coolly, "Oh, I care, Spring. Didn't I just give you your long-hoped-for freedom from me? And didn't I just take all the blame for your condition so John would marry you without embarrassment when we both know the real circumstances?"

"You are loathsome!" she cried, voice quivering.

He smiled. "Yes, I do try to live up to your expectations of me." He moved away and left her standing alone in the middle of the room.

She felt totally bereft, empty, devoid of feeling. Numbly, she walked to the kitchen and watched him, astride Aphrodite, make the hill, the breeze blowing the blue-and-white scarf out behind him.

*   *   *

David arrived back to Saunders's Haven one week before the baby was born. He and Pap had stayed away two weeks longer than originally planned.

Mary had tried to console Spring into understanding David's mood, but she couldn't even convince herself, much less Spring. Ever since Lorna's baby had come, David was not himself.

There was no improvement in Spring's relationship with David, not that she expected any. He had, after all, made it quite plain to everyone that he no longer wanted anything to do with her. She felt so big and uncomfortable and utterly unloved as well as unlovable. Her heart was so heavy in her chest that it seemed to hurt physically.

It was almost the first day of the new season, Spring's twentieth birthday, and no snow had fallen, which was extremely rare, since early January. Almost all the previously fallen snow had melted in the valley of the Haven, but remained in the higher elevations, so it was with surprise that a blizzard hit them two days before her birthday.

Hap had gone out to the line camps, and Mary and Pap had gone to the Samuels for the day. Spring awoke in the early morning with a dull backache. She could hardly move, and the baby kicked and jabbed mercilessly. She managed to turn to her other side and saw that David was gone from the bed.

All the nights past, they had shared only one thing: a place to sleep. She didn't know why he stayed there with her, but he had. Renewed sadness settled over her, and she fell back to sleep.

Later, a mild cramp across her middle awakened her, and at the same time, she heard the clock strike twelve. There was a low fire burning on the grate, but the room was fairly dark. Which twelve had the clock struck?

The cramp went away, and Spring pushed back the covers.

She had no desire to do anything, so she went to look out the window. There was so much snow falling that that was the cause for the darkened room.

She went to wash up and decided against the laborious chore of dressing. Slipping on her robe, she went to the kitchen, realizing she was alone in the house. That was nothing new. Halfheartedly, she drank some tea and then set about cleaning up the kitchen. David had left his breakfast things in the sink.

Wondering what to do with her time, she began to bake some bread and to prepare a stew for supper. Along about two o'clock, another pain rippled across her swollen stomach. She busily ignored it, but when another came an hour later and again in the next half hour, she became anxious and not a little frightened. Her time must be upon her.

David was nowhere in sight, and she knew Pap was gone to Henry's. Even if she could've reached their cabin through the drifting snow, there was no one to answer her knock.

The contractions were not hard ones, and far enough apart to let Spring continue with her work. Besides, she didn't want to think about the impending hours if she could help it. At five thirty, she had the stew simmering on the stove and warm, freshly baked bread ready for dinner.

Six thirty brought David stumbling into the house, leaving melted snow on the hardwood floor. He hung his coat, scarf, and hat by the fireplace to dry and then sat down to eat. He made no comment to Spring over the fact that she was not dressed.

The pains were coming every twenty minutes and were harder, but not so much so that she couldn't hide them from David. In fact, she thought if she stripped off her clothes and ran around the room, he wouldn't notice.

After eating silently, he retired to the living room to make shells for his rifle, and Spring put the kitchen in order. Another contraction seized her, and she held on to the sink, biting her lip. That one was the hardest one yet, and only fifteen minutes from the last one. As soon as it was over, she went into the storeroom. She neatened up, and without warning, for she expected a longer interval, another contraction wrapped itself around her.

Clutching herself, she sank to the floor and waited for it to subside. When it did, another took her breath away immediately, causing her to remain on the floor. She decided to stay there awhile, until she could be sure of rising without trouble. A minute passed, and Spring was able to rise; however, she was compelled to lean against a flour barrel. She gritted her teeth and pressed the back of her hand to her mouth. She remembered other discomforts in her life, from headaches to the nausea, to being hit by the Indian Black Claw, to the whip's lash. Nothing seemed to compare to this. How could she ever get past David to the bedroom? She didn't think he would care about her predicament, but she didn't want to appear weak in front of him.

Somewhere in the back of her mind, Spring thought that if she ignored what was happening to her, and no one else knew of it, it would somehow go away. Realistically, of course, she knew this could not be. All these thoughts raced through her head as she was steadily becoming weaker and constantly being wracked with the stabbing, shooting pains.

David was ever conscious of Spring, especially when she was close by. Everything in his life that had any meaning to him had some way of disappearing on him, and she would soon be gone too. It would be easier if he made himself not care, so when she and the baby rode away with John, he would be able to take it.

He realized he hadn't heard her puttering in the kitchen for quite a while, and all was quiet in the house. He continued working, but his curiosity finally got the better of him, and he got up to see what she was doing. One glance in the dining area and the kitchen told him she wasn't there. Only one other place to look. He saw the lantern's glow in the storeroom, and he strode over and looked inside.

What he saw made his heart lurch and his gut tighten in a knot. Spring was huddled on the floor, knees under her, her head on her arms, a small pool of water under her.

"Spring, how long have you been in labor?" he asked urgently, his worry taking over his calm constraint of the past months.

She raised her head and tried to stand. "It's nothing . . . oh . . . I'll just go to bed." Her eyes were enormous, fearfilled, belying the calm of her voice.

Two steps brought him to her side. "I asked how long?" He helped her up and swept her into his arms.

"I think the first pain was about noon, but they've gotten closer since about five or so. I'm not ready, though."

He laid her on the bed. "You may not be, but the baby is. Your water broke."

"My water?" She remembered a warm gush on her legs.

"God, aren't you women taught anything?"

However, Spring was no longer listening, for her nemesis had taken hold of her in a firm, relentless grip. Her back arched, and her fingers clenched. And David watched.

"There is no one to help you, Spring. You know Pap and Mary aren't at home. I'll have to deliver you," he told her between her pains.

She looked at him, like an animal trapped, in alarm. "No, no, I can't."

He took her hand and spoke gently. "I've delivered babies before at the Indian camp and have seen many born, besides the animals I've helped. Trust me." The thing he did not say was that he'd never had to help anyone he loved, and that would be so much more difficult for him.

"I can't do it," she said helplessly. "It's too big. Go away, David. It doesn't matter. Your problems will be over sooner if you . . . oh God." She shut her eyes, and every muscle tightened.

"Spring, Spring," David tried to speak through her curtain of pain. "I'm not going to leave you or the baby. Let me help you. I know you're frightened, and I understand why. But if you try to relax and we work together, we can do it. Spring, did you hear me?"

Mutely, she nodded. Then he explained everything that would be happening to her, damning himself silently for his insensitivity in not going over all this at an earlier time, especially after Lorna's experience had brought such fear to her.

Hour after hour dragged by with no progress. The pain had reached a certain level, with the contractions about seven minutes apart. Every time one occurred, Spring breathed deeply, squeezing two of David's fingers in her small palm, never uttering a sound. Throughout the night, and into the dawn, Spring's strength continued to drain.

David did not know what to do to help her. The baby was quite large for her small frame. He remembered once at the Indian camp when a baby's head had to be crushed in order to relieve the mother. In the end, they both died.

It did not surprise him that she didn't cry out. She had always borne either grief or pain stoically. But it would have made him feel a lot better if she did.

Finally, about noon, the suffering of his beloved became so acute that he was truly terrified. He couldn't bear to see her twisting and arching on the bed. But there was no one else to be with her, so as he had been fairly adept at doing lately, he put his feelings aside.

"Spring," he said, smoothing back her hair, "the pains are coming much closer now, every two minutes. I don't think it'll be much longer."

"I can't do it, David. It's too . . . too . . . hard. It's . . . I'm sorry, so sorry. I . . . I . . . oh, damn, oh!" She fumbled for his hand.

"Yes, dearest, you can. Scream, darling," he begged her.

She shook her head from side to side. "I will not," she said through her teeth. Another came, and David tore back the covers and pulled up her gown, putting her in the proper position for delivery.

"Bear down, Spring. Push, honey! You can do it." But she had no more strength. Wave upon cataclysmic wave of monstrous pain distorted her body, until she thought she would go out of her mind. Her hair and body were drenched with perspiration, and her usually bright tawny-green eyes were dulled into vagueness.

Suddenly, David tore her gown from her misshapen, agony-ridden body and pulled her from the bed. Spring's body was limp against him, her head falling back.

"Don't give up on me, damn it, Spring. Hold on, little girl." He supported her as he had her squat by the bed, with one knee and one arm. The other hand he held between her thighs. "Now, push on the next one. Hear me? All right, honey, just once. Do it once, little one. Go push. That's it. I can feel the head now. Rest a bit. Get ready for the next one. Take a big breath, Spring. All right, now push again." He encouraged her time after wrenching time, until finally, with a mighty push with hidden strength, Spring pushed their squalling son out into David's hands. He quickly wrapped him up and then assisted the new mother back into bed.

A little later, he brought the cleaned baby to her and laid him in her arms, where he began to nurse hungrily at her breast. Spring gazed down at the wrinkled little human. He had a minute fringe of reddish-brown hair around the sides of his head. One small perfectly formed hand kneaded the full breast as the rosebud mouth tugged at the nipple.

David had never seen a more beautiful sight. He knelt by the bed and gathered the two most important people in his life into his arms.

"Thank you, Spring. You did it. I knew you could. You were wonderful. Thank you for my son." He kissed her hollow cheek. Her eyes were vacant, deeply set, and circled in purple. She could hardly keep them open.

"You saved me again, David," she said slowly, lethargically. "For the life of me, I don't know why."

He took the now-sleeping infant and cradled him in his arms, gazing at him in wonder. "You are exhausted. Do you want to sleep?"

She nodded and pulled the blanket up under her chin. "I could sleep forever," she said and gratefully closed her eyes.

It was five days before Pap and Mary could leave Henry's, and instead of stopping at their place, their horses plowed their way on down the hill to the red-and-white house.

"Hi, come on in," David invited, taking their wraps.

"Quite a storm, huh?" Pap commented. "Mary's been so anxious about Spring. We came on down to see how she is. You too, of course."

"No doubt." David laughed. "Come on. Spring's been very lazy lately. She's in bed." He led them to their bedroom, where Spring was propped up, folding some clothes.

"Hello, sweetie," Mary greeted. "What are you doing in bed?"

"Come see, Mary." She held out her hand to her friends, and they rounded the bed. In an oakwood cradle David had been making all day in the barn when Spring began her labor lay their son, sleeping peacefully.

"Oh my heavens, Pap. The baby is here. When did it happen? How?" Mary bent over and took the babe in her arms.

"Actually," David said, "he came the day before Spring's birthday."

"I'm sorry I wasn't here," Pap apologized.

"That's all right," Spring replied. "David did a fine job."

"Not a hard time, then?" Pap asked.

"Well . . ."

"No," Spring interrupted David. "Everything went fine."

David eyed her quietly. In the past quiet days alone together, he was constantly marveling over her resilience. And the love she had for their child was heartwarmingly obvious.

"He looks like a fine, husky boy," Mary put in. "Must have weighed quite a bit. Have you named him?"

They had agreed most amicably on *Zachary* for his given name. Spring wanted *Allan* for her father as his middle name, and David went along with her on that.

"*Zachary* is a strong name for this strong fellow," Pap said.

"I must say," Mary commented, wiping a tear from her eye, "that you, Davey, and Spring made a beautiful little boy from . . . from your being together. Pap and I truly hope he has a beautiful life too."

"Thank you, Mary," David replied. "Whatever can be done for him, will be."

"How about a drink to celebrate?" suggested Pap to David.

He glanced over at Spring, and she smiled at him. "You have a right to celebrate, David. Go on."

Over drinks in the dining area, Pap asked, "How did it really go? The doc in Denver said she may have problems with a first child."

"She never told me that. You didn't either. I thought I was going to lose her. We had to do it squaw-style. But you know Spring. She would never admit it was hard. She never uttered one sound of pain. It was incredible. I don't really know how she did it. I didn't realize, Pap, how scared she was up at Lorna's. As it was, she had every reason in the world to be afraid."

"Well, what now?"

"What do you mean?"

"Are you going to let her go off with that murdering scoundrel with your son?" Pap slammed his glass down on the table

"What can I do? She told him she still wanted to marry him. We all heard her."

"He won't treat your son right," prophesied Pap.

David eyed Pap silently, his lips forming a hard line. "No, probably not. I doubt he'll treat Spring well, either, but who am I to talk?"

"You at least love her," Pap stated.

"No, not any longer," denied the younger man.

"You don't fool me, Dave. Not for one damn moment. I just wish you'd get off your hellish pride and ask her to marry you."

"I won't take her freedom away. I won't ever do that to anyone again," he said vehemently.

"You realize you're throwing away the best thing that ever happened to you? Can you even stand to think of that man with her?"

"Shut up, Pap!"

"Just the thought—"

"I mean it, Pap. Shut up," he hissed through his teeth. "I can only live my life! My way."

"That doesn't mean it's the best way, you know."

*   *   *

David saddled up the horses and tied the food supply and bedrolls on to them. He was taking Spring up to the Rim canyon cabin for the night, leaving Zachary with Lorna to nurse him. Spring would be leaving the day after their return, with John. John had sent a note with Drake, saying when he would be up to get her.

The cabin was quite rough, having only one room with a small fireplace, one thin bed, two chairs, and one table. It sat under two towering evergreens on a sloping mountainside, overlooking a wide canyon that stretched for miles west and east. In the bottom, a river chased itself over huge granite boulders that had fallen into the gorge over eons of years since creation.

Spring stood gazing out over the scene, the wind blowing her sun-dazzled hair in its ribbon tied behind her head. She had regained her previous slimness, though her breasts remained full, and her gracefulness was every bit as apparent as it had ever been.

David walked up behind her after bedding the horses down for the night. He wasn't really sure why he had brought her up here, except that this would be their very last time together.

"It's beautiful up here, isn't it?" he asked.

"It's so massive!" she exclaimed. "I really can't take it all in, all the majesty. And look at that sunset." Their eyes moved west to the golden halo of the sun as it shimmered in the purpling skies. They stood silent until they heard the sun go down. She looked up at him and said, "I'll never see another sunset without thinking of you, David. You've shown me so much."

He looked away and heaved a sigh. "Come on, it's getting chilly. I'm hungry too."

Supper over, they sat on a small mat he had brought with them in front of the roaring fire. Nights were still quite cold in the mountains, especially in the higher elevations.

They sat for a long while, and then he leaned back on his arms, his legs stuck out before the flames. From this angle, he could see the delicate curve of her profile, the small curve of her nose, the strong chin, the long lashes brushing her cheeks.

"White Feather and Lily are dead," he said without preamble.

"What? When? What do you mean?" she asked, turning shocked eyes on him.

"I found the Indian camp where they were for the winter. Many of them had the smallpox, and many had already died."

"Oh, David," she said compassionately, remembering his calling out to them not to leave him. She touched his arm. "I'm so very sorry. Were they d—"

"No, both were alive, yet very ill. Both died in my arms, two days apart."

He spoke so nonchalantly that she said, "You don t seem too upset."

"The time for my tears is past," he answered.

Again she remembered how he had cried out in his fever for White Feather and Lily, imploring them not to leave. Yes, he had grieved for them, she knew.

"You were lucky not to get it yourself."

"I had the smallpox when I was younger, about seventeen. A light case."

She was silent and then started when he leaned forward and took her hand. He played with her tapering fingers, smoothing them, curling them, and then flattening them in his palms.

Again, he spoke with no show of emotion. "You know, everyone I've ever been close to has left me in some way. My mother could've taken me with her. It would have saved me a lot of pain physically and emotionally. Of course, you know how Isabel left me. And now White Feather and Lily are gone. Day after tomorrow, you'll be gone, too. I understand why you are going, Spring, and I hope you understand why I can't attach myself to anyone ever. But for now, will you let me hold you and love you? It has to last me a lifetime."

*   *   *

Later, lying entwined in each other arms, flesh to flesh, Spring felt totally consumed by him. David had taken sole possession of her, as if he could not get enough. His lips and hands had been everywhere on her body, worshiping every inch. Her wanting of him had been as desperate and full of yearning as his was of her. At the peak of the sublimity of it all, Spring had cried out in exquisite, sweet pain and arched almost violently against him. When he was done, he shuddered convulsively, whispering her name over and over, knowing he would not have another chance to. He even told her he loved her still, despite what he had told her before. She strained to hear as well that he would marry her, but the words never came.

Late afternoon of the next day brought them by the Samuels. But David made no effort to guide the horses that way.

"Aren't we going to stop for Zach?" Spring asked.

"He's down at the Haven. There's going to be some changes once you leave. They need more room up here, so Hap and Pap and Mary are moving into Henry's for a while to help him build onto their place. Lorna is moving into my house with her babies. I go into the bunkhouse."

"This place is really growing," Spring admitted, feeling a tug at her heart for all these close friends she would be saying good-bye to.

"Yes, when Penny has her baby, Zachary will have quite a group to grow up with."

Spring rode for several seconds, and then the import of his words sank in. "I don't understand about Zachary having friends here. He won't be here."

"Yes, he will be, Spring. I'm not letting you take him away from everything that will be his someday."

Spring reined in her horse across Aphrodite's nose, causing David to stop. Her stomach felt sick with fear, especially when she saw the look of confident affirmation on David's cold face. She would never understand how he could be so intensely loving to her and yet give her that hard, icy stare. "You can't mean that. A child belongs with his mother. I'm nursing him. I carried him all those months. David, please, I'm begging you. Don't do this to me."

David spoke to her gently, for he didn't want to hurt her. "I'm not doing it to you, Spring. I'm doing it for Zach. You don't think John will tolerate a child of mine, do you? I can't prevent you from doing what you want, but I can keep my son away from that bastard."

She ignored his words and said caustically, "That's not true. You are doing this for yourself, your own selfish self. I have to take him with me. I'm nursing him."

"Lorna has said she'll take over that responsibility."

Lorna! Suddenly Spring felt betrayed. "But he's mine, David!" Tears welled up and spilled over onto her hot cheeks.

"He's as much mine, Miss Ames. You forget we both enjoyed creating him. He's staying with me."

Spring was furious, but she made a last attempt to dissuade him. "Last night you said you didn't want any attachments. Zachary will become an attachment."

David shrugged, pushing his gray hat back onto his head. His gaze was unrelenting. "I suppose I meant the female adult type. At any rate, he stays here."

David made a move to leave, to end the conversation, for he could no longer bear to see the anguish in her face. Spring was beyond reason, and she took her little riding crop, raised it, and lashed him across the face. David jerked back, placing his hand to his face. Blood smeared his hand. He wiped it slowly from his face with a handkerchief.

His eyes iced over, but his lips curved in a brilliantly hard smile. "Well, my dear, I guess one good whipping deserves another."

"Oh!" she screamed at him. "I hate you now more than I could say! I hate you!" She threw the crop at him, wheeled her prancing horse around, and galloped off to the Haven.

David followed at a slower gait. He wanted to be sure the tears were gone from his eyes before he reached home.

*   *   *

It almost seemed as if Spring was working her way through a reception line at a funeral. Everyone was lined up in front of the white house with the red trim to say farewell, and everyone appeared stricken with grief.

There were tears in Penny's eyes as Spring kissed her and wished her well with her baby. BJ shook her hand, saying he would miss her.

Hap embraced her. They had shared many wonderful musical moments together. She told him to keep practicing the piano.

She stooped to kiss and hug Jacob. She hugged Henry too. The tears on Lorna's guilt-ridden face brought forgiveness into Spring's. "Take good care of my baby, Lorna," she whispered.

"I will, Spring, and I'm sorry."

Spring smiled at her and moved on to Pap. "Thanks for everything, Pap. You've been wonderful to me, and I'll never forget you."

"I hate to see you go, sweetheart. We all love you."

"That's debatable," she said with a quivery laugh.

Then, turning to Mary, she was enfolded in the older woman's arms.

Mary sobbed, finally managing to blurt out, "How can you leave us, darling? I'll miss you so . . . almost like a daughter to me."

Spring stepped back, swallowing the lump in her throat. "I can't express what I feel for you, Mary. I wish things had been different. I love you."

Quickly, she moved away. David stood a few feet away, holding their six-week-old son. One glance at John told her he was anxious to put this emotional display behind him. "I'll be right along, John," she told him, walking over to David. She took her child and held him to her breast. He immediately looked for nourishment. She kissed his softdowned head. He looked up at her with David's eyes at their most tender.

"You best be off," David said to her.

"I don't want to leave Zachary." Her voice quavered. *Or you,* she cried silently.

"You are welcome to stay here," he reminded her.

Spring responded, "Without marriage?"

"Without marriage."

"I can't."

"Well, don't worry," he said, gently. "I'll take good care of our son. I love him, Spring. I've loved him from the moment he began."

"Are you going to tell him I deserted him like your mother did you?"

"No," he answered, taking Zachary into his big arms. "I would never malign you to him."

She took a deep breath and turned away. John motioned for her to come.

"Take care, little one," David said.

She turned back, tears glistening in her eyes. "I want you to know, I don't regret anything, David Saunders. Not one moment of anything we've shared." Again, she turned, but for the final time.

"So long, Venus," she heard him whisper.

Spring straightened her back and brought her head up proudly. That was the hardest thing for David to see her do.

Chapter 23

"Spring? Spring Ames, is that you?"

Spring looked out of hollow eyes, one purpled and swollen. She hid her face in the torn knitted shawl she always wore.

"Go away," she whimpered.

"I most certainly will not," Molly insisted, pulling Spring under her arm and away from the outside alley wall of the squalid hotel she was resting against. "You'll come with me." And Molly helped Spring into her shiny black carriage.

Molly did not ask the sorrowful-looking creature any questions but hustled her to her private rooms and into a tub of steaming water. She supervised the process herself, and was therefore able to observe how incredibly thin the once-beautiful girl was. She had seen her with bruises the first time, but those had only been confined to her face. These covered not only her eye and cheekbone, but the green-and-purple marks spread across her jawbone as well. Her lips were cut and chapped.

Her upper arms and wrists showed bruises obviously made from fingers crushing into the delicate skin, and there were like marks on her neck and throat. The worst injuries of all were ghastly contusions across her breasts, ribs, and buttocks area.

Spring's once-lovely and graceful hands, from which golden notes had fallen, were red, torn, and bleeding.

Once in Molly's bed, in the silken sheets, she ate heartily, as though half starved. Then she made a move from the bed.

"Where do you think you're going?" Molly demanded, pushing Spring gently back against the pillows.

"I've got to go back. John will be very upset if I'm not in the room when he gets there." Actually, Spring relished being pampered after the months of physical torture she had endured.

"John? You mean that murdering devil you were going to marry? Don't tell me you did!"

Spring gave a harsh, bitter laugh. "Heavens no! He got me here under false pretenses. Said we'd be married, but once here, the first thing he did was beat me. Then he raped me."

"It's a good thing you didn't marry him. Then you'd be stuck with him. Why don't you leave him?" Mary asked hotly.

"I can't. He says he will kidnap Zachary and kill him if I leave him." Spring nervously twisted her hands, and tears filled her eyes. It seemed she cried all the time now

"Who's Zachary?" Molly asked, leaning against the footboard.

"My baby. Mine and David's. David kept him."

"Ah, I see." Molly was quite adept at reading between the lines. And she already knew much of the first part of Spring's association with David. "How long have you been down here?"

"About four months. Four months of pure, unadulterated hell."

"Whip would take you back, you know."

Spring knew that was true, but despite everything, she hadn't gotten rid of her pride. She could never go back lower than she left. She expressed as much and then said, "Besides, he won't marry me. I can't be his whore." Realizing what she'd said, she apologized. "I'm sorry, Molly, I didn't mean anything by that."

Molly smiled. "Don't worry about that. But, Spring, you are John's whore."

"I don't know what to do, Molly," Spring's voice became agitated. "I've got to protect my baby, though I'll never see him again. He's so beautiful. I wish David had let me keep him."

"Aren't you glad he didn't?"

"Yes, he was right. He's always right, even about those terrible things he told me about John. John plotted the whole thing—my abduction by the Indians, but he didn't plan on David coming for me. He didn't know Mrs. Butler had told David all about it before she died. He says he hadn't meant for my father to be killed, but some of his followers became too enthusiastic. He laughs when he tells me the story, which is often. He takes all my money I get from the bank. I don't think he knows David owns it, or that David made arrangements that I would only get a little each month. John doesn't understand why, and I pretend not to, so he made me get a job washing dishes." She held out her reddened and disfigured hands. "He takes that money too and uses it to drink and gamble. Then he comes to our room . . ." She shrugged her shoulders helplessly.

"You were a teacher," Molly said. "Why don't you let me get you a position at the orphanage. I'm sure they'll pay you more. That way, John won't mind you changing jobs."

"That would be wonderful, Molly, if you could arrange it for me. I suppose I could get some stuff to cover these bruises"

"We'll fix you up fine. Even Whip wouldn't recognize you now."

"Ha! I doubt he ever even thinks of me, Molly."

The madam stared at her young friend as she struggled into her shabby clothes. Then she went out, tears brimming, to see what she could do to help.

Spring was wrong about David. From the moment she disappeared into the granite-cliffed pathway, the light went out of his life. If it hadn't been for Zachary with the rosy, cheerful face, the intense blue eyes, and chestnut hair that glowed in the sunlight as his mother's did, David would very likely have spent every waking moment with a bottle in his hand. As it was, for the first two months, after dinner, he drank himself into a stupor. He listened to no one on the merits of fatherhood or the example he needed to set for his son.

During the days, he dragged himself from his unkempt bed, nauseated and with a pounding head, to try to work about the place, making little progress.

He took no pleasure in the springtime—the bright warm sun, azure skies, multicolored mountain slopes blanketed with all variety of wildflowers. On many occasions, he expected to see Spring come into view, her arms laden with the treasures of the hillsides. On a few occasions, he actually did see her, and even ran in her direction, calling her name, until she evaporated before his eyes. But this happened only after particularly bad bouts with the bottle.

It took one night of walking the floor with a colicky baby, after being pulled bodily to his feet by Henry, for David to mend his ways. He was met at the back door by a worried Lorna, because Zachary was screaming in pain.

Then, during his days, he, and he alone, took care of Zach, except for feeding time. Then he took him to Lorna. When she became ill, Penny took over after her little girl was born.

David was so turned in on himself that he didn't realize it was not a good situation for anyone.

After the night of caring for his fretting son, David was much improved, at least on the outside. He no longer drank, he kept himself clean, and he took Zach with him wherever he went. If it was riding to some home to work, he put him into a back carrier as a papoose. If he worked around his own place, repairing buildings or tack, there was Zachary in a wicker basket beside him.

However, David was not over the loss of Spring, and he yearned for her, to hear of her. Yet when Pap suggested he or one of the other men go into Denver to make inquiries, David was negatively firm. His conviction was that the less he knew, the less he would want to know. But he was wrong.

He took Zachary to all the places he had been with Spring, and he talked constantly about her, but only to the uncomprehending baby. Zach would open his large blue eyes, however, and stare wide-eyed at his father and give him a toothless grin, winning David's heart over and over. No, there wasn't a day that went by that he didn't think of Spring.

John was not happy that Spring had renewed a friendship in Denver. It gave her a sense of independence he didn't want her to have, especially since Molly was a friend of Whip Saunders. But he couldn't leave because that was where her money was.

He had been genuinely frightened one evening when Hairy Harry had accosted him with a knife at his throat outside Molly's house. John was threatened with sure death if he didn't let Spring have the teaching job at the orphanage, and most importantly, he was to stop beating her.

It wasn't that John hated Spring. Indeed, he felt sorry that David had "raped" her and she had to carry his child.

But something in his own mind snapped when he was with her, knowing Whip had bested him. For some reason, he felt he had to make ugly what Whip had found lovely. And the fact that she did not respond to him in any way but was completely passive did not help the situation.

So it was that Spring began a short-lived career teaching the youngest children at the orphanage. It was located not on the best side of town but on the more seedy side, the old Denver.

The summer was drawing to a close, and it was unseasonably warm. There was an influx of Indian women and children, some of whom came to the home for handouts. Some of the women left their children there for good, saying good-bye in the early cool mornings, never to return. Some of these children were ill when brought in, usually with cold symptoms of coughing and sneezing. There was no doctor in attendance, and many of the illnesses went unchecked.

Spring enjoyed the work, spending long hours there. The longer she was there, the less time she spent in the dreary little room she shared with John. She also had less time to think of Zachary and, yes, David.

She usually was quite exhausted by day's end and was relieved when John left her alone. But more often than not, he did not. The situation with him, the verbal and physical abuse, though better hidden, was intolerable. Some days it was all Spring could do to just be able to move one foot in front of the other. She knew somehow that a break had to be made, but she did not know in what direction it would take.

Several weeks, after coming to the orphanage, Spring walked to the hotel in a dusky, warm twilight. Her head had been aching since noon and had gotten progressively worse. She went immediately to bed to fall asleep deeply.

A few hours later, she was jostled roughly awake by a whisky-breathed John, sweating and unwashed for days.

"Wake up," he mumbled, shaking her shoulder.

"What?" Spring tried to focus in on him.

"I say, wake up, damn it!" John rolled her over. He began to kiss her wetly, thrusting his tongue into her mouth.

She jerked away, coughing.

"John, please, I don't think . . ." Her head seemed to split in two; it was pounding so viciously. She tried to stem the coughing, unsuccessfully.

"You don' wha', you lil' bitch? Don' wan' me touchin' your pure white body?" He slapped her head back against the dank pillows. She had never turned him down before, and this was the ultimate humiliation. The fact that she was resisting him now brought out the worst in him.

"It's not that," she began.

"I bet you nev' turned down ol' Whip, did ya?"

"John, I'm ill."

He didn't hear her. She felt her ribs crack under his fists. She knew now she would have to leave. That is, if she was still alive when he was through.

*　　*　　*

Joe brought his horse to a halt outside of the barn door. He walked in and paused, waiting for his eyes to adjust to the dimness inside. Then he saw hay falling over the edge of the loft and David with a pitchfork in his hands.

"Hey, Dave," Joe called by way of greeting.

David rested on the implement and peered down. "Hi, you are back sooner than I expected."

"Yeah, well, I'm not really through. But I thought you'd want to know, I've seen smoke coming from the direction of the Rim for two, three days now."

"Hmm," David said, pushing his hair back. "I don't mind someone taking shelter for a night, but not taking up permanent residence. Think I'll go up and take a look. We can ride together partway."

He came down from the loft, and after making preparations and cuddling a grinning Zach, he and Joe set off for higher places.

When David rode up to the cabin, the sun had already disappeared, though a lingering glow haloed the mountain ridges. No smoke was visible, nor was there any sign of life. He led Aphrodite to the shed on the side of the cabin and sighted a gray horse tethered in one of the stalls. He unsaddled the black and put feed in her box. He saw the other animal's box was empty, and there was no water in the bucket. In fact, it was dry. Obviously, it hadn't been fed or watered for a day or two.

It was very dark inside. No fire or lamp burned. He did not discern anyone at first, but as his eyes became accustomed to the blackness, he noticed a huddled, blanketed form lying in front of the cold hearth. It did not move. He lit the lantern on the table and held it over the figure. He nudged it with his foot. *Not dead, anyway,* was his thought.

Kneeling, he rolled the body over, and then drew back in horror. The face was completely distorted by bruises and swellings, and there were red blisters all over it. He stared at it, and nausea swept over him. The lamplight had shone its glow on the person's hair. Despite its lackluster, there was no doubt that this was Spring.

David quelled his rising stomach and leaned over the prone woman. Her breathing was shallow and labored. He pulled her to a sitting position and thumped her back several times.

Sharp pain tore through Spring's body, which brought her to a semiconscious state. Then she was wracked with violent coughing, freeing herself of the mucous and phlegm that had filled her breathing passages. After this, she was sick in the old cracked chamber pot David took out from under the bed.

David held her slack form against him, and then laid her back on the floor. He pillowed her head with his blanket.

Her head rolled back, revealing her slender, once-delicate ivory throat. Deep purple and red marks covered it from ear to ear, discernible finger shapes visible.

"Oh, God," David whispered to himself, "I sent her away to that." Then his eyes went to the red blisters, and he knew what they were. He unbuttoned the shabby blouse she wore to examine her more fully. Right away he saw more purple marks and greenish-yellow ones across her upper chest and breasts, and he knew she had been beaten mercilessly. Upon closer inspection, he saw full teeth bites on both breasts, where they had broken the skin. Such rage filled his being that he could scarcely think.

However, besides the physical abuse Spring suffered, she was very ill. There were more blisters on her arms. He had seen these before. Spring had the smallpox.

Spring felt David working over her. She did not open her eyes, but she knew it was he. It seemed wherever he touched her, though with the utmost tenderness, it hurt excruciatingly.

At last, she spoke through her stiff, cracked, and swollen lips. "Me, again. causing you trouble."

Tears smarted his eyes. "I'm going to kill that goddamned bastard!"

She moaned. "Not now. I need you."

"No, not now. You must get well." He removed the grimy clothing she had worn for the past several days and covered her with a blanket. Everywhere on her body were old and fresh evidence of the misery of her afflictions. The only bones he discovered broken were two or three ribs on her left side. They could not be bound until the smallpox had healed.

Spring was too ill to care that he examined her daily with careful scrutiny, that he saw her at her most wretched, coughing, sneezing, and losing everything that passed her lips.

Her body was emaciated, almost wasted; she had been so long without wholesome food. The breasts he had taken such pleasure in were now as flat as a young boy's. Blisters now covered her entire body, and she itched constantly. David hated to do it to her, but in order for her not to scar her face or her body, he tied her wrists loosely to the bedposts when the itching was at its peak.

One day, he heard a horse approaching and he went out to find Joe reining in.

"Go away, Joe," David warned. "Spring's here. She has the smallpox."

"What about you?" Joe asked.

"I've had it. Listen, you can bring me some supplies."

He reeled off a list of things he needed to make Spring more comfortable.

After Joe went on his way, David returned to the cabin.

It was quite warm inside, yet Spring was consumed with chills. Her eyes were bright with fever. He covered her with all the available blankets and then lay with her, as she had done once for him. He spoke softly to her, telling her how much he loved her and would never let any harm befall her again. He rocked her gently, and finally, she quieted and was able to sleep.

Joe brought the supplies the next day, leaving them a distance away. Neither man wanted the germ to be carried back to the Haven.

The next several days, Spring's condition worsened. She couldn't talk; she was rarely conscious, and only long enough for David to force a few sips of water down her parched throat. He constantly bathed her with tepid water and alcohol to bring down the fever and dry up the blisters.

Ten days at the Rim brought them to the ultimate peak of the illness. Spring lay burning with fever, her skin hot and dry to the touch. She thrashed about, kicking the blankets off. There was nothing for David to do but continue his bathing of her.

He could not help but remember the fragile whiteness of her skin as she stood proudly above him in the silvery moonlight. How beautiful she had been. Now his eyes roved over the battered, pock-maked woman. If she lived, the pox would disappear with little scarring. The ugly bruises, too, would heal; but how would her mind be? He thought of his mother and what her reaction to his father's beatings had been. Suddenly, the bitterness he had always felt toward his mother fell away. Looking at Spring, he finally realized why his mother had left him. With him along during her escape, she may not have survived, and that was most important at the time, to get away.

"David?" Spring suddenly whispered. "I'll never see Zachary again, will I?"

"What do you mean, my darling? Of course, you will."

She clutched feebly at his arms. "No, no," she cried out, arching her back. "It's over for me!"

"Spring, stop it. I need you. Zachary needs you." He looked at her desperately as she shook uncontrollably, and then, unexpectedly, relaxed on the narrow bed. She no longer twisted and turned, and a fine mist spread over her. "I was wrong, Spring, to ever let you go. If you would, I want to marry you. Spring? Spring?" He leaned over and could barely discern quiet breathing. She was asleep.

After that, Spring, true to her name and nature, made a fairly rapid recovery. The blisters dried up and dropped off. David was able to wrap her ribs tightly just for comfort. He took her outside for the sun's medicine for hours at a time. She ate hungrily at every meal he prepared. And she, at last, became a semblance of the old Spring.

One day, finishing a picnic lunch, he insisted she lie down, with his thigh as a pillow, to rest in the sun.

"I finally feel like a human again," she commented. "At least as much as I can."

He gazed down at her and brushed wisps of the auburn hair back with his fingertips. "Why did you come up here? How did you ever get up here in that condition?"

She closed her eyes and sighed. "This was the last happy place I was. I thought it was a good place to die. I used what strength I had to get here. I stole that horse. I went by the house one day very early. No one was about. I knew I couldn't stop. I knew I had the smallpox."

"It's a wonder that son of a bitch didn't kill you!" he bit out. "I hate him with all I have in me."

"David," she said, moving to look up at him, seeing his firmly set jaw. "You mustn't have such hate. Let it go."

"How can you say that?" he asked, incredulous. "If I ever see that . . . him again, I'll kill him, I swear!"

She reached for his hand and pressed it to her lips. "Please, David, don't think about him. Everything you ever told me about him is true. I'm sorry I didn't believe you, that I hit you with that parasol. I was stubborn and paid for it. Let's put it behind us." She had explained earlier why she felt she had to stay with John.

"Your stubbornness was not so bad, for you to be so unjustly punished. It's hard for me to be so forgiving." He slid down beside her and gazed into her eyes. He put his arms around her.

She stiffened and turned away. "No, no," she began.

"And now you are afraid of me too in this way," he said softly. "You know I've never hurt you when you've been in my arms."

She shuddered. "I know how awful it can be now. When I think of all he did, what he forced me to do, the pain of his hands and his body . . ." She began to cry softly.

David cradled her with worshipful tenderness.

"Hush, my dearest Spring. It's all right. Try to remember how we were together."

"I do, but I felt whole and worthwhile then. Now I'm nothing but a piece of flesh with no heart or soul. David, I can't. It's too awful."

"I can wait for you. You are worth waiting for. I do love you so." He kissed her temple and then kissed her salty tears away. "Yes, you are worth everything to me. I want to marry you right away, if you would like to."

At long last, the words she had hoped for sounded in her ear, breathlessly. But too much had happened to her. She didn't think she could be the way she used to be with him.

"I've wanted to hear you say that for a long time," she said. "But too much has come between us. I'm different. I don't think I could be a proper wife to you. I don't want to be like Isabel."

"You aren't. I love you. I'll wait 'til you're ready."

Chapter 24

Spring walked up the back slope of the hill behind the red-and-white house. When she reached the summit, she gazed all about her. This was her favorite spot anywhere at the Haven, because it afforded her a chance to see all around her. She could view the peacefulness of the house nestled in its little valley, the neat fences of the corral, the smoke rising from the fieldstone chimneys of the house. She could sometimes see various ones working about the barn or yard. The hills were verdant, velvet green, rolling and folding into one another, the sky a sapphire blue holding a bright circle of golden sun. Farther west was the Samuels' place. She could not see it from this point, but she could visualize it in her mind, now grown by two rooms. To the south, she could just make out the whitewashed structure of BJ and Penny's home. Smoke could be seen rising had they not been down the hill.

She stretched and sat down among a field of buttercups and lilacs and held her face to the sky. Today she was happy, and she now knew that with a few ups and downs, she would remain that way, in Saunders's Haven.

Closing her jade green eyes, she remembered back over the long autumn and winter months. Things had not gone well for her. Sometimes she did not know if she could stand making everyone around her so miserable. For that was the way she had been—miserable and depressed. And everyone had felt that way for her.

The first thing that happened to make the welcome home unpleasant was that Zachary cried when she picked him up. He did not know her; she was a stranger to him, and he squirmed and struggled to get down. Finally, David had to take him from her. He had tried to talk to her about it afterward as she sat on the edge of the massive bed, but she had said it didn't matter. Later, when she was bathing in the tub behind the closed door, he heard her sobbing uncontrollably.

She tried to play the piano, but she had no feeling for it. It was as if she hadn't had a lesson in her life. Her fingers were so rough and sore that nothing came out sounding right. She couldn't concentrate on her reading that she enjoyed so much, or do simple mending.

While the weather permitted, she walked about, mainly alone, except for the faithful Suzie at her side. David would stand and watch her, his heart wrenching at the lonely figure she made. When winter set in, she wandered about the house puttering. She didn't have any interests.

All were kind to her and tried to bring her out of her depression. One day, however, Mary really lit into her by saying how lucky she was to be alive and having a loving man like Davey to care for her and a beautiful son, and friends who cared about her.

Spring turned on her angrily. "I'll tell you how lucky I am," she shouted. She proceeded to tell her every sordid detail of her life with John, leaving out nothing. She told her things that she hadn't confided even to David. Mary, for all her fairly worldly ways, was sick with horror, and it had been all she could do to keep from putting her hands over her ears to keep the gross words out of her mind. Later, telling Pap about it, she said, "At least she got angry. That's some form of emotion. That's better than nothing at all, I guess."

Naturally, Pap told David everything Mary had told him, word for word.

One Saturday morning, when Spring entered the kitchen, she overheard David saying something about getting even with "that man, if you could call him such!" Mary was cutting his hair, and it lay in blond swatches all about his booted feet. Snow was blowing against the windows.

Spring looked at him and saw that his eyes, which had remained calm and warmly blue since he had nursed her back to health, were once again iced over in the old way. Because she had talked to Mary in so graphic a manner two days previous, Spring had felt somewhat better about things in general, and so she was able to approach David.

She stood by his chair and put her arm around his neck, drawing his head to her now-filling-out breast. She pressed his head against it, oblivious to Pap and Mary.

"David, please. I don't want you to hate, so leave it alone. It's behind us, behind me, now."

He slipped his arm around her waist. "You alone are bearing the burden of what's happened to you. I don't think that's fair. John has always been between us, one way or another, and until something is done, he'll always be there. And he's not behind us, it's not behind you. We can't even love each other because of him!"

She stepped away and looked at the three people, a lost look on her face. "Well, can we not dwell on it?" she asked.

"Yes," he answered, his face softening. "We cannot dwell on it."

Spring walked back to the front room to sit on the new sofa that had been added to the furniture in her absence.

It faced the fireplace, their chairs on either side of it. Zachary was playing with wooden blocks she had asked David to make for him. She watched him smack them together in his chubby hands. He had grown so.

David had changed too. He was less commanding in his ways, giving her choices instead of orders, less overbearing in his attitude toward her, as if he realized she was no longer a child but a woman in her own right. It was too bad that she didn't feel that way about herself any longer. However, she was not above appreciating the change. It made her respect him as never before.

Spring heard a wild bird's cry and peered up into the sky, shading her eyes. She was glad for a reprieve from her memories, for some of them were extremely painful. There in the distance, she saw the eagle, Freedom, wheel and dive, then glide away over the treetops.

Freedom, she thought. What was that anyway? She had wanted freedom from David and this valley, and it only got her a form of slavery. David had given her freedom, and she had been caught in a web of self-despair and abhorrent circumstances. And yet, when she thought about it, he had always tried to teach her right thinking, and in right thinking, one gained freedom. She now knew she was free.

She went back to her thoughts of the past months. Little Zach had become accustomed to her, but he did not come to her on his own. He began to walk in his tenth month, and he climbed on everything. She remembered how he struggled and struggled to get up on the piano stool. She had watched to be sure he didn't fall and tried not to clap her hands in glee when he finally attained it. Then, with pleasure, she saw and heard him pluck a few notes.

Talking to him softly, she had picked him up and placed him on her lap, and sitting at the piano, she picked out a few simple tunes she thought he would enjoy. That was the beginning for them. All afternoon, she played and played, holding him until, at last, she realized the heavy load on her chest was that of a sleeping head. From then on, however, Zachary went to her without reservation, and when he wanted her to play, he would go over to the shiny instrument and reach up, mumbling, "Ano? Ano?"

Spring smiled to herself, remembering how she had run out to the barn after putting Zach to bed for a nap, exclaiming to David over their son's interest in the piano. David had grinned and taken her hands. She was getting better in many ways. Then her smile faded, for she recalled the obstacles they had had to pass for themselves.

David and she had shared a bed since he brought her back to the Haven. But whenever he made any kind of movement toward her, or she thought it was toward her, she stiffened and turned away. She never saw the hurt or sorrow or anger aimed at John in his face. He kept these well hidden from her.

Slowly, though, he forced her to lie in his arms. He held her night after night, until she could relax and come to expect that from him.

The scars and bruises were completely gone, her well-fed body was becoming beautiful and lovely once more, and it was very difficult for him to lie next to her and not take her in the way that he loved her. One night, after crawling into bed beside her, he lay staring at the ceiling, thinking of what he was going to be doing the next day. Spring expected his normal embrace, and when it didn't come, she moved next to him, placing her arms around him.

He turned to her anxiously, trying to stem his passion, and kissed her hungrily. She pushed on his chest, turning her head away.

"No, no, David. I can't. I'm sorry." She turned from him, and he silently chided himself for his lack of control.

Holding himself on one elbow, he gently rolled her back to him. "Listen to me, Spring. I've been, I think, very patient with you. I will not force you to do anything you don't want to do. The thing is, I really feel you do want to get back what we once had. It's kind of like falling off a horse. You have to try it again to lick your fear of them. Don't be afraid of me. I love you, my darling. I won't hurt you." He then kissed her gently on the forehead, the nose, her eyelids, her lips, and the soft hollow of her throat.

Then he stopped and lay back.

"I don't know why you put up with me," she said in a small voice.

"I love you, Spring, more than words can say." He paused. "You know, you have never told me how you feel about me. Not once."

"I tried to, once, just before you left to see Lily and White Feather. But you stopped me." She thought a moment and then sighed. "Now, it's hard to say. I mean, I knew once that I hated you. And then I think I showed you how I felt. I couldn't have done that, so willingly and all, if I hadn't loved you. I wanted to stay here forever with you and marry you."

"And I was afraid to get married," he stated flatly.

"No, and I didn't think you cared enough about me, if you didn't want to marry me."

"I didn't want to take away your freedom. That's what you wanted."

"Only in loving and living together in the proper way could I be truly free here," she had told him.

"But you always said you loved John, you wanted him."

"Only because you didn't want me, completely. It was my foolish pride talking."

Cross purposes. That was what they had been working at. Neither had really understood what the other had wanted or needed, and it had led them to be farther apart than ever.

Now to work back to what they did have and more. "But how do you feel about me now?" he asked, going back to his original question.

"I'd love to love you again. But I don't even love myself, and I think, until I do, I can't love you or anyone."

He enfolded her against his warm chest. "Oh, my Venus. I couldn't love you if there wasn't anything there to love. You know how hard to please I am. And you please me very much."

"Thank you for your faith. I'll keep trying."

And so each night, David held her and kissed her, until she was responding with her own kisses. When he felt she was holding nothing back from him, he slowly began to make love to her, reawakening her senses to his tender and considerate caresses. Blushing, Spring recollected a week ago when she found she didn't want to stop him from going farther, and she cried out against his shoulder to take her and love her and hold her forever and never let her go. David couldn't keep himself from taking her passionately after all the time that had passed, but she had been well taught over the weeks, and renewed in spirit, and she gave back to him all that she received. And over and over she whispered, "I love you, dear David. I love you."

Suddenly Spring shuddered in the warm sunlight, for their reacquaintance was almost snuffed out in a fraction of a second three days ago.

She had been working in the bathroom, putting it to rights, after giving Zachary his bath and sending him off to Penny's for the morning to play. Drying her hands on an apron, she entered the bedroom and found John, or what resembled him, standing by the door holding a gun on her.

His beard, which had been matted and unkempt when she last saw him, had been shaved off, and his face was hollow cheeked, his skin sallow and deeply scarred. His brown eyes were wild and menacing, and Spring's heart pounded in her chest as he took two steps forward.

"I knew I'd find you here, you little bitch. I'm going to take you from that righteous bastard once and for all!" He waved the weapon in her face.

Spring tried to swallow, but her throat was so dry she could scarcely speak. Trying to clear it, she managed to say, "John, now, be reasonable . . ."

"Reasonable! Look what you did to me."

"What . . . what do you mean?"

"You were the one who gave me these!" He gestured at his scars.

"You had the small pox?"

"Damn right, and I'm going to kill you for it too. Now no one will look at me. But first, I'll have you, like the good times we used to have. Remember?" He advanced on her.

She stepped back and tried to stall him. "John, it's not my fault you got the disease. I tried to warn you, and you thought I didn't want you. I was only trying to protect you!"

"Ha!" he laughed derisively. "You never cared about me. It was always Saunders. He always got everything I wanted."

Spring saw David in the doorway but tried to keep her eye on John. As David advanced behind him, a floorboard squeaked, and John whirled around, pointing the gun carelessly. An explosion split the quiet air, and David fell back onto the floor.

Without thinking, Spring dashed forward, and, using both hands balled into fists, she knocked the gun out of John's hand. It went skittering across the floor. With a roar of rage, John began kicking David, who attempted to roll away from the offending boots. Then another shot rent the air, and John toppled on top of David, never moving again.

When David could see around the dead body, he saw Spring's outstretched hand holding the smoking revolver at her side.

A look of utter peace filled her face.

"It's over now, David," she said. "He is no longer between us."

*   *   *

Spring glanced up and saw David mounting the hill, his left arm in a sling. The sun glistened on his light hair, his eyes shone warmly from his suntanned face. He sat by her. "The minister is here, little girl. Are you ready to marry me?"

"I've always been ready," she answered, smiling. "The question is, are you?" She touched his hand.

"Yes. There were many times these past two years that I was sure you were the last thing I wanted, but when you weren't here or near me, my life here wasn't. Life did not exist for me. You, like the springtime renewing the earth each year, have renewed my life and spirit. You have a way of restoring my soul each time I see you. Each morning I awake, I know you'll be there, and I can greet the new day with happiness."

She cupped his hard cheek in her delicate hand. "And you, my love, by marrying me, have given me my freedom to love you. I do love you."

They leaned together and pressed their lips to each other, tasting the sweetness and feeling the unselfish devotion each had for the other. Leaning back, Spring giggled.

"What is it?" he asked, smiling.

"Oh, I was just thinking about that silly parasol and how it went sailing over the sidewalk at the fort. I was such a child then."

"I remember I said your name was absurd. Absolutely absurd. Now, I think it's perfect. You are the freedom of spring."

Together they walked down the slope to be joined one to the other, in all ways, always.

The End.

About the Author

Melinda Heald, an elementary schoolteacher in California, specializing in language arts, brought reading and the written word to many children. She has written eight novels in various genres and several children's stories. She is published. She collects dolls and enjoys making jewelry. Travel consumes much of her thought and time, and she has visited all but one continent. Family gives her much joy and contentment. Originally from Maryland, Melinda now resides in Arizona.

CPSIA information can be obtained
at www.ICGtesting.com
Printed in the USA
FFOW03n0347040618
46993397-49265FF